D0175646

How to
Talk to Your Kids
About
Really Important
Things

Specific Questions and Answers and Useful Things to Say

How to Talk to Your Kids About Really Important Things

For Children Four to Twelve

Charles E. Schaefer and Theresa Foy DiGeronimo

Jossey-Bass Publishers
San Francisco

The TV Survey "Rated 'E' for Excellent By The Experts" in CHILD Magazine, December/January 1992, is reprinted by permission of CHILD Magazine. Copyright © 1992 CHILD Magazine.

Substantial discounts on bulk quantities of Jossey-Bass books are available to corporations, professional associations, and other organizations. For details and discount information, contact the special sales department at Jossey-Bass Inc., Publishers (415) 433-1740; Fax (800) 605-2665.

Jossey-Bass Web address: http://www.josseybass.com

Printed in the United States of America

Library of Congress Cataloging-in-Publication Data

Schaefer, Charles E.
     How to talk to your kids about really important things : for children four to twelve : specific questions and useful things to say / Charles E. Schaefer, Theresa Foy DiGeronimo. — 1st ed.
          p.   cm. — (A joint publication in the Jossey-Bass social and behavioral science series, the Jossey-Bass education series, and the Jossey-Bass health series)
     Includes bibliographical references.
     ISBN 1-55542-611-5 (alk. paper)
     1. Parent and child.   2. Communication in the family. 3. Parenting.
4. Children's questions and answers.   I. DiGeronimo, Theresa Foy.
II. Title.   III. Series: Jossey-Bass social and behavioral science series.
IV. Series: Jossey-Bass education series.   V. Series: Jossey-Bass health series.
HQ755.85.S33   1994
306.874—dc20   93-35548

FIRST EDITION
PB Printing   10 9 8 7 6

To my children, Karine and Eric,
who have made "family talks" an enjoyable challenge —
never a burden.
C.E.S.

To my husband, Mick,
my partner in parenting and life.
T.F.D.

Acknowledgments

We would like to thank:

Alan Rinzler, our editor, for recognizing the need for a book about talking to kids and for offering his own parental insights;

Dr. Karen Hein, director of the Adolescent AIDS Program at Montefiore Medical Center, New York City, for reviewing the chapter on HIV/AIDS;

Wendy Hollis, children's librarian at the Hawthorne Public Library, Hawthorne, New Jersey, for her help in compiling the suggested readings.

Contents

Part II
Concerns of Youth   157

Introduction

What children don't know *can* hurt them. That's why we have written this book—to help you talk to your children about really important things.

We realize that no one source can tell you exactly what to say in every situation, but in each chapter of this book, we offer you a unique collection of advice, information, and sample dialogues—all based on our years of clinical practice, parental experience, and scholarly research.

We hope this book will be a valued resource in the years to come, when you talk to your children about their experiences and help them through crises. We also realize that every family situation is unique; we know that in addition to so-called traditional parents, there are gay parents, foster parents, adoptive parents, working parents, and guardians. So we want to say at the outset that nothing in this book should be considered gospel or the "only best way." We're sure, however, that the guidelines we supply can be adapted to your family's belief system and life-style and that they will give you a strong base on which to build a tradition of open and honest communication.

Why Should You Talk to Your Kids?

Children are naturally curious about birth, death, and everything in between. They will eventually find the answers to all their questions—but from whom? If you want to be your children's primary source of information, let them know that right from the start by talking to them openly, matter-of-factly, and honestly about the many issues that are important in their lives.

Strive to be an "askable" parent—that is, someone your children feel will not judge, tease, or punish them for asking questions. An askable parent responds to questions with words and actions that say "I'm so glad you asked."

Children intuitively sense how receptive their parents are to talking about certain subjects. If you avoid talking about emotionally sensitive topics—like death, adoption, or an alcoholic parent—they learn to keep their concerns to themselves. If you ignore "embarrassing" issues—like pornography, homosexuality, and masturbation—your children will get their information (or misinformation) from someone else. If you slight the importance of such life experiences as moving to a new home, starting school, or staying at the hospital, your children will assume you just don't understand their fears.

Open communication is a most powerful parenting tool. The information in this book will help you use it often and wisely.

When Should You Talk to Your Kids?

The content of this book is directed to meet the needs of children ages four to twelve. These are the formative years, when children are developing the foundation for basic beliefs, values, and attitudes. This is also the period of time when children are usually most open to and interested in receiving parental guidance.

It is ideal to initiate conversations about important issues while your children are still young. This creates a pattern of honesty and openness that is quite difficult to establish once kids reach their teen years. By that time, teens have already found other sources for the answers to their questions.

How to Talk to Your Kids

The way you talk to kids is as important as what you say. Each chapter in this book contains specific guidelines appropriate for the given topic. But always keep in mind these ground rules:

Know What You're Talking About. To be effective in giving advice or counsel, you have to establish yourself in the eyes of your child as an expert on the subject. So before offering advice on a topic such as sex or alcoholism, you should read up on these topics. At the end of most chapters, you'll find suggested reading lists for parents and children. Read through some of these books *before* you broach the subject with your kids. Your opinion will be more credible if you offer supporting evidence instead of just stating your view.

Be Trustworthy. Be forthright about what you know and honest about what you don't know. Avoid exaggerating the truth to make an impression or distorting the truth to spare your child or yourself discomfort. Let your children learn that they can trust what you tell them.

Be Brief. Don't beat around the bush; get right to the point. You will keep your child's attention and respect if you can avoid the tendency to give a lecture or a lengthy, involved argument.

Be Clear. Use simple, concrete language geared to your child's level of development.

Respect Your Child's View. Ask your children what they think about issues rather than just telling them what to do or think. Remember to listen to and respect children's opinions so that you talk *with* them rather than *at* them. Respect also involves giving children reasons for behaving in a certain way. Reasons help develop a child's thinking powers and independence of judgment.

Why, when, and *how* you should talk with your kids is what this book is all about. We won't argue, debate, or lecture on the many controversial theories and practices inherent in some of the topics. We strive solely to give you the words you need to talk to your kids.

As you've surely noticed, this book is authored by two people. Charles E. Schaefer, a professor of psychology at Fairleigh Dickinson University in New Jersey, has spent many years talking with children and their families in his clinical practice and with his own two children. He is also a nationally renowned author of thirty books on parenting and child therapy. These experiences have taught him the importance of open communication and the value of old-fashioned family talks on topics our grandparents and even our parents thought too private, insignificant, or taboo to mention.

Theresa Foy DiGeronimo is a writer and mother of three. Her day-to-day parenting experiences have given her opportunities to "test" Schaefer's advice and challenge him to offer realistic and practical dialogues that really work with kids.

Because the authors have worked closely in writing this book, the pronoun *we* is most often used; however, the occasional *I* is the voice of Dr. Schaefer offering his clinical expertise.

Together, Schaefer and DiGeronimo have written six parenting books (several of which have been translated into other languages and published internationally). The authors are delighted to offer you this seventh title together. We know from first-hand experience that talking to kids can sometimes be difficult, awkward, and even frustrating. But we also know that the end result is well worth the effort.

If you can talk to your young kids often and openly about any subject in the world, they'll quickly learn that they can trust you with their secrets and fears. As your kids grow, this trust will enrich your relationship and encourage them to look to you, not the streets, for the information they need to stay safe and healthy.

With this goal in mind, we hope this book will become a trusted resource that you can pull out on all those days down the road when you'll need to find just the right words to talk to your kids about really important things.

January 1994   Charles E. Schaefer
                                   Hackensack, New Jersey

                                   Theresa Foy DiGeronimo
                                   Hawthorne, New Jersey

Part I

Major Crises and Big Family Changes

We like to think of childhood as happy and carefree. But in reality, no stage of life is completely free from stress, and childhood is often a most susceptible time. Children's worries and fears are more deeply felt and less readily forgotten than those of adults, who have developed greater coping skills, wide social supports, and a broader perspective based on more lifetime experiences.

It's certainly true that some stress and change is necessary for a child's growth and development. But if stress becomes severe and/or chronic, it can result in psychological and physical disorders. How reassuring, then, to know that the words and factual information offered in the following chapters can help your children cope effectively, so that no lasting emotional disturbance results from situational crises.

The timing of parent-child talks is a key factor in determining their effectiveness. By forewarning your kids as specifically as possible about forthcoming family changes, you give them what might be called "psychological immunization." The start of school, a new sibling, a new home, a stay in the hospital, and divorce are all less threatening if the child knows what to expect and is involved in making plans for the event.

Some life crises, like a natural disaster or the death of a loved one, can happen quite suddenly, allowing no time to prepare. In these cases there is a special need for open and honest communication of thoughts and feelings. Children also need the facts. They'll want answers to questions like these: What happened? How will it affect me? Will I be okay? Honest answers to such questions can be a kind of psychological "stitch in time" and can prevent serious problems from developing after the trauma.

Stress is an unavoidable and even necessary part of our children's lives. But the dialogues offered in the following chapters will help your kids put that stress in perspective and keep it from becoming unmanageable or destructive.

Adoption

Marge and George have two beautiful children. Both are happy, healthy, and very much loved, but in one way they are quite different. Two-year-old Catherine has dark curly hair, dark eyes, and a large body build. Four-year-old Jake has blonde fine hair, blue eyes, and a slight body build.

"We know they look very unlike brother and sister," says Marge with a laugh, "but we don't think of Catherine as our 'biological' child and Jake as our 'adopted' child. Each one is 'our' child."

"Because we seldom think of Jake as adopted," adds George, "we were caught off guard the morning he asked us a question that we should have been better prepared to answer. Jake wanted to know, 'How come Catherine has brown hair and brown eyes like you and Mommy, but I don't?'"

"Suddenly, I had this very strong desire to lie. I realized right then that I didn't want to tell Jake he was adopted."

The National Council for Adoption estimates that there are about sixty thousand adoptions by U.S. parents each year. It's a good guess, then, that somewhere at this very moment a family like Jake's is talking about what it means to be adopted. What will the parents say? How should the subject be handled? What information should be shared and what should be left unsaid?

The answers to these questions are in some respects unique to each personal situation. However, there are some general aspects of adoption that lend themselves to preparation, which can ease the tension of talking about this complex and sensitive subject and can foster the growth of strong family ties.

The Many Faces of Adoption

By broad definition, adoption means taking legal parental responsibility for a minor child. However, the circumstances and needs of every adoptive family are entirely unique and can't all be addressed in this single chapter. Therefore, we have chosen to focus on talking to children adopted in infancy under the rules of confidentiality. Certainly, interracial adoptions, adoptions of older children, adoptions of related children, and open adoptions all require dialogues that are not specifically included here. Still, many of the questions that children in such adoptive circumstances will ask are universal, and the guidelines for talking to all adopted children remain constant—these you will find here. Please take advantage of the resources listed at the end of the chapter to find more detailed information for special situations.

The Controversy

A generation ago, many parents tried to keep adoption a secret from the children. Fortunately, this practice is rare today. Many adoptive parents who chose to live this lie say they passed the years in constant fear that a relative or a stray document would betray them, or that the truth would slip out after their death. Children who found out about their secret adoption "by accident" say the shock of this discovery caused them extreme upset and anguish. There is no doubt that it's essential to a family's sense of security and trust and to the child's sense of self that the adoption be discussed openly.

The controversy now focuses on *when* children should be told they are adopted. Some researchers propose that children should not be told about their adoption until they are old enough to ask questions about it. It has been suggested that early telling satisfies an adult need, but does not serve the emotional needs of the child.

We don't agree. To a very young child, adoption and birth mean the same thing: *how I got here.* Saying to infants and toddlers "I'm so glad we adopted you" simply makes the word *adopt* a friendly and loving term that can be explained in further detail as the children grow and begin to ask more questions.

Early telling also ensures that the parents will be the ones to tell their children about the adoption. Waiting too long to tell increases the likelihood that someone else—perhaps someone insensitive or cruel—will break the news.

Of course, when to tell your children they are adopted is a personal decision that you will make for yourself. But we strongly believe that adopted children should know something about their birth history before they enter kindergarten. Waiting any longer sets the stage for a traumatic revelation that could hurt the child and weaken the bond of family trust.

How to Talk About Adoption

How you talk about adoption is in many ways as important as *what* you say. You might follow these guidelines whenever the subject comes up.

Maintain a Calm and Kind Emotional Tone. It is essential that your feelings of love, understanding, and respect get through, no matter what facts you're discussing. This is generally easy to do at first. But later, when your children ask the same questions over and over, or challenge your answers, or cry "You're not my real mother," it becomes a bit harder to remain calm, loving, and understanding. Still, especially in those circumstances, it's important to try.

Be Open, Matter-of-Fact, and Honest.   False or evasive responses can be confusing and may discourage further probing. When children are not given honest answers, they may imagine something far worse than the truth.

A friend of my daughter's, for example, was told by her adoptive parents that "adopted" means "special." When this young girl entered school and was referred to the "special" education program for a learning disability, she made an association that she carried around for years: "Adopted people have trouble learning in school."

Keep your Responses Short and Simple for the Young Child.   Try not to tell more than the child wants to know. A colleague once confessed a mistake he made in his eagerness to say just the right thing to his newly adopted son. One night the boy had asked him, "Where's my mother?" This new dad went on in great detail explaining what he knew about the whereabouts of the birth mother. When he was finished, the child looked very sad and said, "Oh, I thought she went to the store." The child had asked about his new adoptive mother and was now completely confused and quite worried by the response.

When you're not sure what your children are really asking, you might ask them to say it again or try to say it another way.

Offer Information in Small Pieces on an Ongoing Basis.   The subject of the adoption should never be presented in one, large, sit-down powwow, when the facts from beginning to end are detailed and then never mentioned again. The concepts of adoption need to be discussed in many stages, to match your child's developmental growth. Offer more and more complex information as you think your child is ready to understand it.

Don't Overemphasize the Adoption. Just as a birth mother does not repeatedly remind her children that they came from her uterus, you don't need to hammer at adoption as the route of entry into your family.

The Language of Adoption

Children need to talk about their adoption, but the words you choose in discussions can color the way they receive the information.

"Real" Parents. Sometimes adoptive parents refer to the biological parent as the *real* or *natural* parent. Avoid these words; *you* are both real and natural to your children. Instead, use the word *birth* parent. You might say, for example, "I have never met your birth mother."

The Chosen Child. It's quite common for adoptive parents to tell their children, "You looked so adorable, we picked you to be our child." Try to avoid using words like *picked, chose,* or *selected.* This leaves children with the possibility that they are members of the family only for external qualities and that if these qualities should fade, they'll disappoint their parents and no longer be desirable.

The "chosen child" phrase also implies that they were available only because someone else chose *not* to keep them. Far better to explain that you wanted a child and so you were thrilled to learn that a child was available for you to love.

Adopted (A Foreign Species?).   You may be proud of your decision to adopt and see no need to hide this fact from family and friends. However, be careful not to use the word *adopted* indiscriminately or inappropriately. There is no need to announce your children's adopted status to mothers at the local playground, to the checkout clerk, or to your children's playmates. This emphasis on qualifying your relationship may make your children feel they are different from all other children.

What to Say About Adoption

Children's understanding of adoption changes with age and experience. In order to deepen their understanding and answer their many questions, you'll need to keep elaborating on the adoptive relationship as your children mature. Only in adolescence will your child fully comprehend the complex issues involved, so remember: talking about adoption is not a single event, but a lifelong process.

Talking to Toddlers

Use the word *adopted* freely when talking to your children from infancy to two years old. Children this age will understand little if anything of what the word means. However, they will learn to associate it with a warm, secure feeling when they become used to hearing it in a happy, loving context. Try these phrases:

"I always wanted a child and now I have adopted you."

"Adopting you is the best thing I've ever done."

"Adopting you answered my prayers."

"The day of your adoption was one of the happiest days of my life."

Talking to Children Aged Three to Six

There are two things you can give your adopted children between the ages of three and six: a sense of belonging and the facts.

Young children love to hear about their infancy. They incessantly ask questions like "Did I cry at night?" "How old was I when I first started to talk?" "Did I like going to the doctor?" Use this interest in the past and combine it with photo albums, baby keepsake books, and the like to lead your children to a better understanding of how they came to be members of your family.

If you have any souvenirs of the adoption, put them together for your children to look at: congratulatory notes, announcements of the child's arrival, pictures of the homecoming. As you talk about these things, the subject of adoption will fall into its place as the beginning of your lives together. This tells young children that they belong in this family.

Like all children this age, your children will now begin asking questions about their birth. Using age-appropriate language and concepts, answer their questions honestly.

"Where did I come from?"

Your children did not come from an adoption agency. They need to know that they were conceived and born like every other child and then adopted into your family.

You might say "You were made by another man and woman and grew inside that woman. You were born to her just like other children are. Those people are called your birth mother and birth father. But your birth mother and birth father couldn't take care of a baby, so we adopted you."

"What does 'adopted' mean?"

"*Adopted* means having a mother and a father who, although they're not your birth mother and father, want to take care of you and love you for the rest of your life."

"Why did you adopt me?"

"We adopted you because we wanted a baby very much, but we couldn't [or didn't want to] make one ourselves. So you came to us through the adoption agency. Now you're every bit as much our child as if you'd been born to us."

"Why didn't my other mother and father keep me?"

"Your birth parents were too young [poor, unsettled, or whatever] to raise a baby, so they made a plan for you to be adopted by parents who would love you and take care of you forever."

Try to emphasize that an adoption was arranged because of the birth parents' circumstances, not because of their feelings. Leading experts in adoption have found that the idea that "I was given away because I was loved so much" can confuse and worry children. They may come to fear that their adoptive parents, who "love them so much," will also give them away in the face of misfortunes like unemployment or divorce.

Talking to Children Aged Six to Twelve

By age six, most children understand the difference between adoption and birth as alternative paths to parenthood. During this period they gradually recognize the permanent nature of the adoptive relationship. More detailed questions about birth parents and the permanence of adoption will now surface.

"What were my 'other' parents like?"

Children will naturally be curious about their birth parents. Give your children whatever information you have without sugarcoating, criticizing, or lying. If you don't know something, say so. If you do know, tell them; children like to know things like ethnicity, religion, physical description, education, and occupation. Children who know this kind of information about their birth parents are less likely to build elaborate fantasies or romanticize the "mystery" parent.

"Do you know anything about my father?"

When your children ask about their birth father, tell them whatever you know factually. If, as is often the case, the birth parents were not married, say so:

"Your birth parents weren't married. That's why your birth records don't tell us much about your birth father."

This is information that should neither be hidden, nor emphasized, nor followed by moral advice. It just is.

"Can adopted children be returned to the adoption agency?"

"Not a child that I adopt." There's no need to give a detailed explanation of the rare circumstances in which adoptive parents and children can be separated. Make sure your children hear you say "You are a part of my life. I love you now and will always, no matter what happens. I could never live without you."

"Can I find my birth mother?"

Don't feel hurt or rejected if your children want to find their birth parent. It's a natural curiosity that does not reflect on your parenting or your child's love for you. Throwing up roadblocks when the subject is first broached will worsen a situation that may only be a passing curiosity or a test of your love.

In her book *Successful Adoption* (Harmony Books, 1987), Dr. Jacqueline Hornor Plumez advises parents to understand that the question is not whether to fight the child's desire to search for birth parents, but how much to help. The answer in part has to do with the age of the child. If the child is under eighteen, many experts discourage face-to-face meetings. Adolescence is too confusing a time, they feel, to be confronted with two sets of parents in the flesh.

But you can still help. Be supportive and understanding. Let your children express their feelings and clarify their goals. Give them whatever nonidentifying information you have and then listen. Most children want answers, not a real meeting. They also are looking for reassurances of your love and evidence that you won't turn away from them if they're honest about their feelings of loss or curiosity.

Responding to Upsetting Remarks

All children say hurtful things to their parents sometimes. This can be upsetting to any parent, but to an adoptive parent these statements may seem especially threatening. If your child lashes out at you in anger, remind yourself of these points:

- Biological children do the same thing.
- This verbal assault has nothing to do with how the child entered the family.

- All children must learn that even loving parents discipline their children.

Then respond in a firm and nondefensive way.

"You're not my real mother. You can't make me do anything."

In the words of Pearl Buck, speaking to her adopted child, firmly reply, "I am your real mother by love and by law."

"I hate you. I wish you never adopted me!"

"Well, I love you, and even when I'm angry at you I'm very glad I did adopt you."

Uncovering Unasked Questions

Some children have lots of questions but are hesitant to ask for answers. Some worry about sounding ungrateful if they ask about their birth parents. Some may have sensed your own anxiety about the subject. Others may assume that if they're supposed to know, you'll tell them. These children need you to create opportunities for talking.

You might say, "Children who are adopted often wonder about their birth parents. Are you curious about this? Because if you would like to know, I'd be glad to give you whatever information I have." Or, "You may have noticed that we don't have any pictures of you in the hospital when you were born. That's because we adopted you a few weeks after your birth. If you ever want to talk about that, just let me know. Okay?"

There's no way you can be completely prepared for all the questions your children may ask you. But there are two general rules that can guide you through the years ahead:

1. Using age-appropriate language and information, be honest.
2. Let your children know that they can ask you *anything.*

Suggested Reading

For Parents

Melina, Lois Ruskai. *Making Sense of Adoption: A Parent's Guide.* Grand Rapids, Mich.: Perennial Library, 1989.

OURS: The Magazine of Adoptive Families

For information, contact OURS, Inc., 3307 Highway 100 North, Suite 203, Minneapolis, Minn. 55422; phone 612-535-4829.

Plumez, Jacqueline Hornor. *Successful Adoption.* New York: Harmony Books, 1987.

For Young Children

Banish, Roslyn. *A Forever Family.* New York: Harper Trophy, 1992.

Bloom, Suzanne. *A Family for Jamie: An Adoption Story.* New York: C. N. Potter, 1990.

Freudberg, Judy, and Tony Geiss. *Susan and Gordon Adopt a Baby.* New York: Random Books for Young Readers, 1992.

Girard, Linda Walvoord. *We Adopted You, Benjamin Koo.* Niles, Ill.: A. Whitman, 1989.

Greenberg, Judith E. *Adopted.* New York: F. Watts, 1987.

Keller, Holly. *Horace.* New York: Greenwillow Books, 1991.

For Children Aged Eight to Twelve

Auch, Mary Jane. *Pick of the Litter.* New York: Holiday House, 1988.

Krementz, Jill. *How It Feels to Be Adopted.* New York: Knopf, 1992.

Myers, Walter Dean. *Mop, Moondance, and the Nagasaki Knights.*
New York: Delacorte Press, 1992.

Powledge, Fred. *So You're Adopted.* New York: Scribners, 1982.

Rosenberg, Maxine B. *Growing Up Adopted.* New York: Bradbury
Press, 1989.

Alcoholic Parent

Joey tiptoed through his back door into the kitchen. He stopped and listened for his cue that would tell him what to do. Every day was different. Some days his mom would be sleeping on the couch; this meant he could stop in the kitchen and have a snack. Sometimes, he could hear her crying; that meant he should go straight to his room and be very quiet. On other days, if Joey heard sounds of anger or rage, he'd head back outside and try to find someplace else to go for awhile. Today, he heard only silence—that was good; it meant he could have something to eat without getting his mother upset.

According to the Children of Alcoholics Foundation, approximately seven million children under age eighteen live this kind of off-balance life with an alcoholic parent. Despite this large population of affected children, most support programs have focused on helping the alcoholic parent. The philosophy has been that the parent is the one who must change if the child is to live an emotionally normal life. This, we now know, isn't the only or best approach to helping children of alcoholic parents. Whether alcoholic parents want help or even admit there's a need for help, the children in these families can be taught to understand and deal with their home environment.

When nonalcoholic parents try to talk to kids about alcoholism, they sometimes feel they are betraying their alcoholic spouse.

It's understandable that you might feel like this. After all, you've joined his or her conspiracy of silence up to this point and it may worry you that saying the word *alcoholism* out loud in your home (and to your children!), will anger, hurt, and insult your spouse. This is a difficult first step to take, and you, too, need support in your decision.

If you're hesitating about talking to your children, get some help for yourself first. Call Al-Anon today; the number is in the telephone book. Their support and information services for family and friends who are affected by someone else's drinking are free and confidential. Let them help you learn how to avoid supporting the drinking, shame, and secrecy yourself, so you can better talk to your kids with honesty and love.

Why Talk About Alcoholism?

Children with alcoholic parents look and act like most other children; they carry on from one day to the next. But professionals who work with these children know that without help they face enduring problems:

- They run a greater risk of developing very low self-esteem.
- They tend to have fewer friends than their peers from nonalcoholic homes.
- They drop out of school voluntarily in larger numbers than any other group of children studied.
- They have more problems with alcohol and drug abuse themselves.

The coping strategies these children develop over the years often set a pattern that follows them into adulthood. As adults they remain unable to trust their own feelings or perceptions of reality. Adult children of alcoholics tend to fear their inability to control both themselves and their relationships. And research continues to find that because their lives were in turmoil when they were young, children of alcoholics feel that any expression of an emotion such as anger—or even joy—means that they lack control.

It's also quite clear that alcoholism runs in families, and children of alcoholics are four times more likely than other children to become alcoholics. For all these reasons, it's very important that *someone* talk to these children about how alcoholism is affecting their lives and how they can cope with it.

How to Talk About Alcoholism

Chris developed a drinking problem when he lost his job. At that time, his daughter, Nicole, was two years old. Now, five years later, Chris is still drinking heavily and no one in his home has yet uttered the word *alcoholism*. As in most families of alcoholics, the problem is cloaked in secrecy and denial. Without ever talking out loud about the situation, everyone knows it's a taboo subject that each family member has the obligation to keep a secret.

The obligation often leads to social isolation for all family members. Embarrassment causes the nonalcoholic parent and the children to stop inviting people into the home lest the family secret be revealed. The family members also tend to become isolated from each other because the alcoholism, although an ever-present problem, is not acknowledged or spoken about. The entire family feels trapped.

Talk Honestly with Your Children.   As a nonalcoholic parent, you can free your children from the trap of secrecy simply by talking to them. On an age-appropriate level, be honest.

To a two- or three-year-old you might say, "Daddy has an ill-ness that makes him very sleepy and sometimes very angry."

After age four, you can introduce the subject of alcoholism and its symptoms in a factual and matter-of-fact way. This tells your children that you're open to their feelings on the subject and you're willing to talk about it.

Encourage Questions and Discussion.   You can offer the facts in answer to your children's questions, of course, but it's also a good idea to invite an open discussion. Wait for a quiet, unhur-ried time (away from the alcoholic parent) to bring up the sub-ject. Tell your children that you feel it's important for them to know why their other parent acts as he or she does.

How to Respond to Your Child's Feelings About Alcoholism

Life in the home of an alcoholic parent tends to be chaotic and unpredictable. Fear, anger, and shame are probably everyday emo-tions for your children. The children may show pseudomaturity because they often have to act as a parent to themselves or youn-ger children. But underneath this maturity there are feelings of deprivation, dependency, and resentment. Reality awareness may be impaired because the alcoholic parent usually denies the prob-lem. Low self-esteem is also common because the children of al-coholics tend to feel that since there is something wrong in their family, there is something wrong with them.

As you observe your child's reactions to the alcoholic parent, look for indications of the feelings described in this section. Look also for opportunities to let your children talk about their feelings.

Guilt

Be Honest About What Is Causing the Parent's Unusual Behavior. Children tend to think it's their fault their parents drink. They often reason, "If I were a better kid, he'd stop drinking." Right from the start of your discussions with your children stress the fact that they are *not* to blame for their parent's problem.

You might explain alcoholism in this way: "Alcoholism is a disease caused by drinking too much alcohol: that's drinks like beer, wine, or whiskey. The disease causes your father to feel many different things, like tired, angry, or sad. It makes him unable to control the way he acts. The problem is not caused by any other person or incident. You are not the reason your dad suffers from alcoholism, in the same way it's not your fault he has an allergy to cats or wears glasses."

Anxiety

Children of alcoholic parents carry around a great deal of worry and concern. They worry that their parents will become injured:

"Will Mommy get hurt when she falls down?"

"Will Daddy get into a car accident?"

"Will she fall asleep while smoking and set the house on fire?"

The tense and hostile atmosphere in an alcoholic household can be more upsetting to children than the actual drinking. The children in these homes worry:

"Will Daddy hit Mommy again?"

"Will Mommy and Daddy fight real loud tonight?"

"Will I get hit if I tell Dad I lost my baseball bat?"

Children have valid reason to be concerned about their own safety. Victims of incest and child abuse often come from alcoholic families.

Here are some things you can do to help your children cope with their anxiety.

Distinguish Between Children's and Adults' Responsibilities. Make it clear that children are not responsible for the safety of their parents; if a parent gets hurt, the parent will have to deal with that problem—not the child.

Establish a Plan of Action for Children if Parents Start to Fight. Instruct your children that they are not responsible for stopping their parents' arguments and should not get involved in the fighting. But offer them an out: you might give older children permission to leave the house when a fight starts, to stay with a trusted friend, neighbor, or relative. For younger children, you might designate one special stuffed animal as the "comfort friend"; tell your child to hug this animal whenever he or she begins to feel worried.

Embarrassment

A child who is ashamed or fearful of his parent's behavior will become embarrassed to invite friends home or to invite the parent to family activities.

Acknowledge Children's Feelings and Help Them Plan Ahead. Acknowledge their feelings by telling your children, "I understand that you may not want your friends to see how your mother sometimes acts. It's okay to feel that way." Then give your children specific actions they can take to relieve these feelings:

- You might give them permission to unveil the family secret. If they arrive home with friends and the alcoholic parent is drinking, encourage them to say, "My father has an illness that sometimes makes him act very unfriendly."
- You can help your child make and keep friends through after-school sports and activities. It's important that children of alcoholics not isolate themselves from activities that will help them get a broader sense of reality than they witness in their homes.
- Establish a plan for helping your older children avoid the embarrassment of coming home with a friend and walking in on an unpleasant scene. Tell your children to call home first. If the alcoholic parent answers the phone it's usually easy to tell if he or she has been drinking, and if the nonalcoholic parent answers, he or she can okay or nix the plan.

Again, emphasize to your children, "Your parent's addiction to alcohol is not your fault. You have no reason to feel ashamed or embarrassed."

Confusion and Insecurity

A regular daily schedule, which is very important for a child, often does not exist in the home of an alcoholic. Moreover, regardless of the child's behavior, the alcoholic parent will change suddenly from being loving to angry. This unpredictability is very confusing to your child. And even you, the nonalcoholic parent, may use so much of your time and energy making excuses for the alcoholic spouse and dealing with his or her erratic behaviors that you have little time to maintain a consistent pattern of daily life. This uncertainty causes your child much insecurity.

You can give your children some of the order and security their young psyches need by supplying them with the facts and by making promises you know you can keep.

Explain the Mood Swings of Alcoholism. Young children get a skewed view of reality in your home; they will begin to think all adults act erratically and impulsively.

Tell your children, "Alcoholism makes your father say things he doesn't mean and do things he doesn't really want to do. If he were not an alcoholic, your father wouldn't yell at you for spilling your milk one day and laugh it off the next day—he would act the same way each time. But alcoholism makes him unpredictable, so we just don't know how he'll act or what he'll say."

This explanation should help your children stop trying to "do the right thing" so Dad won't get upset. As you know, there is no "right thing" in the home of an alcoholic.

Offer Some Consistency. Despite the chaotic atmosphere in your home, find some routines that your children can follow. Establish a bedtime that they can count on. Set a story hour that's guaranteed. Even if it's only once a week, promise them a special time with you that they can count on for undivided, loving attention. Make promises only when you're sure you can keep them. The alcoholic parent usually promises the moon and seldom delivers. So from you, at least, let them learn to trust a promise.

Anger

There is usually much anger among family members in the alcoholic's family. Your children surely feel angry at the alcoholic parent for drinking, and they may be angry with you for lack of support and protection. Sometimes, when children finally gather the courage to speak out against the parent who has hurt them, their cries for help are met with scoldings like these: "Don't you dare talk about your mother like that." Or, "Don't raise your voice to me. I get enough of that from your father." Or, "Don't tell me you're angry. Tell him." These reactions encourage your children to hide or to ignore these feelings.

Give Children the Freedom to Express Their Rage. Encourage your children to tell you how they feel. Let them know that it's safe to cry to you. Empathize with their anger. Give them some kind of release valve, like pillows to punch and opportunities for physical exercise. Say to them, "I know you're angry and I understand why."

How to Answer Children's Questions

Once your children realize that it's okay to talk about your spouse's drinking problem, they'll feel free to ask you questions. A few common questions and suggested answers adapted from the Al-Anon pamphlet *Youth and the Alcoholic Parent* follow. Use them as a guide to help you open up about your family problem and to help your children understand what alcoholism is, how it affects their lives, and how they can best cope with it.

"Why can't Mom just stop drinking?"

"Your mother may want to stop drinking (even if she doesn't admit it), but her desire for liquor is so strong that she can't control

it. That's why it's called an addiction. When the addiction becomes this strong, alcoholics usually can't stop by themselves; they
need help."

"Why doesn't she get help?"

"Maybe your mother knows that she drinks too much but is
ashamed to admit it. Few alcoholics will admit their problem. Or
maybe she has tried to give it up in the past and failed; many alcoholics give up trying to quit because they think they can't. But
no one can help her until she's ready to accept that help."

"Can I help her stop drinking?"

"No, you can't. Begging, crying, pleading, silence, and even
tears won't work. Those things only make your mother feel more
guilty and ashamed—these feelings lead to more drinking."

"Isn't there anything I can do?"

"Yes, you can learn to deal with your mother the way she is
now. You can feel free to talk to me about your feelings and your
worries. You can accept the fact that you aren't responsible for your
mother's drinking and that, no matter how much you want her
to stop drinking, you can't make her."

"What if she never stops drinking?"

"There is always hope that your mother will reach out for help,
but she must do it herself. There is an organization called Alcoholics Anonymous that she may join one day. It is a group of alcoholics who help each other give up drinking and stay sober. But
even if this never happens and your mother continues to drink,
yours is the only life you're responsible for. What your mother does
should not make you give up trying to enjoy life."

"Why does my mother sometimes beat me
and yell at me and then say she loves me?"

"Alcoholics often take out their anger on those they love most. They react in ways that don't make any sense to us, but that's a symptom of their disease. What you need to know about your mother's temper is how to cope with it: try to stay out of her way when she's angry and don't argue with her when she's been drinking."

Talking to your children about an alcoholic parent is not an easy task. But not talking about this family situation puts your child at grave risk for enduring emotional problems. If you read through this chapter and decide that you do want to talk to your children about alcoholism, keep this thought in mind:

Children should not assume responsibility for changing the behaviors of the alcoholic. Your goal in discussing the problem is to give your children a new way of thinking about the situation and to make them feel better about themselves and their own lives.

Suggested Resources

Al-Anon Family Group Headquarters
P.O. Box 182
Madison Square Station
New York, NY 10159
212-683-1771

Children of Alcoholics Foundation
555 Madison Avenue
New York, NY 10021
1-800-359-COAF

National Clearinghouse for Alcohol and Drug Information
P.O. Box 2345
Rockville, MD 20852
301-468-2600

National Council on Alcoholism
12 West 21st Street, 7th Floor
New York, NY 10010
212-206-6770

Suggested Reading

For Parents

Al-Anon Family Group Headquarters Staff. *The Dilemma of the Alcoholic Marriage.* New York: Al-Anon Family Group, 1986.

Balcerzak, Ann M. *Hope for Young People with Alcoholic Parents.* Center City, MN: Hazelden, 1981.

For Children Aged Four to Seven

Kenny, Kevin. *Sometimes My Mom Drinks Too Much.* Milwaukee: Raintree Childrens Books, 1980.

Vigna, Judith. *I Wish Daddy Didn't Drink So Much.* Niles, Ill.: A. Whitman, 1988.

For Children Aged Eight to Twelve

Adler, C. *With Westie and the Tin Man.* New York: Macmillan, 1985.

Brooks, Cathleen. *The Secret Everyone Knows.* Center City, MN: Hazelden, 1989.

DeClements, Barthe. *No Place for Me.* New York: Viking Kestrel, 1987.

Death of a Loved One

The diagnosis hit like a bolt of lightning—advanced ovarian cancer. Adria was only thirty-eight years old, and she had three young children.

"Dear God," she cried from her hospital bed, "I want to watch my children grow. I want to comfort them when they're hurt. I want to be here when they need me."

But she knew her God had other plans. After the initial shock, tears, and cries of disbelief, Adria spent much of her time preparing for her death. She and her husband, Todd, talked long into many nights about who would watch their children while Todd was at work, how he would manage the house without her, and who would become the children's guardian if Todd should also die.

In practical matters, Adria and Todd were prepared for the end. Then, very early one morning, after Adria had been taken to the hospital, the doctor called. Adria had passed away in her sleep during the night; her suffering was over. As Todd looked down into the quizzical eyes of his children, who had gathered around him as he hung up the phone, he knew there was one thing they hadn't prepared for—what would he say to his children? How could he make them understand death? How could he talk to them when his own grief was so great?

In hopes of protecting their children, many parents try to shield them from experiencing the loss, expressing sorrow, and sharing in the family's mourning upon the death of a loved one. Nevertheless, one of the most important lessons you can learn from this chapter is that children have the same needs as adults—to mourn and to accept what has happened.

How a Loved One Who Is Dying Can Help

As death approaches, it's not uncommon for the dying loved one to shy away from children. "I don't want them to see me like this," some say. "I want them to remember me as happy and healthy," say others. Although understandable, keeping children away from the death bed makes the eventual acceptance of death more difficult.

If at all possible, your children should be allowed to stay in touch with the loved one who is dying. This gives them a chance to share their feelings and say loving farewells. In fact, a dying parent, grandparent, sibling, or friend can provide a unique opportunity to prepare children for the impending death.

Encourage Children to See and Help the Dying Person. If at all possible, let your children have continual contact with the loved one, along with opportunities to "do for" the person. Let your children purchase small items, such as magazines or chewing gum, for the ill person. Let them prepare special treats or foods. Encourage your children to ask the person, "Is there anything I can do for you?" This lets children feel they are doing something to relieve the person's pain and suffering.

Let Your Children Visit a Loved One Who Is Hospitalized. Preventing children from visiting does not protect them;

on the contrary, it can lead to feelings of abandonment. When children feel they're being ignored or deserted, it leaves room for the imagination to build fantasies more frightening than reality.

School-age children will not be overwhelmed by seeing a sick loved one if they are adequately prepared with simple and specific explanations of the hospital setting. It's important to describe hospital equipment and machines in terms of the helpful role they play. You might say, for example, "The tube in Daddy's arm gives him food because he feels too sick to eat the way he usually does." Equipment such as a syringe or a blood pressure gauge can be given to children to inspect so they can become familiar with medical apparatus and feel comfortable in the hospital environment.

If the sick person's appearance is notably different, point this out and relate it to the disease process familiar to your child. Remind your children, "Remember when you were very sick with a stomach virus? You stayed in bed in your pajamas and you didn't wash your hair for a few days, and you didn't want anything to eat?" Then explain, "Well, your sister has been sick in bed for a long time, so she looks very thin from not eating, and her hair isn't styled the way she usually wears it. But even though she looks a little different, she'll be very happy to see you."

Encourage Children to be Physically Close to the Loved One. If medically safe, behaviors like sitting on the bed and touching and hugging should be encouraged. These things help normalize the situation and make it less frightening.

Breaking the News

Tell Your Children of the Death Promptly and Simply. When possible, begin by talking about things the children have experienced or noticed already: "You know, don't you, that Mommy has been very sick lately. She's had to go to the hospital several times." Next, give the facts of the death: "The doctor just called to tell us that Mom died this morning."

Comfort by Touching. Communicate by your touch that the children are not alone in this, that you are there. Hold your children close to you, stroke their hands soothingly, and offer your comforting hug.

Immediately Offer Reassurance. Tell your children that although you are sad and upset, you are strong and will be able to take care of them. If a child asks if you will die too, say with confidence, "I'm going to live a long life. You'll very likely be grown up and have your own family by the time I die."

Children and Mourning

Children as young as three and four seem able to mourn the loss of a loved one. However, it's hard for most preschoolers to mourn since it's difficult for them to tolerate intense sadness or anger. That's why they may initially deny and avoid experiencing the loss.

If your children don't express sorrow or they pretend nothing is wrong, you can help them confront their repressed thoughts and feelings. If after their father's death, for example, your child says, "I want to wait until Daddy comes home before I eat dinner," that's an opportunity for you to help her face reality.

You might say, "Daddy won't be coming home for dinner any more because he's dead. It's hard to believe because we're so used to having him here." Then move to assure your child of your continued presence and love: "But I'm still here and I've made an extra special dinner just for you. Come on, let's eat."

Typically, children don't begin to show their grief until they feel assured that their needs for care and protection will be taken care of. Even then you may find that your younger children need to experience their grief in small doses. That's why they may cry for awhile and then they'll suddenly want to play—they have a short "sadness span."

Your older children will feel sorrowful for longer periods of time and will be more able to verbalize their grief. Still, they need your help to manage their painful thoughts and feelings.

Guidelines for Helping Children Mourn

The best thing you can do to help your children cope with the loss of a loved one is to help them confront and accept the death. Encourage your children to cry if they want to and to talk about their thoughts and feelings; this will bring their grief to the surface.

Take the Initiative in Expressing Grief.   If your children are hesitant to express their grief at first, you may be able to help by verbalizing their obvious feelings and letting them know you have those feelings too. You might say, "I know you miss Nana very much. I really miss her, too."

Acknowledge and Accept Children's Feelings.   Children are more likely to talk about their emotions and their concerns about death if they are confident that whatever they feel is acceptable and normal. The child who feels angry at the deceased for leaving should be able to say "I hate Jeffrey for dying" without hearing back "What a terrible thing to say!"

Another child, who feels guilty for having somehow caused the death, may insist, "It's all my fault," and will benefit from understanding rather than criticism.

A child overwhelmed with fear of abandonment may wail, "Now I'm all alone with no one to take care of me," even though you are obviously nearby and ready to love and care for the child.

Don't dismiss or ridicule these feelings. Accept them as sincere emotions that are valid, and don't in any way negate the child's loving relationship with the deceased.

If your children make these kinds of statements, first just listen. Let them finish what they have to say without being cut off with an admonishment like "Don't say such a thing." Hear them out to the end. Then echo their sentiment to show you understand how they feel. You can admit, "Sometimes I feel angry, too." Or, "You sound like you're feeling guilty about Grandma's death." Or, "It can be real scary when someone you love and depend on dies."

Provide Nonverbal Outlets for Feelings. Verbally inhibited children may express their grief in a variety of nonverbal ways, such as sleeplessness, nightmares, clinging behavior, and difficulties at school. If your children seem unable to express their thoughts verbally, give them an outlet through play or art activities.

Puppets and dolls are wonderful vehicles for "talking" about death. Guide your children to imagine that one of the puppets or dolls has died and ask, "How do you think the other one feels about that?" If your nonverbal child shrugs "I don't know," continue: "Do you think he feels sad? Or angry?" Keep asking questions and supplying your own answers until your child feels comfortable joining in the game.

You can also use artwork to "talk" about the loss of a loved one. Encourage your children to draw pictures of the deceased. A simple portrait can be framed as a loving tribute; drawings of a special occasion shared with the loved one can prompt happy memories; even imaginative pictures of the bird's-eye view from heaven can help children express their thoughts and feelings.

Writing stories and letters to express feelings is another way of helping children give sorrow words. (Younger children can dictate their tales to you.) Suggest to your children that they write a good-bye letter to the loved one. Or, you might ask them to write a story about their happiest memory of the deceased. Your older children may even find comfort in writing in a daily diary that allows them to record any thoughts or feelings they need to express.

By encouraging these activities, you demonstrate that you understand the many feelings that accompany death. This attitude will teach your children that talking and thinking about death are a natural part of mourning a loved one.

Talking About Death

When you talk to your children about the death of a loved one, you will no doubt be dealing with your own grief as well. It's unrealistic to expect that you will always say the right thing at the right time. But the following suggestions will give you some simple ideas that can help children accept death.

Give Age-Appropriate Explanations of Death.   Always be truthful and open about the facts of death, but remember that your children's ability to understand death varies according to age.

Children aged six and younger cannot really understand the full meaning of death, especially the finality and universality of it.

Children aged six to eight are beginning to grasp the finality of death and tend to associate it with ghoul-like creatures and ghosts.

Children from from nine or ten through adolescence are beginning to realize fully that death is irreversible and inevitable.

See the chapter entitled "Death" in Part II for a full presentation of how you can best gear your discussion of death to your child's comprehension level.

Reminisce. Deliberately remember the deceased in detail. Even though it may be painful to do this at first, initiate loving, evocative conversations about the loved one who has just died. Refer to past experiences to make it easy for your child to reminisce. You might say at the dinner table, "Remember how Grandpa always loved this meat loaf?" Look for opportunities to bring the deceased person into your daily conversations.

A memory book is also a good way to reminisce about a loved one. Gather special mementos like pictures and cards with your children and put them together in some kind of scrapbook. If your children can draw pictures of the deceased or write stories about things they did with him or her, add these to the collection. This kind of physical memory-making helps children pass through the mourning process and also serves as a priceless remembrance your children will cherish always.

Openly Express Your Love and Support. Although you cannot shield your children from painful feelings, you can help them bear these emotions more easily. In the early stages of mourning, children need reassurance that they are loved; this restores a sense of security to their world. During those difficult months after a traumatic loss, one of the best ways to show you care is by your presence. Be sure your unlimited support and affection are readily available to your children. This isn't the time for your kids to "be brave" or "carry on"; it's time for mourning.

Don't Hide Your Grief. It's important for your children to see you express your grief on occasion. Explain that "all people cry when they feel sad, and that's okay."

A friend who lost her husband very suddenly in a fatal car crash once told me, "I just can't talk to my kids about their dad because every time I try, I start crying." If you find that talking about your loved one brings you to tears, don't let that make the subject taboo in your home. Admit your feelings to your children and tell them, "Sometimes when I talk about your dad, I get all teary because I miss him so much, but still, I do like to think about him and talk about him. Don't you?" This will give your kids permission to also talk about the deceased, even when it makes them feel like crying.

Explain Your Philosophical and Religious Outlooks. As your children grapple with the pain of death, help them see the natural and positive side as well. You might explain that love does not die when a loved one dies. Tell them, "The spirit of someone you love does not die. It lives in your heart and your memory. It belongs to you always and is your treasure."

Studies have found that if a family is religious and has a transcendental value system, these beliefs can help family members better cope with death. Talking about your belief in a deity and an afterlife can comfort children and help them accept death. Certainly, the loss can become more bearable if your children believe that one day they'll rejoin their loved one.

Children at Wakes and Funerals

Wakes and funerals serve the valuable function of allowing the living to acknowledge, accept, and cope with the loss of a loved one. These rituals can give children three things: (1) a sense of closure, (2) the opportunity to share their loss with other mourners and be comforted by them, and (3) time to face the reality of death.

Whether or not your child should attend the wake and funeral depends on the age of the child and the situation. A preschool child may be confused and frightened if some adults present are expressing uncontrolled grief. Some young children may have nightmares about dead bodies or fears about going to sleep for some time after seeing an open casket. So unless a preschooler is particularly mature, it may be best to keep the child home during the wake and funeral.

If your children are old enough to understand the ritual of the wake or funeral and want to participate, being present can help make death less mysterious and frightening to them. Our experience indicates that children over five are usually sufficiently mature to attend a wake or funeral if they wish. Kept from these occasions, they are apt to feel left out. They may think themselves deprived of an opportunity to share their feelings and actively experience the grief process.

Before making your decision to bring your children or leave them home, explain what wakes and funerals are all about, give opportunities for lots of questions, and then whatever the child's feelings about attending may be, they should be recognized, discussed, and valued.

The following questions and suggested answers are the kinds of preparatory information your children will need.

"What's a wake and funeral?"

"Wakes and funerals are ceremonies in which we say good-bye to those we love who have died."

"Why do people have wakes and funerals?"

"The reason we have wakes and funerals is so that people who grieve a person can come together to share their feelings. They have a chance to tell others that they loved that person, they will miss her, and they will always remember her."

"Will [the deceased loved one] be at the wake and funeral?"

"Yes. Her body will be at the wake in a long box called a casket. You'll be able to see the body, but because the body is dead, it can't move or talk or know you're there. At the funeral, the lid of the casket will be closed so we won't be able to see the body, but it will be inside."

"What will I do at a wake?"

"You'll stay close by me all the time. We'll first look at the body in the casket and whisper our good-byes. Then we'll stand or sit nearby and say hello to all the people who come to share their love and sorrow."

"Do I have to go?"

"Many people find wakes and funerals a good way to say good-bye. But some people find them much too sad; they like to say good-bye in a different way, perhaps alone and away from others. You decide. If you'd rather not go, that's okay and no one will be angry with you. If you do attend, I will be with you and will help you feel as comfortable as possible. Whatever you decide, I know you loved [the deceased] and you will miss her as much as I do.

Living through the loss of a loved one can be a very difficult time for everyone in your family. But this kind of emotional trauma can have positive and maturing aspects for your children if you remember to fill these basic needs:

- The need to feel involved and important
- The need for information that is clear and age appropriate
- The need for reassurance and love
- The need to reminisce
- The need to know that all people faced with the loss of a loved one feel sad
- The need to express all feelings without fear of reprimand or ridicule

Suggested Reading

For Parents

Colgrove, Melba, Harold Bloomfield, and Peter McWilliams. *How to Survive the Loss of Love.* New York: Bantam, 1977.

Kushner, Harold S. *When Bad Things Happen to Good People.* New York: Schocken, 1981.

La Tour, Kathy. *For Those Who Live: Helping Children Cope with the Death of a Brother or Sister.* Omaha, Neb.: Centering Corp., 1987.

For Children Aged Four to Seven

Carlstrom, Nancy White. *Blow Me a Kiss, Miss Lilly.* New York: Harper & Row, 1990.

Carson, Jo. *You Hold Me And I'll Hold You.* New York: Orchard Books, 1992.

Caseley, Judith. *When Grandpa Came to Stay.* New York: Greenwillow Books, 1986.

Clifton, Lucille. *Everett Anderson's Goodbye.* New York: Holt, Rinehart & Winston, 1983.

Hines, Anna Grossnickle. *Remember the Butterflies*. New York: Dutton Children's Books, 1991.

For Children Aged Eight to Twelve

Hamilton, Virginia. *Cousins*. New York: Philomel, 1990.

Hermes, Patricia. *You Shouldn't Have to Say Good-bye*. San Diego, Calif.: Harcourt Brace Jovanovich, 1982.

Marino, Jan. *Eighty-eight Steps to September*. Boston: Little, Brown, 1989.

Martin, Ann M. *With You and Without You*. New York: Holiday House, 1986.

Death of a Pet

The bunny was a surprise present for Diane and her brothers.

"I remember my dad calling to us early one morning," recalls Diane, "saying, 'Look who's outside!' What a thrill it was to peek out and see this tiny white rabbit standing so still against the new spring grass."

All the children clamored to be the first outside, but Diane was closest to the door from the start—and she won the race. The memory is still vivid: "I was the first to touch his soft fur," she remembers, "the first to pick him up and feel the rapid beating of his heart and to look into his frightened glass-pink eyes. This was my first and most beloved pet."

One month later, Whitie (the name chosen by unanimous family vote) grew too large to be kept inside. Since warmer weather had arrived, it seemed like a good time for Whitie to move into the backyard cage Diane's dad had built for him. Outside was definitely the best place for Whitie—back and forth he'd hop to the edge of the yard and back to Diane for a hug. He'd jump from spot to spot looking for the best greens to eat, returning shortly for a drink and his favored carrots.

One morning, as usual, Diane ran out to see Whitie before school. But on this morning, he didn't nuzzle his nose against the screen to greet her. He lay very still and heavy. "Thinking back," says Diane, "I remember noting a disturbing glance pass between my mom and dad when, hearing my screams for help, they ran out to see Whitie lying lifeless." Diane accepted her parents' explanation that the rabbit was very ill and needed to visit the veterinarian. Her mom offered to take him to the vet as she hurried Diane off to school.

It was several years before Diane heard the truth about what happened to Whitie after she left for school that day. It seems the rabbit was quite dead when Diane found him that morning, but no one wanted to tell her. Her dad dug a grave behind the shed, buried the rabbit, and told Diane that Whitie was staying at the vet's where the doctors were trying to make him better.

Well, life went on and Diane eventually stopped asking about Whitie (who, as the story was repeatedly told, was eternally "trying to get better"). "I know that my parents lied about Whitie's death," reasons Diane, "because they wanted to protect me from getting hurt. But to this day, I don't know if I feel more foolish for having believed the 'getting-better' story for so long, or angry for having been betrayed by the two people I never thought would be dishonest about something so important."

Getting Through the Stages of Grief

It's quite common for parents to try to shield their children from the hurt caused by the death of a pet or cherished animal. But too often the effort to protect turns, instead, into a type of conspiracy of silence that leaves a confused child to mourn alone. The grief children experience over the loss of a loved animal is quite real, and that feeling needs to be acknowledged. In quality and intensity, grief for a pet can be much the same as grief for a well-loved human. In fact, the stages of grief children experience are the same whether a pet or a person has died. Even as you're grappling with your own feelings of loss, keep in mind the following stages of grief your children will be experiencing.

Stage One: Shock and Numbness

When the pet first dies, your children will feel shock and numbness. During this period they may have difficulty accepting the fact that the pet is dead, and children younger than eight may have trouble understanding exactly what "dead" is. The following dialogue, between a parent and a five-year-old whose pet dog died in his sleep during the night, will give you an idea of the kinds of things you can say to your children to help them accept the reality of what has happened.

"Mommy, Tora won't get up."

"That's because Tora is dead, Karine."

"Dead? What do you mean 'dead'?"

"Dead means that Tora has stopped breathing and his heart has stopped beating."

"How come?"

"Because sooner or later everything that lives has to die."

"Now make Tora better."

"I'm sorry, honey. I can't make Tora better. This isn't like when your scooter broke and I fixed it. Or like when you had a stomachache and Daddy gave you medicine to make you feel better. This is different. When you're dead you can't be fixed."

"Why?"

"Because that's the way things are. Eventually everything dies. Remember how we planted seeds in the garden last spring?"

"Yes."

"And remember how they grew and became beautiful flowers and we enjoyed looking at them?"

"Yes."

"And then after a while all the flowers wilted and never came back. Remember?"

"Yes."

"Well, that's what life and death are all about. Tora used to be a little puppy. Then he grew up to be a big dog and had lots of fun with us for a while. Then he got older, and now he's dead."

Older children may want and need more specific and factual information. In that case, it's appropriate to talk about the cause of death. You can explain how illness or traumatic injury affects health. This way the death of your pet can become a learning experience.

It will take a while for your children to understand and accept what you say about the death of their pet, but this kind of explanation gives them information to think about and it will help them move on to the next stage.

Stage Two: Raw Feelings

The second stage of grief involves feelings of extreme unhappiness. Also, during this stage, your children may lash out in anger at the vet or even at themselves for failing to save the pet.

Show Respect for the Loss.   When your children express their sorrow or anger, respect this display of grief. It's best not to minimize the loss by saying, "It's just an animal." It's not just an animal to your child; it was a friend and confidant and object of affection.

Also, this isn't the time to try to ease the magnitude of the loss by saying, "We'll get you another cat." Another cat can never replace the uniqueness of the lost animal. In this second stage, it's important to recognize what the pet meant to the child and not to rush the mourning process by getting a new pet too soon.

Accept Children's Expressions of Emotion. Don't suggest to your children that it's weak or foolish to repeatedly cry and talk about the deceased animal. Encourage your children to let their feelings out. The freedom to express feelings—be they sorrow, anger, guilt, or whatever—is very important to the grieving process.

When your children verbalize their feelings, you can be most helpful if you simply listen and give feedback that lets them know you understand. If, for example, your child tearfully says, "Every time I look outside I expect to see Shane come running across the yard," you might respond, "I know how you feel. Sometimes I get so sad when I look at the places where he used to be."

Stage Three: Acceptance and New Beginnings

The final stage of grief is reached when the child has accepted the loss of the pet and has reached the state of resolution and re-organization. At this time, your children will clearly understand that the pet will not be coming back and they will have accepted the finality of that fact. Your children may indicate their readiness to reorganize their lives without their pet by admitting, "It would be nice to have a cat again." Now, children will feel that a new pet is not a replacement for the old one, but an animal with whom they can start a whole new relationship.

The length of a child's mourning period can't be predicted. Some children can go through these three stages in just one week. But if the child-pet bond was really close and long-standing, it may take eight to ten months, which is about the same amount of grieving time expected when a human loved one dies.

Whatever the intensity of feelings and the manner of mourning, the death of a pet is a milestone event in your child's life. It can be a valuable experience if you take the time to talk about this sometimes taboo subject and let your children know that you respect their feelings. Talking about the death of a pet is a good way to help your children understand death and prepare them for later losses.

Suggested Reading

For Parents

Nieberg, Herbert, and Arlene Fischer. *Pet Loss: A Thoughtful Guide for Adults and Children*. New York: Harper & Row, 1982.

For Children Aged Four to Seven

Dabcovich, Lydia. *Mrs. Huggins and Her Hen Hannah*. New York: Dutton, 1985.

Keller, Holly. *Goodbye, Max*. New York: Greenwillow Books, 1987.

Kroll, Virginia L. *Helen the Fish*. Niles, Ill.: A. Whitman, 1992.

For Children Aged Eight to Twelve

Orgel, Doris. *Whiskers, Once and Always*. New York: Viking Kestrel, 1986.

Rogers, Fred. *When a Pet Dies*. New York: Putnam, 1988.

Stolz, Mary. *King Emmett the Second*. New York: Greenwillow Books, 1991.

Viorst, Judith. *The Tenth Good Thing About Barney*. New York: Atheneum, 1971.

Dentist or Medical Doctor Visit

"Why do I have to go?"

"What will the doctor do to me?"

"Will it hurt?"

"Ma, I don't want to see the doctor!"

These questions tumbled one after the other from the little four-year-old as she sat in the doctor's waiting room. I listened in, curious to hear how her mom would answer the questions.

"Shhhh!" hissed her mom. "You're going to see the doctor and that's that. It will be our turn soon."

Looking very frightened, the child continued to whine as she clung to her mother's arm for comfort.

I don't think this mother was being intentionally cruel to her child. Surely her daughter had been to the doctor before, and perhaps this mother had grown tired of answering the same questions over and over. But it's precisely this repetition of factual information that eases the fear some children associate with visits to a dentist or doctor of medicine.

This mother could have easily calmed her daughter's fears. She might have taken some time to prepare her for what would happen during the visit and she could have suggested some simple coping techniques to ease her worries.

There are several ways that you can help ease the concerns of your young children who are especially fearful of or unfamiliar with doctors or dentists. If your children seem fearful of doctors, take some time before the visit to prepare them for what will probably occur.

Establishing a Positive Attitude

Fear is a contagious thing. So if you have your own fears about going to a dentist or medical doctor, you'll have to put them aside before talking to your children. If you're frightened by your child's illness, express your concerns to your spouse or a friend—but not to your child. If the sound of the dentist's drill makes your hair stand on end, put on a smile and make it stick when you talk to your kids about dental work.

You can convey a positive feeling about medical and dental care if you can keep all your discussions about health upbeat. When the subject of illness or cavities comes up in your family conversations, always present the doctors' roles in a positive and supportive way. You might say, "I remember when I was so sick [or had a cavity] last year, the doctor knew just what to do to make me feel better. I was so glad I went for some help."

Also, try to avoid disciplining with threats related to personal care. One mother I know always urged her children to brush their teeth with the warning, "If you don't brush, you'll have to go to the dentist to get your teeth drilled. Then you'll find out what real pain is all about." Naturally, when it was time for her kids to visit the dentist, they didn't want to go, and became even more fearful when they were reminded, "Don't cry to me. It's your own fault for not brushing your teeth like I told you to."

We all probably say things like "If you don't wear your hat, you're gonna get sick and it will be your own fault if you have to go to the doctor." But next time, think twice about using this kind of motivation.

Once you've settled your own feelings about medical and dental visits, it's time to talk to your kids.

Preparing Children for a Visit to a Medical Doctor

Before visiting the doctor, discuss what's going to happen. Talk to your little ones who are unfamiliar with medical procedures about what they can expect. Review the detail of the visit even with older children who will benefit from the reassurance of repetition. Here are some things you might say:

• "The nurse may tell you to take off all your clothes except your underwear."

• "The doctor may ask you to step on a scale so he can weigh you and measure your height. This won't hurt at all."

• "The doctor may use an instrument called a stethoscope. This is simply a tube that lets the doctor hear the sounds of your heart and lungs. This does not hurt at all."

• "The doctor may use a small flashlight to look into small spaces like your ears. This won't hurt you at all."

• "The doctor may take your blood pressure by pumping up a special cuff around your arm. This will give you a tight feeling around your arm for just a short time [demonstrate by lightly squeezing the child's arm], but it doesn't hurt."

• "The doctor or nurse may give you a shot with a needle. The shot will hurt for a minute or two, but it's very important to have this because the medicine you get from the needle will help protect your body against germs that could make you sick."

• "The doctor may take a blood sample by sticking your finger and taking out a little blood. The doctor will examine this blood to make sure that everything is okay. It will hurt when your finger is first pricked, but only for just a second."

Add any other details you know will be a part of your visit. If this doctor gives children some kind of treat at the end of the visit, be sure to emphasize this positive point.

Preparing Children for a Visit to the Dentist

When you schedule a visit to the dentist, the fear your children may feel probably comes from the unknown aspects of this adventure. Dental visits don't usually occur as frequently as visits to a pediatrician, so your children may need some time to process all the facts you can give them. You might tell them details such as these:

- "You're going to the dentist next Thursday. This is a doctor who takes care of teeth. This doctor wants to help you keep your teeth strong and healthy."

- "When we get to the dentist's office, you'll sit in a chair that's kind of like the recliner we have in the living room, but it's more fun because the doctor can make it go up and down."

- "The doctor will put a big bib on you. Everybody—even Mom and Dad—gets a bib at the dentist's. This keeps the patients' clothes dry while the doctor is cleaning their teeth."

- "There will be a bright light shining down on you. This helps the doctor see all your teeth."

- "The doctor puts her dental tools on a little tray by your chair. This tray holds things like little hand mirrors, metal toothpicks, and cotton balls."

- "The doctor will ask you to open your mouth real wide and then she'll put her little mirror into your mouth to look at all your teeth."

After you set the stage, discuss the procedures the dentist will follow. Mention the use of the X-ray machine and the process of teeth cleaning.

If you know your child needs a filling, explain what this means. Give the facts about tooth decay and tooth repair. You might say something like: "Sometimes our teeth get small holes in them called cavities. If these holes aren't filled in by a dentist, they become bigger and deeper and they start to hurt. To fix a cavity, the dentist will put some cream on your gum by the cavity. Then you'll feel a pinch [don't necessarily mention "needle"], and then your tooth will fall asleep."

You don't have to use the words *pain* or *needle* or say "be brave" in connection with a visit to the dentist. The newest dental techniques are rarely painful if the patient is relaxed and not overly fearful.

Teaching Children Coping Strategies

If, for whatever reason, your children seem genuinely afraid of the doctor, you can help them better deal with the inevitable visit by teaching them a few simple coping strategies.

Role Play Together. Role playing helps young children practice going for a medical or dental exam. When you first introduce this game, suggest to your children that you pretend you're the doctor and they're the patient. Welcome them into your "office" and begin the exam. Then suggest switching roles—you be the patient and let your children be the doctor. This gives your children a feeling of control and hands-on practice with what's going to happen. You might also encourage your children to play doctor with their dolls and stuffed animals—they too need to stay healthy.

Practice Positive Self-talk. In stressful situations we all too commonly say negative things to ourselves, like "I can't do this" or "This is going to be awful." This kind of mental conversation increases stress.

Teach your children how to relax by saying nice and encouraging things to themselves. Before going to the doctor's, help your children practice saying things like "This is a good dentist [doctor]. I'm doing well. I can handle this. I'm doing great!"

Remember Deep Breathing.   The short, quick breaths we take in stressful situations reduce our oxygen intake. This can cause light-headedness, hyperventilation, and other stress-related symptoms. You can teach your children to calm themselves before they enter the doctor's office simply by taking a deep breath and letting it out slowly. If they do this about five times, they'll begin their exam in a more relaxed state.

Try Guided Imagery.   One more stress-reduction trick is really a little mental game your children can play anywhere, anytime. Teach them to think about a relaxing, fun place while they're in the dentist's chair or on the physician's examining table. Help them imagine going to the baseball field, the lake, or the amusement park—anywhere that makes them feel happy and unafraid. This really does ease the discomfort of stressful situations.

Final Tips

A visit to a medical doctor or a dentist can be upsetting for some young children, but it's an inevitable occurrence that can't be avoided. So, the best you can do is reduce the feelings of apprehension and fear by giving your children some control over the situation:

- Give them an opportunity to talk about their fears.
- Be honest about what's going to happen.
- Teach them a few simple coping skills to help them relax.

Suggested Reading

For Children Aged Four to Seven

Berenstain, Stan, and Jan Berenstain. *The Berenstain Bears Go to the Doctor.* New York: Random Books for Young Readers, 1981.

Berenstain, Stan, and Jan Berenstain. *The Berenstain Bears Visit the Dentist.* New York: Random Books for Young Readers, 1981.

DeSantis, Kenny. *A Doctor's Tools.* New York: Dodd, Mead, 1985.

DeSantis, Kenny. *A Dentist's Tools.* New York: Dodd, Mead, 1988.

Forsey, Christopher. *At the Doctor.* New York: F. Watts, 1983.

Kuklin, Susan. *When I See My Doctor.* New York: Bradbury Press, 1988.

Rogers, Fred. *Going to the Doctor.* New York: Putnam, 1986.

Disasters—Accidents and Natural Catastrophes

Gloria and her seven-year-old son stood shivering in the night air. They watched the flames that hugged their home reach toward the sky with ever-growing strength and intensity. They watched the streams from firehoses attack through windows and doors, but the water seemed to retreat fearfully as it ran back out the front door, cascading down the steps and out to the street.

"When I think about that night," remembers Gloria, "standing there watching everything go up in flames, I'm always surprised by how numb I felt. I didn't cry or yell or panic. I just stood there staring. Jacob, too, was very quiet. The only thing I remember him saying was, 'Ma, what about all my baseball cards? Are they gonna be ruined?' Funny how in the face of total destruction, baseball cards was on the top of his list of worries."

Losing his entire baseball card collection to a fire that he had no control over probably bothered Jacob more than his mother could imagine. Indeed, because of their sudden, violent, and destructive nature, disasters such as fires, earthquakes, tornados, floods, and hurricanes, can leave lasting psychological scars on children who survive them.

If your family should experience a catastrophic tragedy, you can lessen the impact on your children, whatever their age, with careful attention to their feelings, fears, concerns, and worries as they proceed through the three stages characteristic of emotional disturbance.

Stage One: Shock and Confusion

In the first stage after a disaster, your children will be in shock, appearing stunned and bewildered. Their attention will be noticeably restricted; you'll notice little responsiveness to outside stimuli like loud noises or major commotions. Their behavior will be reflexive and automatic; this means they will respond to your directions like robots, without comment or question. You may also notice that your children appear to lack any feelings about what has happened. Although physical signs of stress such as shaking, sweating, or clinging may be evident, your children may shift to a neutral gear emotionally until they can process what has happened.

During this first stage, understand that your children are overwhelmed by their feelings. Your physical presence will be more important than words at this time. But when you do talk to them, be comforting and reassuring, with comments like, "I'm here with you. Everything is going to be okay. We made it through."

Immediately in this first stage, you'll need to monitor your own stress reactions. It is a well-established fact that children whose parents cope well with calamity experience less severe and usually temporary reactions. Remember: if you react hysterically, so will your children. If you react with concerned calm, so will your children. Of course, you may have your own emotional upsets after a disaster, but do keep in mind that you can help your children adjust and go on with their lives if you can keep your outward signs of distress under control.

On the other hand, when your children do witness your disturbed reaction, be honest about your feelings. It's good for your children to see that you too are shaken by the event to an appropriate degree and yet can talk about it and put it in some degree of positive perspective.

To do this you might say, "I can't help but cry over what the hurricane did to our beautiful house and neighborhood. But I know that we're all very lucky to be alive and healthy and that's what's most important."

Or, "I feel so angry and so sad at the same time when I look at the damage the flood did to our house. But I know we can get new furniture and rugs and get everything back in order real soon."

Or, "I'm really upset about losing our apartment in the fire, but now I'm looking forward to finding a new and even better apartment. Apartments can be replaced. The main thing is that we're safe."

Stage Two: Emotional Response

When the initial stresses have ceased or when you and your children have escaped immediate danger, then your children will begin to gradually experience the total impact of the tragedy. These are some common symptoms you might see in your children during this post-traumatic second stage:

• *Fears and anxieties.* There is often continuing anxiety about recurrence of the disaster. Because of this, your children may show an exaggerated sense of dependence on you: they may want to be with you at all times; they may cry if they don't see you; they may question your every move for fear you'll leave their side.

• *Sleep disturbances.* Your children may experience sleep disturbances that are related to the extreme sense of dependency they feel at this time. Their concern over being away from you will show itself in a resistance to bedtime or the refusal to sleep alone. The ongoing fears and anxieties may also cause recurrent nightmares.

• *School avoidance.* It's not uncommon for children to refuse to go back to school after a disaster. This confuses parents, who view school as a place where friends gather and normalcy remains. But to children who have experienced a catastrophic tragedy, school is a place where they can't be near their parents, on whom they are extremely dependent at this time and who may be injured if the disaster recurs during school hours. Fear of abandonment is common among disaster victims and frequently leads to intense separation anxiety.

• *Anger and resentment.* Children may erupt uncharacteristically in explosive anger tantrums. They may break and throw things or strike out at loved ones. The anger is rooted in confusion: they can't understand why something like this would happen to them, and they are angry that they weren't protected from danger.

• *Regression.* To express their need to be cared for, protected, and comforted, some children will regress to babyish behaviors. Thumb-sucking, bed-wetting, clinging, whining, and even crawling are not unusual reactions by children of any age.

Relieving Stress During Stage Two

When you talk to children of any age during the second stage of recovery, your goal is to relieve their stress. You can do this by following these guidelines:

Give the Facts. It's important for you and your children to acknowledge that something disastrous has happened. Children, especially, are most fearful when they do not understand what's happened around them. So give your children accurate information about what happened and why. Share what you know about the truth of the disaster and its likely impact on the family. Your children will want to know when their lives will return to normal. Be honest about this and avoid giving false assurances. In many instances, the victim's world will never be the same, and statements to the contrary will instill false hope. So give an accurate appraisal of the situation.

"Why is this happening?"

If your children ask, "Why are there hurricanes [floods, tornados, and so forth]?" tell them, "A hurricane is something caused by nature, like the rain and the snow and the wind. Sometimes the force of nature can become very strong and destructive, but it's not anyone's fault. It just happens, and although we can prepare ourselves so we stay as safe as possible, there's nothing that can be done to stop these things from happening.

Your children might start questioning the random nature of the universe and ask, "Why did the hurricane hit our house but not Timmy's house?" You can tell them, "There is no definite reason. Nature has no exact plan for what it does. The force of a hurricane just zigzags around, and this time, our house happened to be in its path."

"Why would anyone do something like that?"

If your family is injured in an arson fire or a bombing, your children may ask about the perpetrator's motives. You might tell them, "There are people in this world who do bad things. This happens for many reasons. Some people feel so full of hate they do things that are angry and violent. Other people are mentally ill and do terrible things without realizing how awful or destructive their actions really are." (See "Television and Media Violence" and "War" in Part Two of this book for additional information.)

"Will it happen again?"

As they recover from the disaster, children will soon wonder, "Will this happen to us again?" Give your children the truth about the likelihood of a recurrence. If you feel that this particular catastrophe could happen again, say so, but be sure to assure your children that you will be better prepared next time. Giving your children concrete ways to protect themselves is an excellent way to relieve the fear of being a powerless victim. If, for example, your family has experienced a flood, map out how you'll monitor the rain and the rising of the river next time, and explain how the town is perhaps uniting to prevent a recurrence by building rain tunnels or higher river banks. Give your children the truth and some hope.

Be Comforting and Reassuring.   Your understanding and support can speed recovery and, in many cases, prevent serious problems later. You might say, for example, "We're all together and nothing has happened to us." Or, "We're going to stay real close to you now and we'll take care of you." In the initial stages of recovery, physically hold your children as often as possible and spend more time with them than usual. By exhibiting courage and calmness, you can give your children the strength they need to face their fears.

It's important for the family to remain together during and after a crisis because you are your child's main source of security. Particularly during times of stress, children need this sense of belonging to and being protected by the family. So, for example, don't leave your children with a neighbor or relative immediately after a crisis, while you go out to inspect the damage. Keep all your children close to you for some time to alleviate their fears of being abandoned and unprotected. According to Anna Freud, the noted child psychoanalyst, "Love for the parents is so great that it is a far greater shock for a child to be suddenly separated from his mother than to have a house collapse on top of him."

Be careful, however, to avoid the two extremes of reassurance. Don't coddle your children and keep them close in ways that will feed their fears. Don't, for example, say, "You poor child. What a terrible ordeal for someone so young. This should never have happened to you. I don't know how you'll ever get over this." Obviously, these words of "comfort" are frightening. Likewise, you won't be able to reassure your children by ignoring the terror they've experienced. Don't say, "Oh, it was nothing. You're too brave to be scared by an earthquake." This implies that children's natural fears are unfounded and should not be voiced.

Encourage Your Children to Talk About Their Feelings.
After a disaster, it's important to be able to share anger and fears with others who show interest and concern, so let your children know that it's okay to cry, yell, or complain. The intensity and duration of children's symptoms decrease more rapidly when their parents are able to take time away from their own concerns after a disaster to talk to their children about what happened and discuss how they feel about the experience.

Some children need no invitation to talk; they need only a willing listener. For these children, try to make yourself available to listen even when you're obviously distressed and upset yourself.

Other children won't say anything unless you help them find the words they need to vent their feelings. To do this, you might start by offering your own feelings: "I'm so angry about losing our beach house in the hurricane. How do you feel about it?" Younger children might find outlets for pent-up feelings in play. Encourage these children to draw pictures that show how they feel. Let them act out the disaster with their dolls or stuffed animals. Give them clay or water toys to recreate the episode. During these play sessions, invite them to explain to you what they believe happened and how they feel about it.

Stage Three: Return to Normalcy

The final stage of emotional recovery finds your child's life returning to normalcy. You can speed this return by making an effort to resume your daily schedule as soon as possible. Even if you are living in a shelter, with friends, or among the ruins of your own home, try to keep things such as meals, play, school, and bedtime on a schedule similar to pre-disaster days. Predictability and order help children feel in control of their environment—a feeling they are groping to recover after a catastrophic event.

You can also encourage your children to help you return the family to normalcy. Ask them to participate in simple, useful tasks as soon as possible. For example, you might ask a child to help clean up the home after a flood, or clean up the yard after a hurricane, or wash down salvageable items after a fire. It's comforting to a child to see things being put back in order and family routines being reestablished.

Dealing with Excessive or Extended Stress Reactions

Most children show only temporary post-trauma symptoms. But a minority will exhibit long-term reactions of a severe nature. At least ten to twenty percent of children who have experienced a trauma will need post-disaster mental health counseling, to counter chronic anxiety, disorientation, depression, personality changes, and the like. If, after a week or two, you see that your child is not able to resume his or her daily schedule or that the child continues to show signs of severe emotional upset, it's time to see a mental health professional. Putting the tragedy in perspective and in the past will keep the incident from causing long-term emotional problems in the future.

Suggested Resources

American Red Cross
Contact your local chapter, listed in the phone book.

Cooperative Disaster Child Care
P.O. Box 188
500 Main Street
New Windsor, MD 21776

Suggested Reading

For Parents

Terr, Lenore. *Too Scared to Cry: Psychic Trauma in Childhood.* New York: Harper & Row, 1990.

Children Aged Four to Seven

Branley, Franklyn M. *Flash, Crash, Rumble and Roll.* New York: Thomas Y. Crowell, 1964.
Lyon, George Ella. *Come a Tide.* New York: Orchard Books, 1990.
Zolowtow, Charlotte. *The Storm Book.* New York: Harper & Row, 1952.

Children Aged Eight to Twelve

Arnold, Caroline. *Coping with Natural Disasters.* New York: Walker, 1988.
Rutland, Jonathan. *The Violent Earth.* New York: Random House, 1987.

Divorce

Their marriage ended as so many do—in small, barely noticeable, silent steps. One night before going to bed, Ted sat down next to his wife and told her he was leaving in the morning. "I just can't live like this anymore," he confessed. "This distance between us is unbearable."

Mary sat stunned and numb. She knew their marriage had ended a long time ago, but still, the finality of this move seemed so abrupt.

The next morning Ted packed his bags and headed for the front door.

"Daddy," called five-year-old Lee Ann. "Where are you going?"

Ted glanced back at his wife and then crouched down by Lee Ann. "Daddy has to go away for a while," he said. "But I'll call you real soon. Okay?" Fighting back tears, Ted stood up and walked out.

"Daddy, wait!" yelled Lee Ann. "Where are you going? When are you coming back?"

Feeling scared and confused, Lee Ann ran back to her mom looking for answers. Holding her daughter tight to her breast, Mary whispered through her tears, "Daddy's not coming back sweetheart. He's not coming back."

Lee Ann had just joined the millions of children of divorce in America. And, as is so often the case, her parents unintentionally said and did things that will cause Lee Ann to suffer problems and negative feelings that could have been avoided with some advance warning or explanation.

For one parent to physically leave is traumatic for children. That's why the importance of preparing children for the separation cannot be overemphasized. When children are properly prepared for the divorce, they can better cope with what is to come, without losing confidence and trust in their parents.

There is no one best way to talk to your kids about a separation or divorce. So much of what you say will depend on your personal circumstance and your child's age. But there are some general guidelines for discussing this very difficult subject that can ease the pain and hurt your children are bound to feel.

When to Tell Your Kids About Your Divorce Decision

Children must be told of their parents' decision to separate and pursue a divorce. Once Ted and Mary came to a final, irrevocable decision that the marriage was over, they should have made plans to talk to their daughter about that fact before Ted walked out the door. Because they didn't prepare her, Lee Ann began her new family life at a double disadvantage: (1) she didn't hear about the decision until after her father was already gone, and (2) her mother had to do all the talking so Lee Ann was left to wonder what role her father really played in this event.

Once you're sure the marriage is over, following these guidelines will help you choose the right time to talk to your children about this decision:

Talk to Your Children When a Physical Split is Imminent.
If you tell your children long before the actual split, they'll spend

too much time worrying and plotting and wondering if there's any way this isn't really going to happen. One to two weeks ahead of the separation is probably best.

Tell Your Children at Home, When You Have Lots of Time to Talk.   Don't break this news in public—at the park, in a restaurant, or the like. And don't tell your kids at a time when you or they have to be out the door for work or school. Give them time to absorb your announcement, ask questions, cry if they want, and look for assurances in your hug.

Talk to Your Children When You've Attained a Sense of Emotional Calm.   No matter how angry or upset you may be about the breakup of your marriage, don't dump your emotional load on your kids. Certainly, you can share your feelings of sadness and upset, but try to stay calm.

How to Tell Kids About Your Divorce Decision

Even in the worst of marriages, the kids are hurt by the final announcement of a separation between their parents. There's nothing you can say to get around the hurt, but how you present the news can ease the intensity of their reactions.

Both Parents Should Tell Children About a Divorce Decision.   When both parents sit down and give the news, children are more likely to accept the finality of the decision. If only one parent breaks the news, the children may think there was an argument and the other parent will soon be back to make up. Telling children about a divorce decision together also lessens the possibility that the children will hear two completely different stories or confusing contradictions from each parent.

If your spouse can't be there when you break the news, arrange for him or her to call or write the children almost immediately after your talk. Whenever possible, kids need to hear this information from both parents. If, on the other hand, your spouse is totally unavailable due to disappearance, mental illness, hostility, withdrawal, or the like, you'll have to handle the discussion alone. In this case, you can explain (without anger or judgment) your spouse's silence by saying something like, "Your dad [mom] has an illness [or whatever] and is not able to talk to you about this right now. But I'm here any time you want to talk."

Tell All Your Children at the Same Time.   The presence of siblings can cushion the shock and provide a sense of support and family continuity. It also gives younger children permission to turn to their older siblings for support and clarification later. You may want to speak to older children alone to offer a more detailed explanation, but the initial announcement should be made with the whole family present.

Be Straightforward.   Children should be informed of the impending separation in an honest, straightforward manner—no lies, no excuses, no false promises. Stating the situation firmly and without hesitation will convey the finality of the decision.

What to Tell Your Kids About Your Divorce Decision

When you talk to your children about your decision to divorce you should attempt to reach three goals:

1. Give assurances of both parents' continued love.
2. Relieve your children of blame.
3. Ease the trauma of the life changes that will follow.

Open your dialogue in a straightforward way. You might say something like, "Mommy and Daddy are not happy living together and we have decided that it is best if we get a divorce and live in different houses. We both still love you very much and we'll always be your mommy and daddy."

After you break the news, your children may begin to ask questions or you may want to supply further details. Usually, the question foremost in children's minds is "Why?"

"Why?"

Children do not need to know all the painful personal reasons for the divorce. Infidelity, substance abuse, alienation, and such are adult reasons for divorce; children need know only that you no longer get along and have made a decision to live apart.

Let your children know that the decision was not made lightly or suddenly. Tell your children, "We have tried for a long time to work out our problems and have put a lot of thought into this decision. We are now finally convinced that we cannot possibly live together any longer."

If your children push you to give more detailed reasons, tell them that the reasons are personal or private and just between the parents.

Then take the focus away from the reasons for the divorce and put it on the children by telling them, "Our decision to separate will have an effect on you so we wanted to talk to you about what's going to happen." This is, after all, what most interests your children.

"What About Me?"

Once again, assure your children that married people divorce each other, but they don't divorce their children. Be sure your kids hear you say, "Our decision has nothing to do with our love for you. You will always be loved and cared for by both of us."

Make sure your children know that even the departing parent still feels great love for them and will continue to offer love, comfort, and encouragement.

Then give your kids whatever specifics you have about any changes in the family structure. Tell them whatever you can in answer to questions like the following.

"Where will I live?"

Explain the details of any change in your child's living environment. Discuss the reason why you may have to move to a smaller apartment, or why you're selling the house, or why you're all moving to Grandma's for a while.

"Where will [the departing parent] live?"

Take your children to the departing parent's new home. Walk them around the neighborhood. Try to make them feel comfortable and welcome.

"Will I ever see [the departing parent]?"

Explain again that both parents still love the child and even the departing parent will make arrangements to visit. You might tell older children why one parent has custody and not the other, or why you've chosen to share joint custody.

"When and where will I get to see [the departing parent]?"

Let your children talk about when and where they'd like to visit the absent parent. You might think about places to visit and things to do on visitation days. Regardless of how you feel about parental visitation rights, always keep your conversations about this subject upbeat and positive.

How Your Kids May React to Your Decision to Divorce

In general, the degree of a child's reaction to divorce depends on how the parents react. The less conflict, hostility, and emotional distress the children witness, the better able they are to cope and adjust. However, despite your best efforts to ease your children through the tough times of a divorce, there are some common, age-related, negative reactions you can expect.

Responses of Children Aged Three to Five

Young children cannot grasp all the complexities of the decision to divorce. In a very simplistic way, many will assume the blame. A young child may figure, "If I had been good and hadn't made Daddy yell at me he wouldn't have left."

Other young children may become fearful of complete abandonment. They reason that if one parent has left, the other might leave, too. Three-year-old Carrie cried every night at bedtime after her mother left home. Her cries subsided only if her dad agreed to sit by her bed until she fell asleep. This fear of losing both parents is why many young children of divorce become very clingy and will cry at even the most temporary separations—such as when the remaining parent goes to work or even to the store. These children worry that they will be left with no parents at all.

Some young children will show their fears and insecurities through developmental regression. After his parent's separation, four-year-old Nathan, for example, searched the house for the security blanket he had given up a year earlier. Confused by the changes, young children will look backward for security and strength. They may revert to behaviors like thumb-sucking, bed-wetting, whining, and tantrums.

If your young children begin to show these signs of distress, give them freedom to express their fears. Indulge their regressions by ignoring them; on their own, most children return to their preregression stage within just a few weeks. Give your continued patience and love by dealing kindly with the sudden fear of separation. If they want to go with you every time you walk out to the mailbox, let them come. This fear of abandonment won't last long.

Also, encourage your children to talk to you about their feelings. Young children can do this best through play. Using dolls or stuffed animals, suggest to your children a game called Play House. Let your children talk for the mommy and daddy dolls. Encourage them to have the mommy and daddy dolls talk to the child doll. The dialogues your children make up will give you insights into what's really on their mind.

Responses of Children Aged Six to Eleven

Older children, who are more aware of what divorce actually means, may express their hurt in a number of physical and emotional ways. Your children may develop headaches or stomachaches. They may suffer nightmares, loss of appetite, or irregular sleep patterns. Most predictably, these older children will show signs of profound sadness and anger.

Their sorrow can be seen in many forms. They may cry a lot. They may regress to a weepy, whiny stage. They may become lethargic or withdrawn. If you ask, "What's the matter?" they'll pull away or sadly report, "Oh, nothing (sigh)."

This mental malaise can affect a child's ability to concentrate and will therefore influence school achievement. If you notice behavior changes in your children, it's probably best to tell their teacher about the divorce. Teachers can become supportive allies if they know the reasons for sudden moodiness or behavior problems.

Anger also has many faces. Older children are developing a strict sense of right and wrong—and divorce seems "wrong." Nine-year-old Janet showed her anger in her irritable response to anything her mother said. If her mom asked simply, "What do you want for breakfast?" Janet would snap, "What do you care? All you care about is yourself." And then stomp out of the room.

Other children may show their anger through a form of passive aggression. Ten-year-old Jason, for example, never spoke harshly to his dad after he moved out of the home, but instead chose to ignore his presence. He pretended he didn't hear anything his father said. He purposely would "forget" he was supposed to be home for a visit. He would "accidently" hang up the receiver if his dad called on the phone. Like many preadolescents, Jason felt a strong sense of loyalty to the custodial parent and directed his anger at his dad who had left.

It's best to handle the reactions of children ages six to eleven with lots of patience and understanding. Although you should maintain whatever form of discipline you used before the separation, try to be patient with your children as they adjust to their new family situation.

Pediatric specialists advise parents to allow angry children to express their feelings openly. The angry response of preadolescent children to divorce, they say, is difficult to modify because it serves a defensive purpose in warding off pain and grief. What you can do is recognize the cause of the anger and always keep your door open.

If your children don't seem willing to talk to you about their feelings, you might initiate conversation by saying something like this:

"Sometimes I feel upset about the divorce. Do you ever feel that way?

Or, "Have you noticed how things have changed around here since your father left?"

Or, "What's it like for you going back and forth between here and your mother's place?"

Don't push too hard for a response, but keep offering your sympathetic shoulder. If repeatedly given the opportunity, most children will eventually talk about what's on their mind.

The following general do's and don'ts will also help your children talk about your divorce decision and accept this change in their lives.

General Do's and Don'ts

Do's

- Encourage your children to verbalize their feelings and ask questions.
- Listen closely to their concerns.
- Discourage children's wishful thinking that this will blow over and that soon they will have both parents

together again in a happy home (even if this is your own wish).

- Remember that telling children once is usually not enough. Repeated conversations give children the chance to digest the painful news and accept the reality of it.
- Repeatedly assure your children that the divorce is not their fault.
- Tell your children that both parents love them now and always will.

Don'ts

- Don't be indecisive. If the divorce is going to happen, say so firmly, allowing no room for leeway.
- Don't blame your former spouse for the breakup (even if the fault is clearly on one side).
- Don't bad-mouth your former spouse in front of the children.
- Don't ever ask your children to choose sides.
- Don't look to your children for emotional support.
- Don't discourage expression of emotions by saying things like "Be brave. Show us how strong you are."
- Don't try to minimize the loss with comments like "Oh, you never saw your father much anyway."

When to Seek Professional Help

Although the majority of parents and children adapt to the changes brought about by divorce, sometimes professional counseling can help families through the transitional time. If you or your children experience symptoms of distress such as long crying jags, serious depression or anxiety, decreased work or school performance, or explosive temper tantrums for more than six weeks, you may find that professional mental health counseling—both individual and family therapy—may help alleviate the pain, prevent future problems, and provide needed emotional support.

Even after the first six months' adjustment period, your divorce will continue to have a major impact on your kids. For the rest of their lives, the breakup of the family will affect holidays, birthdays, graduations, and the like. You will continually need to make a real effort to keep talking about feelings and concerns as your children's ages and needs change.

Suggested Resources

The Divorce Resource Center
P.O. Box 98
Flushing, NY 11361
718-224-5947

Suggested Reading

For Parents

Johnson, Laurene, and Georglyn Rosenfeld. *Divorced Kids: What You Need to Know to Help Kids Survive a Divorce*. Nashville: Thomas Nelson, 1990.

Kalter, Neil. *Growing Up with Divorce: Helping Your Child Avoid Immediate and Later Emotional Problems*. New York: Free Press, 1990.

Rogers, Fred, and Clare O'Brien. *Mister Rogers Talks with Families About Divorce*. New York: Berkley Books, 1987.

For Children Aged Four to Seven

Brown, Laurene Drasny, and Marc Brown. *Dinosaurs Divorce: A Guide for Changing Families*. Boston: Joy Street Books, 1986.

Christiansen, C. B. *My Mother's House, My Father's House*. New York: Atheneum, 1989.

Haxen, Barbara. *Two Homes to Live In: A Child's Eye View of Divorce*. New York: Human Sciences Press, 1978.

Helmering, Doris Wild. *I Have Two Families*. Nashville: Abingdon, 1981.

For Children Aged Eight to Twelve

Adler, C. S. *Tuna Fish Thanksgiving*. New York: Clarion Books, 1992.

Cleary, Beverly. *Dear Mr. Henshaw*. New York: Morrow, 1983.

Cleary, Beverly. *Strider*. New York: Morrow, 1991.

Danziger, Paula. *The Divorce Express*. New York: Delacorte Press, 1982.

Dying Child

Little Brett, who had been napping on the couch, awoke to the sound of her mother's tears. Linda had been crying all afternoon and now her eyes were swollen nearly shut. Her heart ached as the pediatrician's words echoed in rhythm with the pounding pain that racked her head: *"leukemia, leukemia, leukemia,"* over and over and over.

As Linda lifted her head off the kitchen table, Brett climbed up onto her lap, nestled against her breast, and whispered, "Mommy, am I going to die?"

Sobbing, Linda hugged her child close to her heart and vowed, "Oh, my darling daughter, no. I won't let you die. I won't."

This happened four years ago. Now, after an exhaustive journey through the medical maze of cancer therapy, the end is very near. The doctors say Brett can hold on only a few days more.

"Mommy," cries Brett, "am I going to die?"

This time Linda has no words of comfort. Holding her daughter close to her aching heart she whispers only, "Oh, my darling daughter."

Talking to a child about his or her death is surely the most painful task a parent can undertake. Emotional trauma surrounds the situation, making it extremely hard for parents to know what to say and do. Quandaries abound: "Should I keep the severity of the illness a secret?" "What's the point of telling a child he's going to die?" "Can she really understand death?" "I can't bring myself to talk to my child about death. I just can't do it."

Despite the difficulty, most of your conversations with your dying child will come from your heart—not from scripted phrases suggested in this chapter. What we can offer you, though, are some insights gleaned from research in this field and lessons learned from other parents in the same heartbreaking circumstance.

The Stages of Grief

Dr. Elisabeth Kübler-Ross, an expert on dying, has described five stages of response that parents can expect to go through when they realize their child is dying. These stages influence how parents talk to their child and what words they say.

Denial

Characteristically, the parents of a dying child show an initial reaction of denial. During this stage they do not tell the child anything about the fatal condition because they believe death will not occur. Instead, they tell themselves there's been a mistake, there'll be a miraculous cure, this isn't really happening.

Anger

When the early feelings of denial cannot be maintained any longer, they are replaced by manifestations of anger and rage. The children often witness angry outbursts as their parents lash out at their physicians, each other, God, or other family members. Parents may easily lose their temper with siblings or, on occasion, even with the child who is sick. During this stage, critically ill children may blame themselves for their parent's anger. Still, parents are unlikely to feel ready to talk about death with their children.

Bargaining

Grieving parents may promise to abandon vices or to under-take heroic service, placating God or benefiting mankind, in return for a cure or even a temporary prolongation of life. During this stage, parents may begin to assure their children that they will re-cover soon and return to good health.

Depression

When the parents of the terminally ill child can no longer effectively deny the seriousness of the illness, depressive symptoms usually develop. In the beginning, the parents are depressed about their child's suffering and disfigurement, if any. As time goes on, the parents feel another type of grief in preparing for the final sepa-ration from the child. During this stage, the children too become very sad and worry about their parents, who, they observe, are often crying.

Acceptance

If parents have had enough time and help in working through the first four stages, they will contemplate the coming end with a degree of quiet expectation. Acceptance should not be mistaken for happiness, but can be perceived as a near void of feelings. It is as if the pain is gone, the struggle over, and there is time for a rest before the child's final journey.

Your Desire to Protect Your Child

As you move through these stages, can you imagine that your chil-dren won't know what's going on? Because it's most common for parents to want to protect their dying child from the distress of this information, they may order family, doctors, and nurses to keep the prognosis from the child. "I couldn't bear to have my son know that he wasn't going to be here to play baseball next spring like I promised him," said one dad, looking back on reasons for keeping the severity of his child's illness a secret.

As natural as this protective attitude may be, it's not the best way to handle this situation. Fatally ill children tend to know more than their parents think they do. These children watch their parents' faces when they talk with the doctors. They listen intently as their parents talk with other family members. They see the tears and observe the false smiles and sorrow-laden actions of everyone around them. Terminally ill children have even been known to feign sleep to gain information about their health.

It seems that despite efforts to keep children with a fatal illness from becoming aware of the prognosis, they somehow pick up a sense that their illness is very serious and very threatening. Therefore, hiding the seriousness of the illness only adds to the child's fears.

What Children Fear Most

The fears of fatally ill children will vary according to their age. Before age five, children fear separation from their parents more than death. These children are not old enough to understand the concept of death so they do not truly worry about the fatal nature of their illness; instead, they worry that "death" means they'll be alone, abandoned by their parents. When you talk to these children it is best *not* to focus on death. Spend your energy convincing them that you will never leave them, that you will be nearby during their medical procedures, that you will be with them whenever they need you. Your comforting presence is what these children need most.

Older children, however, do have some understanding of the concept of death. Recent research has found that contrary to earlier belief, children six years old and older, with a fatal prognosis, are not only aware that they are dying but can express that awareness with words relating to death. Although it's true that these children are most outwardly anxious about operations, body intrusions, and needles, they also sense that they are very ill and could die. They are eager to have their parents help them talk about the illness, death, and dying.

Why Talk to Dying Children About Death?

In their book *The Damocles Syndrome,* psychologist Gerald Koocher and psychiatrist John E. O'Malley describe the results of a study they did of 117 childhood cancer survivors and their families. They found that "the earlier a child was told the diagnosis, the more likely he or she was to be well-adjusted. . . . Directness and openness in all matters associated with the illness seem to foster better adjustment among childhood cancer patients." This finding is repeated throughout the medical literature. Talking about critical and terminal illness helps children deal with it.

In another study, families of children who had died of a serious illness at age six and older reported that open communication about the illness resulted in increased feelings of closeness to the children. Families whose children died without discussion of the illness or of the imminent death usually expressed the wish that they had spoken more openly with their child. These parents described feelings of incompleteness. They never had the chance to say good-bye. The researchers also found that open communication with children about their illness and concerns can even help decrease feelings of isolation, fear, and loneliness.

You should definitely talk to your dying child about the diagnosis and prognosis. Honest discussion may well result in better psychological adjustment by the child and by you as well.

How to Answer a Dying Child's Questions

Many terminally ill children want to discuss their approaching death. If your child brings it up, you should try to discuss it with honesty, love, and acceptance. Truth is more supportive and beneficial to a child than deception or denial.

"Am I going to die?"

If a seriously ill child asks this question, you might answer, "I can understand that you worry you might die. I have thought about it too. You have a serious illness, but right now the doctors tell us that there are still things to do and medicines to take that can make you feel better."

When a child who is very close to death asks about dying, and there is clearly no hope left, you should say, "The doctors have no further way of curing the sickness, but they will make sure you will be comfortable until you die."

Then get ready to answer questions you may have never really thought about before. You may find, for example, that the concrete image of the grave may become the focal point of your child's questions:

"Will I feel cold in the winter if I'm in the grave?"

"Will I be able to open my eyes?"

"If it rains a whole lot, will I get wet?"

"What if someone digs me up?"

You'll need to answer these questions honestly: "Your body no longer functions after death—you feel, see, taste, and smell nothing."

Then turn your child's attention to the fact that real love does not die when a loved one dies. Tell your children, "Your body dies, but not your spirit. Your spirit will live on in our hearts and memory and thoughts. You will always be close to me, and my thoughts and memories of you will be my treasures forever."

If you are religious, you can offer your child a more comforting view of life beyond the grave. You might say, "You will be going to a new life in heaven—one of happiness, peace, and love." Surely then, your children will want to know all about heaven.

"Will I be able to see you from heaven?"

"Will I have wings like the angels?"

"When you come to heaven will we live together again?"

The answers to these questions have fueled debate among theologians since the beginning of time. Because there are no absolute facts in this area, don't hesitate to answer from your heart, even when you're not really sure if your answer is "correct."

Finding Support Systems

You don't need to endure the loss of your child alone. Many resources are available to help you talk to your child about his or her condition and to help you and your child cope with its reality. Ask for help from your child's physicians, a bereavement counselor, or the hospital social worker.

Children's Hospice International can give you more information about support systems. Unlike hospice programs for adults, which are devoted solely to cancer victims, children's hospices accept youngsters with any terminal illness. They offer comfort and freedom from pain to the patient, and they can help families nurture each other during the child's last days. For more information, contact: Children's Hospice International, 501 Slaters Lane, #207, Alexandria, VA 22314 (703-556-0421).

Suggested Reading

For Parents

Buckingham, Robert W. *A Special Kind of Love: Caring for the Dying Child.* New York: Continuum, 1983.

Dailey, Barbara A. *Your Child's Recovery: A Parent's Guide for the Child with a Life-Threatening Illness.* New York: Facts on File, 1990.

Kübler-Ross, Elisabeth. *On Children and Death.* New York: Macmillan, 1983.

Lingard, Joan. *Between Two Worlds.* New York: Lodestar Books, 1991.

For Children Aged Four to Seven

Cohn, Janice. *I Had A Friend Named Peter.* New York: William Morrow, 1987.

For Children Aged Eight to Twelve

White, Ryan. *Ryan White, My Own Story.* New York: Dial Books, 1991.

First Day of School

Imagine how you might feel about taking a long-awaited trip abroad. From a distance, the idea sounds wonderful and exciting. But as the date of departure comes closer, you might begin to worry.

"What if the plane crashes?"

"What if I get separated from my tour group and can't find my way back to the hotel?"

"What if I can't manage the change in currency?"

By the time the day of your trip arrives, you may find yourself wishing you weren't going at all. This anticipatory anxiety is what many children feel when the first day of school finally arrives.

The timing of a child's "first day of school" has changed quite dramatically over the last decade. With more parents working and more schools focusing on kindergarten readiness, child-care centers, nursery schools, preschools, and kindergartens open their doors on the "first day of school" for children ranging in age from two to six. But at any level, the psychological task involved in this "first day" experience is the same—learning to cope with fear of the unknown and fear of loss through separation.

Although nothing can completely remove the apprehension that young children feel when they first begin school, their fears can certainly be eased if you give them plenty of opportunities to express their feelings and concerns.

Planning Ahead

Keeping the analogy of a trip abroad in mind, it's understandable why children need to know exactly what's going to happen in school. Your fear of traveling would certainly be compounded if you were told only that you were going on a long trip and you'd have fun. That's exactly how your children will feel if you tell them only, "You're going to school and you're going to have fun."

Children need honest and detailed answers to questions such as these:

"Who is my teacher and where is my class?"

Most schools offer a pre-enrollment visit for prospective students and their families. Take advantage of this opportunity. It gives your child a great deal of information about the classroom, the teacher, and other students. This kind of visit reduces fear of the "unknown" elements.

If your school doesn't offer an orientation program, or if you're unable to attend the one the school has scheduled, call the school and make a special appointment for you and your child to visit. If the school won't allow a pre-enrollment visit, find another school.

"What will I do at school?"

You can build your children's sense of security if you can tell them exactly what they'll do in school. Saying "You'll play games and you'll learn things" is too vague to be reassuring. Contact the teacher and ask for a rundown of a typical day. Then you might be able to offer your child specifics like these:

"Well, first all the children come into the classroom and put their sweaters, coats, or book bags in the cubbies that are along the wall. Then they sit in a circle on the floor by the piano. The teacher helps them sing a song and then she shows them where that day is on the calendar." And so on.

You can also use this information to help your children "re-hearse" going to school through playacting, as explained later in this chapter.

"How long will I stay there?"

Typically, time is a scary aspect of school for many young children—especially because they can't yet judge how long "a few hours" really is. To a young child, the statement "I'll pick you up in three hours" sounds a lot like "You'll never see me again."

It's also not a good idea to downplay the length of time with comments like "You'll be in school for only a very short time. The day will be over before you know it."

Here are a few ideas to help your children better understand how much time they'll be away from you:

• Draw a picture of a clock and color in the time period your children will be at school. Even if your children can't tell time, this gives them a concrete picture of how their time in school re-lates to the entire day.

• If you've made after-school arrangements for your children, tell them all the details about who, when, where, and how long. Color these after-school hours on your clock picture with a differ-ent color.

• Take a calendar and help your children color in the days of the week from Monday through Friday. This will again give them an image of when they'll be in school and when they'll be at home with you.

"Where will you be while I'm at school?"

Children often worry about their parents when they're apart. Some are concerned you'll do something fun while they're at school and they'll miss it. Other children worry about their parents' safety and well-being. Tell your children where you'll be and what you'll be doing while they're at school. Give details like these: "I'm going to drive to work right after I leave you. Then I'll be doing my job at work at the same time you're doing your job at school."

Reducing Your Child's Fears

As the first day of school approaches, your children may lie in bed and worry.

"What if I have to go to the bathroom? I don't know where the toilet is!"

"What if I can't find my classroom?"

"What if I make a mistake?"

"What if I trip and fall and everyone laughs at me?"

"What if I forget how to say my name?" And on and on.

Coping with Regression and Anger

Although not being able to cope with unknown or new experiences is common to us all, the ways we express our fears are quite varied. You may find that your children show their fears by regressing to behaviors like thumb-sucking, baby talk, bed-wetting, whining, clinging, even crawling. Or, they may withdraw and become very sullen and quiet. If any of these things happens, try to be patient, ignore the behavior, and continue to offer a positive outlook about school.

Fear may also show itself in anger or temper tantrums. If you notice an increase in back talk or tantrums as the first day of school approaches, again, try to accept it as your child's attempt to deal with the upcoming life change. Continue to follow your normal disciplinary routine for such problems, but keep in mind that an increase in the frequency or severity of misbehavior may be related to apprehension about school.

If your children do regress in their behaviors or become irritable, take these actions as a signal that your children need reassurance. *Don't* say, "You'd better cut this out because your teacher won't put up with this stuff." This only fuels their fears.

Instead, you might calmly comment, "I know this kind of behavior won't last long and you'll soon be acting like your old self again."

Addressing Specific Worries

Some children have fears that are quite specific. If you can get your children to tell you what they are afraid of, you may be able to help them overcome their fear. If, for example, your son persists in worrying that he won't be able to find the bathroom, and if he won't be appeased by assurances like "Your teacher will show you where the bathroom is," indulge his concern. Take him to the school and show him the bathroom; let him see what it looks like and show him how to get there from his classroom. If this reduces his first-day-of-school jitters, it's worth the trip.

Pinning Down Elusive Fears

Sometimes it takes a while for children to realize what it is they're afraid of. Five-year-old Clark, for example, spent his summer excitedly awaiting the start of kindergarten in September until suddenly, one week before opening day, he changed his mind and couldn't explain why. Clark had been in a private preschool for two years and he loved it; his older sister was already in his "new" school, and he was happy about joining her. Then it started— whining and crying. Each night at bedtime, Clark wanted his mother to stay in his room until he fell asleep. If she tried to leave his bedside, he'd grab her arm and beg her to stay. He continually cried, "I don't want to go to school. I don't want to go." But no matter how much his parents questioned him, they couldn't uncover the reason for his change of heart.

Finally, on the Friday before the first day of school, Clark started crying and blurted out that he was worried about having no friends in the new school. None of Clark's preschool friends lived in his neighborhood, and it was true, he knew no one who would be in his class. "Here it was three days before school," remembers Clark's mom, Nancy, "and Clark finally tells me what's bothering him. At first I didn't know how to fix the problem because I didn't know anyone going to kindergarten either." But, wanting Clark to feel happy about going to school, Nancy called some of her neighbors and friends until she found the name and number of another child who would be starting kindergarten with Clark.

Nancy called the child's mother and explained her story. "She was really understanding," recalls Nancy. "We arranged for the children to meet the next day at the park and then I had them both over to our house for lunch." Apparently, that was all Clark needed. That night he went to bed happy for the first time in a week saying he couldn't wait to go to school to see his new friend again.

Ways to Help Children Express Their Feelings

If your children are showing signs of fear, encourage them to talk about their feelings; then maybe you can pinpoint the source and find a way, beyond verbal assurances, to ease their mind.

Some children truly may not know what they're afraid of. Still, with your help, even vague fears can be eased. The books for children listed at the end of this chapter can help young children visualize other children like themselves going through and mastering the same experience—and this can be very comforting.

You can also help your children face their worries through playacting. Using dolls, puppets, or stuffed animals, you and your children can set up a classroom and enact the first day of school. Or, encourage your children to play school in much the same way as they might play house. With friends or siblings let your children choose their parts as students and teachers. Give them pencils, crayons, paper and watch the drama unfold.

Dealing with Separation

In addition to fear of the unknown, feelings of loss through separation are perfectly normal emotions for both parents and children on the first day of school. Although the fear is normal, you do have some control over the degree of anxiety your children may experience. As you read through the following scene, see if you can detect behaviors that are making the separation process more difficult for this parent and child.

Since Brittany's birth three years ago, Joan has been a stay-at-home mom. Now she and her husband have agreed that it's time to put Brittany in preschool while Joan goes back to part-time work.

On the first day of school, Brittany began to scream and run after her mom as she began to leave the school. No matter how Joan tried to console her, Brittany wouldn't calm down or listen to reason. Eventually, the teacher had to pry Brittany from Joan's leg and carry her, kicking and squirming, back into the classroom.

Joan cried all the way to work.

When she returned that afternoon, Joan found Brittany sitting comfortably next to her teacher listening to a story. But when Brittany saw Joan at the door, the little girl ran to her in a burst of tears. Joan dropped to her knees and tearfully hugged and kissed her daughter. "It's all right now. I'm back," she whispered. "I missed you, too, but I'm back now. Let's go home." Then like the white knight rescuing the damsel in distress, Joan picked up Brittany in her arms and carried her to the car.

The next morning, Brittany again cried and carried on when she arrived at the preschool. Joan stayed for awhile, hoping to help her adjust slowly to the separation, and the teacher skillfully engaged Brittany in a fun activity to distract her from her fear. When Joan saw her daughter contentedly playing with blocks, she quickly left before Brittany could start crying again. Because Joan didn't have to go through the separation scene again, she felt happier about the arrangement as she drove to work. She didn't know that when Brittany realized her mother was gone, her crying was longer and more intense than it had been the day before. When Joan returned, she and Brittany repeated the anxious and tearful reunion of the day before.

Notice any problem areas?

Children can't become independent beings when they experience trickery or emotionally upsetting separation and reunion scenes. They need honest explanations and experiences to teach them that parents and children can't always be together. When they are apart, both can feel happy and confident. And they will always come back together again.

You can help your children accept separation by following these basic guidelines.

Stay Calm.   Emotions are contagious, so display the feelings you want your children to catch. Don't fret and worry, or look anxious or hesitant. Remain cheerful. Smile, say good-bye with confidence. No matter how loudly your children scream and beg, keep smiling.

Don't Drag Out Your Good-byes.   Explain to your children that you're going to leave them with the teacher at school and tell them exactly when you'll return. You might say, for example, "I'm leaving now, but I'll be back in time for us to have lunch together."

If allowed, you might want to stick around for a while to make sure your children are well settled, but once you decide it's time to leave, give your children a few minutes warning. Then smile, say your cheerful good-byes, and leave. Don't drag out your departure with one more kiss and another assurance of your love. Don't get to the door and then come back to calm the cries. This encourages children to believe that if they cry hard enough you might change your mind.

Don't Discourage Tears.   It is unreasonable to ask your children to stop crying or to be brave. Let them cry. It's their way of expressing how they feel and your opportunity to offer understanding. Say, "I know you feel sad when I leave, but I must go, and I'll see you again after school." This assures children that you aren't ignoring or misinterpreting their feelings, and it helps them accept the separation as inevitable.

Never Sneak Out.   It's very tempting to dodge out the back door when your children are distracted for a moment—but don't. Eventually, children will notice your disappearance, but then they have no way of knowing that they haven't been abandoned forever. Always be honest and direct. Say, "Good-bye. I'm leaving now and I'll be back at three o'clock." Then leave.

Return with a Smile.   When you return, your children (who probably have been quite content while you were gone) may burst into tears, run to your arms, and cling to you for dear life. Or they may completely ignore you. Either response is perfectly normal, but you should continue teaching the lesson of separation by remaining cheerful and calm. A parent who gets teary and exclaims "I missed you so much. Are you okay? Did you miss me?" teaches the child that there really is danger in being alone. Focus on the positive by saying something like, "Your teacher said you had fun playing with blocks today."

Fear of the unknown and fear of loss through separation inevitably accompany many parents and children on the first day of school. If you use the techniques suggested in this chapter and find that they ease the strain of this experience, mark these pages for future reference. You may want to use them again if your children decide to go to college. You'll find that these same fears return when they leave your home for their last "first day" at school.

Suggested Reading

For Parents

Ames, Louise Bates. *Don't Push Your Preschooler.* Rev. ed. New York: Harper & Row, 1981.

Balaban, Nancy. *Learning to Say Goodbye: Starting School and Other Early Childhood Separations.* New York: New American Library, 1987.

Ryan, Bernard. *How to Help Your Child Start School.* New York: Perigee Books, 1980.

For Young Children

Berenstain, Stan, and Jan Berenstain. *The Berenstain Bears Go to School.* New York: Random Books for Young Readers, 1989.

Delton, Judy. *My Mom Made Me Go to School*. New York:
    Delacorte Press, 1991.

Grindley, Sally. *I Don't Want To!* Boston: Joy Street Books, 1990.

Hamilton-Merritt, Jane. *My First Days of School*. New York:
    Simon & Schuster, 1982.

Hathon, Elizabeth. *We Go to School*. New York: Random House,
    1992.

Martin, Ann M. *Rachel Parker, Kindergarten Show-off*. New York:
    Holiday House, 1992.

Park, Barbara. *Junie B. Jones and the Stupid Smelly Bus*. New York:
    Random House, 1992.

Rogers, Fred. *Going to Day Care*. New York: Putnam, 1985.

Schwartz, Amy. *Annabelle Swift, Kindergartener*. New York:
    Orchard Books, 1988.

Hospital Stay

Jonah had suffered from ear infections since birth. As soon as one would clear up, another would begin. "Whenever I heard the first sniffle of a cold," remembers his mother, "I knew he'd be back at the doctor's for an antibiotic." Finally, just before his third birthday, the pediatrician suggested that Jonah have tubes put into his ears to aid fluid drainage and end the chronic infections.

"We knew that in the long run, tubes were the best way to handle the problem," says Jonah's dad, "but we were also worried that the hospital experience would be very traumatic for him. We didn't know what to say or how to prepare him."

Hospitalization can be a stressful and anxiety-producing experience for young children. In some circumstances, it can cause emotional and behavioral problems that last long after discharge. Fortunately, there are some very simple dialogues and strategies you can use to minimize the harmful effects of a hospital stay.

Dealing with Your Child's Fears

Your children's fears of the hospital grow from four common roots: (1) fear of the unknown, (2) fear of separation from you, (3) loss of control and autonomy, and (4) lack of coping strategies.

When you talk to your children about their hospital visit, keep these four factors in mind.

Overcoming Fear of the Unknown

Professionals who work with children in hospitals agree that children who come prepared tend to exhibit less anxiety, adjust better, recover more quickly, and have less difficulty when they return home. That's why it's very important for you to tell your children everything before they arrive at the hospital. It's far better for children to face the situation and endure a small amount of anxiety with you at home, than to suffer the overwhelming distress that can come from finding themselves in a strange environment, not knowing what's going on.

Before discussing an upcoming hospitalization with your children, make sure you have the information you'll need to answer their questions.

Take a Hospital Tour.   Many hospitals offer children and their parents preadmission tours of the pediatric and surgical units; find out if your hospital has such a program and if so, sign up! Many of your children's (and your own) questions and concerns will be addressed on this kind of tour.

On a recent hospital tour, I found it most interesting to watch the various parent and child interactions. (The way both of you act during such a tour will give you some insight into how you'll respond to the actual hospital stay.) Some children and parents on this particular day, found the whole experience fascinating— they peeked into every corner and asked many probing questions. But many others mechanically marched from place to place with faces full of fear and apprehension.

One youngster clung to her mother and cried the entire time. Trying to take the edge off her own fear with humor, this mom quipped, "I don't think she's going to make it through this." The other parents laughed, but the child was noticeably saddened to discover her mom didn't believe she could handle this experience.

One dad with a whining child tried to rid the boy of fear with commands. "Stop acting like a baby in front of all these people," he ordered. "You know you have nothing to worry about. Now stop it right now." Not surprisingly, the boy cried louder.

A third set of parents abruptly left the group and went home when their child refused to follow along on the tour.

Although it's true that children respond to the hospital in varied and unpredictable ways, we can predict that without positive, detailed, and supportive preparation, these fearful youngsters will experience a traumatic hospital stay.

Ask Your Doctor Questions. If your hospital does not offer an organized tour with an informed medical guide, call your child's physician. Explain that you need detailed information about the upcoming hospitalization because you'd like to prepare your child for the experience. You can use the following list as a guide to the kinds of questions you'll need answered:

1. Exactly what is physically wrong with my child and how will it be treated in the hospital?
2. Is there any preadmission testing? What kind? Will it be done on a day previous to admission? Will blood testing involve a finger prick or will blood be drawn from a vein in the arm?
3. On the day of admission, will we first go to a bed in the pediatric unit or will we go directly to the procedure or surgical area?
4. Can children bring a security item (like a blanket or teddy bear) with them?

5. If surgery is needed, what type of anesthesia will be used? Will it be delivered by injection or mask?

6. How long can I stay with my child before the medical procedures begin? (Some hospitals now allow parents right in the operating room until the anesthesia takes effect! Others won't let parents even in the holding area.)

7. Where do parents wait during the procedure?

8. Are parents allowed in the recovery room? If not, where and when will I meet my child?

9. What is the hospital's policy on parents "rooming in?"

10. When will my child be coming home?

When you have the answers to these questions, you're ready to prepare your child for hospitalization. Keep in mind that kids want to know concrete facts that affect them directly. There's no need to explain the wonders of modern medicine or the latest technological advancement. Just the facts.

Explain When, What, and Why. The first thing you'll want to discuss is what will happen and why. Medical and surgical procedures can sound quite complex and frightening to even the most sophisticated patient. Talk to your child in simple words and be sure to explain exactly what the scheduled medical procedure is all about.

If your child is going in for a tonsillectomy, for example, you might start by saying, "On Monday you'll be going to the hospital so the doctors can remove your tonsils. This will keep you from having all those sore throats you've been getting lately."

Tell About Preadmission. Most hospitals require admission registration, blood testing, X-rays, and any other preparatory tests or procedures a day or two before the actual hospital stay. If this is the case, tell your child all about it.

Explain, "In the admitting office, a woman or man will ask us a lot of questions about things like where we live and what our phone number is. Then we go for some tests."

If blood will be drawn, say so and add, "The technician will take only a very small amount of your blood. It will hurt like a sharp pinch for a second but then it will stop hurting very quickly."

If your child needs an X-ray, you might compare the X-ray machine to a camera. Tell your child, "The X-ray pictures let the doctor see inside your body; X-rays don't hurt at all."

Rehearse the Day of Hospitalization. On the day of hospitalization, your child will benefit most from what's called "anticipatory guidance." This is a preparatory strategy that helps a child master a potentially traumatic experience. Before arriving at the hospital, tell your child exactly what he or she can expect. Using the answers to the questions in the list above, take your child step-by-step through the hospital stay. It's important to tell children everything—from the fact that they'll take off their clothes and put on a hospital gown to any post-procedure discomfort they might feel.

Be Honest. It's always advisable to be as honest as possible about the hospital and any discomfort your child will experience. One of your child's first questions will be "Will it hurt?" If any aspect of the medical procedure will be painful, say so. Discuss all unpleasant aspects such as needles, intravenous fluids and medications (IVs), bedpans, and restrictions. Then also talk about the positive aspects, such as going to sleep during the operation, having friends visit, receiving get-well gifts and cards, and having your ongoing presence.

Use a Calming Tone.   Your children will take their cue about
how to act from you. Talk about the hospital visit in a calm, matter-
of-fact way. Assure your children that you understand they might
feel frightened, but quickly emphasize the positive by mentioning
something like how much you trust the doctors' and nurses' ability to help your children get well. If you exhibit a high degree of
anxiety about the hospitalization, it is almost certain that your
children will feel a heightened sense of anxiety too.

Use Role-playing.   Play experiences utilizing dolls, stuffed
animals, and doctor kits can be very useful in helping children
release, understand, and master their feelings of uncertainty. Encourage your children to play doctor; you might even play the
role of a fearful patient and let your child be the doctor who
calms and reassures you. Playing doctor gives children freedom
to talk about their concerns, and role reversal opportunities give
children back some of the control they forfeit in the hospital
environment.

Help Your Child Find Information in Books.   Books with
pictures and simple descriptions of another child's hospitalization
can decrease children's fears and may answer questions they didn't
know how to ask. The books listed at the end of this chapter can
be used to acquaint your children with the feelings and medical
procedures they themselves will soon experience.

Express Confidence.   Always assure your children of your
confidence in their ability to get through this. Tell them, "I don't
expect you to like this, but I know you're going to do just fine."
Also, express confidence in the medical personnel. Tell your chil-

dren, "Dr. Smith is a fine physician, and I fully trust her ability to take good care of you."

Overcoming Fear of Separation

Your child who is under the age of six is mainly frightened of being separated from you. You are your child's major support and security system, so you should stay with your child whenever possible during the hospitalization period.

Many hospitals allow parents to sleep in the room with their hospitalized child; be sure to ask because it will mean a lot to your child if you're able to be nearby throughout the night. At times when you can't or aren't allowed to be with your child, explain why and state exactly when the two of you will be together again.

Fear of abandonment in the hospital is a very real concern for many young children. So don't scold or ridicule your child for clinging to you or crying when you leave. Instead, assure the child that lots of kids feel afraid when they're alone in the hospital. Then, again, express confidence in the medical staff, who will take good care of the child, and in the child's own ability to get by until you can be together again.

Helping Children Cope with Loss of Control and Autonomy

Children soon realize that they have little say over what happens to them in the hospital. This loss of control can be frightening, especially for children older than five. To help your children overcome these feelings of helplessness, try giving choices whenever possible. You might say, for example, "Do you want to stay in your room or go to the playroom?" "Do you want your temperature taken while you're in the bed or sitting on the chair?" "Do you want the shot in your right leg or left leg?"

The Need for Coping Strategies

Your children's ability to cope with anxiety-producing situations has been developing slowly over the years every time such a situation occurs. When something they don't like happens, they might deal with it by fighting back, running away, arguing, or denying its existence. In the hospital environment, however, your children will find that their usual coping skills aren't effective. So now what?

Before their hospital admission, teach them a few simple coping strategies that they can use to reduce their fear of this experience.

Use Guided Imagery.   During an unpleasant procedure, an injection for example, tell your children to talk or think about something that's pleasant, such as a birthday party or summer vacation.

Explain Positive Self-talk.   You can teach your children to say positive thoughts to reduce anxiety. Practice phrases like these:
"I can handle this."
"It's not that bad."
"It will only hurt for a little while."
"The doctors and nurses will help me if I get too uncomfortable."

Practice Some Relaxation Exercises.   Relaxation exercises can reduce tension. Teach your children how to breathe slowly and deeply whenever they feel afraid. (Add a smile to this exercise for a guaranteed spirit booster.) You can also teach your children how to tense and relax different muscle groups when they're upset.

Show Children How to Combine Strategies.   Some coping techniques work well when used together. While they're making and releasing a fist, for example, help your children breathe
deeply and think thoughts like, "relax," "stay calm." This use of muscle tensing, deep breathing, and self-talk will work together to help
your children reduce the stress of their hospital experience.

Lastly, don't use this experience to teach the importance of
independence and bravery in the face of adversity. Let your children lean on you for support during their time in the hospital.
Use lots of comforting body language to tell your kids that you
understand their fears: hold their hand, let them sit on your lap,
keep your arm around their shoulders. If hospital regulations allow, encourage friends and family to visit and bring encouragement and support (and of course cards, gifts, and balloons!). If your
child's recovery requires an extended hospital stay, bring toys, books,
dolls, and stuffed animals from home. Anything that increases comfort, reduces anxiety.

Suggested Reading

For Children Aged Four to Seven

Bucknall, Caroline. *One Bear in the Hospital.* New York: Dial
   Books for Young Readers, 1991.
Hautzig, Deborah. *A Visit to the Sesame Street Hospital.* New York:
   Random Books for Young Readers, 1985.
Rogers, Fred. *Going to the Hospital.* New York: Putnam, 1988.

For Children Aged Eight to Twelve

Carter, Sharon. *Coping with a Hospital Stay.* New York: Rosen
   Publishing Group, 1987.
Howe, James. *The Hospital Book.* New York: Crown, 1981.

Mental Health Professional

Nine-year-old Brandon's easy-going, happy personality seemed to vanish after his parents divorced. In its place were anger and resentment. His protest took the form of belligerence and hostility; he began striking out at anyone who tried to offer sympathy. Brandon's mom, his teachers, his grandparents, and even his best friend had all tried to talk to him about his attitude, but suggesting a possible "problem" only made him angrier. Six months after this personality change first became noticeable, Brandon's mother decided that she had waited long enough for her son to get over his disappointment about the divorce.

"He was getting worse instead of better," she said. "Brandon would blatantly break any rule I set. If I said 'Be home at six o'clock,' he'd shuffle in at seven. If I said he couldn't go out to play until his homework was done, he'd throw his books on the floor and walk out the door. I couldn't reach him anymore, so I wondered if he needed professional help, but I knew he'd hate me even more for suggesting such a thing."

There are many reasons a child may be in need of professional counseling. Almost any issue discussed in this book—sexual abuse, drug abuse, divorce, moving, a new baby, an alcoholic parent, the death of a loved one, and so on—may trouble a child to the degree that he or she becomes excessively fearful, depressed, withdrawn, angry, or rebellious. Such a child needs a mental health checkup, whether the child thinks it's a good idea or not.

Talking to your children about going to a mental health professional (for example, a psychologist, psychotherapist, or psychiatrist) is very much like talking to them about going to a medical doctor. Your goal is to prepare them in advance of the visit and to convey your expectation of a positive outcome.

Preparing for a Visit

The primary reason for preparing your child for a visit to a mental health professional is that a satisfactory evaluation or therapy session depends heavily on the child's cooperation with the professional. Without advance preparation, many children resist the visit and become quite fearful or angry about it.

Ask the Mental Health Professional Questions.   Before you mention the subject to your child, make an appointment with a mental health professional and ask for some information about your visit so you'll be prepared to answer your child's questions. Explain to the therapist that you want to prepare your child for the visit and need to know what the child can expect at the first meeting. For example:

Will you, the parent, stay with the child?

Will the child undergo psychological testing? What kind?

What will the child be asked to do?

Will it be a talk or play session?

How long will the appointment last?

Tell Your Child About the Visit and the Counselor. Once you have this information, set aside some quiet time to tell your child about the appointment. In a firm and matter-of-fact

fact way you might say, "I've made an appointment for us to see Mrs. Jones about [controlling your temper, your inability to pay attention in school, or whatever the problem is]."

After you've announced your plan, explain just what a counselor does: "Mrs. Jones is specially trained to help people understand their problems and feelings. She doesn't take your temperature or give you a shot. She simply talks with you, asks you to talk about your thoughts and feelings, and sometimes she may give you games, puzzles, or pictures to play with."

Discuss the Purpose of This Visit.   You may want to say, "I'm concerned about you. This problem doesn't seem to be getting any better. It keeps coming back and it doesn't seem to be under your control. I think it might help to get a consultation just to find out if it's really something to be concerned about, and if so, what can be done to help you."

Describe the Visit Itself.   Try to give the child an accurate preview. For example: "I've talked with Mrs. Jones and she's explained that on the first visit I will stay with you when you first meet her and you and I will talk about what we feel may be a problem. During the second half of the visit, which will last about an hour all together, you and Mrs. Jones will talk in private." (Fill in the details as they have been explained to you.)

Add a View of the Outcome.   To give your child a sense of the purpose of counseling, you might say something like this: "This therapist may be able to help you feel more relaxed and teach you how to feel good about yourself. These are things I've tried to do, but now I see that I can't help you alone. We need to talk to somebody specially trained in understanding how children feel and act."

Handling Resistance

Without intervention, a child's ongoing psychological problem can cause great family upset, leaving everyone feeling angry and full of despair. Often counseling is considered only as a last resort. This is unfortunate because when therapy is presented to children as an act of desperation, they will associate going for help with punishment.

You can expect resistance if you suddenly say to children, "That's it. We're taking you for a psychiatric evaluation to find out what's wrong with you!"

It's also inappropriate to threaten your children by saying, "I'm going to have to take you to a shrink because you won't listen to a thing I say."

Instead, seek professional mental health counseling before the problem reaches crisis proportions and present your decision to seek help in a firm but caring way.

If your child resists the idea of professional mental health therapy, continue to show that you're concerned, not angry.

A child who resists your suggestion is likely to reply, "But I don't want to go see a psychologist. I'm not nuts. Do you think I'm crazy?"

To this you might reply, "I understand you don't want to go. Most of the time you do act reasonably. But there are times you act troubled. Many people go to therapists, and very, very few behave in a 'crazy' way. We don't think you're crazy, but we are concerned about you and would like some advice. If you had a stomachache or toothache, we would go with you to a doctor. In the same way, when you have some emotional difficulties, it's our duty to see that you get help."

Is It a Secret?

Although you may suspect that we don't have a completely unbiased view of the mental health profession, we do sincerely believe that taking a child to a mental health professional is a sign of an intelligent and caring parent. However, we should caution that you can sabotage your decision by trying to keep it a secret. Talk openly about your decision to your child's siblings and other family members who are in close contact with your child. Knowing that you're not ashamed of seeking help will allow everyone to view psychotherapy as a positive experience.

If your child has resisted the idea of counseling or seems upset by your decision, be sure to tell him or her about how you feel before you tell anyone else. In a private moment, say, "What goes on during the counseling session is your own business and you don't have to talk about that. But going to a therapist is nothing to be ashamed or embarrassed about, so there's no reason to keep this a secret. It's good for your sisters and brothers to know that you're smart enough to get help when you need it. In fact, maybe they'd like to come with you sometime."

How to Find a Mental Health Professional

When you decide to seek professional help for your child's problem, there are a number of sources you can turn to to find appropriate treatment:

1. *Your school psychologist.* Public schools generally employ a child psychologist who can help you either begin a psychological evaluation or refer you to another source.

2. *Community mental health clinics.* Some cities and other smaller communities have county or publicly financed mental

health clinics. Often these clinics use sliding scales to set fees that clients can afford.

3. *University clinics.* If you live near a university, call the department of psychology and ask for information regarding child-development clinics. Often, universities offer outpatient counseling for many of the problems commonly encountered by young children.

4. *Medical referrals.* You can call your local hospital, community clinic, or your pediatrician and ask for a referral to a mental health professional. Explain your child's problem specifically because mental health professionals often specialize in areas such as drug abuse, insomnia, bed-wetting, and the like.

5. *Consult telephone information listings.* Look for the number of your state psychological association. Representatives from this association can help direct you to the appropriate mental health professional in your area.

6. *Check the resources suggested at the end of this chapter.* Organizations listed there can direct you to an appropriate mental health facility or professional in your area.

Suggested Resources

American Academy of Child Psychiatry
3615 Wisconsin Ave. NW
Washington, DC 20016
202-966-7300
Provides general reference services and offers information on all
  aspects of child psychiatry and mental health including social
  policy, legal issues, training, etc.

American Psychoanalytic Association
1 East 57th Street
New York, NY 10022
212-752-0450
Answers inquiries and makes referrals.

Child Development Research Institute
Frank Porter Graham Child Development Center
Highway 54
Bypass West 071A
Chapel Hill, NC 27514
919-966-4121
Answers inquiries, provides advisory services, conducts seminars and
workshops, distributes publications, makes referrals.

Pediatric Projects
P.O. Box 1880
Santa Monica, CA 90406
213-459-7710
Advocates mental health care for chronically ill, disabled, children,
and their families.

Psychology Society
100 Beekman St.
New York, NY 10038
212-285-1872
Answers inquiries, provides counseling, conducts seminars, makes
referrals.

Moving to a New Home

Myra and Tom can laugh now about their moving day blunder, but at the time it was a scary experience. "We were all so busy that day," Myra remembers, with a glance at Tom, "that we really didn't take much notice of Glen's sulky mood."

"At the time he was only seven years old," adds Tom, "and there wasn't that much he could do to help. All I knew was that every time I turned around, he was under my feet. I don't remember exactly what I said, but I'm sure it was something like, 'Will you get out of my way and go find something constructive to do!?'"

When it was time to leave, Tom jumped into the cab of the moving truck and Myra followed behind in her car—each thinking Glen was with the other.

"Thankfully," says Myra still blushing from the memory, "we had agreed to meet at the gas station a few blocks away to fill up before the two-hour drive to our new house. And that's when we realized we had left Glen behind."

"He was sitting in the closet still sulking when we found him," laughs Tom. "Glen likes to tell the story like it was a real *Home Alone* adventure."

"But it wasn't funny," says Myra, interrupting Tom's laugh. "We felt just awful. Even though we were under a lot of stress ourselves, I think we should have been more careful about the way we spoke to Glen."

Moving to a new home certainly is a stressful experience for everyone. It's also a common one. Recent figures estimate that almost sixteen percent of all American families move each year—that's well over ten million children on the move! Moving falls into the "major crisis" category for many children because generally they're creatures of habit. They like to do the same things in the same way day after day. They like to know exactly when and where their activities will take place. They like to keep order in their daily routines because order is one of the few things that gives them a sense of control over their own lives. Moving weakens this sense of control, but talking honestly and frequently about the move can give them back a sense of security. As Myra and Tom found out, what we say, and even how we say it, during this busy time can greatly affect our children's feelings about moving.

How to Answer Children's Questions

Most questions that children ask about moving to a new home can be answered with simple but thoughtful responses. Before you answer any questions, however, check your own attitude.

Like magnets, your children will be drawn to your attitude and will hold to it as tightly as if it were their own. So, once you tell your children about your decision to move, try to convey a positive outlook. You can, and should, let your children know that you, too, are sometimes worried about making the move—that concern about facing a new experience is a normal feeling. But if you're very unhappy about the move, try not to let your children see you wallow in discontent. Let it be optimism that you pass on through your answers to their questions.

"Why do we have to move?"

Your explanation of why you have to move depends, of course, on your personal situation. But whatever the reason for moving, make sure your answer is detailed enough to satisfy your child's desire to fully understand your decision. If you respond, "Because my new job is far away," your child will be left wondering, "What does that have to do with me?" If you say, "Because we need a bigger house," your child will still want to know, "Why?" If the move is necessitated by a divorce, this too is a confusing reason to have to move.

Explain your decision to move by giving details appropriate to your child's age and needs. (You probably don't need to describe the argument you had with your boss that made you decide to look for another job.) You might simply and honestly say, for example, "We're moving because my new job is far away. This job is a better job for me. It will pay me more money and make me happy. But if we don't move closer to where the job is, I won't be able to spend much time at home with you. We're moving because I want to be able to come right home to you after work every day."

"Where are we moving to?"

"Where?" is a straightforward question. Try to avoid a vague answer. Even the imaginative mind of a child will have trouble picturing very general responses such as, "We're moving to a very nice house in a wonderful town." Or, "We're moving just a few towns away to a place you'll really like."

In answering this particular question, actions (and pictures) speak louder than words. If possible, include your children in making plans for the move so they can *see* where they're going. For example:

- Take them with you when you go hunting for your new house or apartment.
- Listen to their opinions.
- Walk with them around the neighborhood.
- Arrange for them to visit their new school.

These activities bring your children into the selection process and reduce their feelings of helplessness and powerlessness.

If your children cannot accompany you on your house hunt, you can still keep them involved:

- Take pictures and videos throughout the search.
- Continuously ask for their opinions and thoughts.
- Once you've selected a new home, take pictures and videos of the neighborhood, school, and recreational areas.

One nine-year-old, who was particularly unhappy about his family's upcoming move across the country, surprised his parents with a complete change of attitude after he watched a video his dad had taken. "Mark loves baseball," says his dad. "One of his biggest complaints about moving was that he'd miss his friends and the games. So on one of my trips to finalize our move, I went to the town field and videotaped a baseball game. Once Mark saw that even on the other side of the country, kids still play baseball, still enjoy friendships, and look and act very much like him and his friends, his fear turn into acceptance." Mark's father found a creative way to tell his son where they were moving—without saying a word.

"Where's my room?"

You may love your new kitchen, or the yard, or the den. But you can bet your kid's main interest is in his or her room. Just as you mentally go from room to room decorating and rearranging your new home, help your children mentally prepare their new room. Here are some ways to do that:

- Describe how it is similar to and different from their present room.
- Talk about the view from their window.
- Measure out the dimensions.
- Map out where your bedroom is in relation to theirs.
- Draw pictures of where the furniture will go. And don't be surprised if your children want to arrange their new room to resemble their old room. This gives them a feeling of consistency and it's an easy way for you to allow them to feel comfortable in their new surroundings.
- Talk about where the toys and games can be stored.
- Let them pick out the paint or posters for their walls.

When moving day draws near, let your children pack their own things, and when you arrive at your new home, try to unload these boxes first and let your children unpack in their rooms while you're busy with the rest of the house. This will keep them from being underfoot, and more importantly, it will give them a feeling of ownership and control.

"What about my friends?"

When your children express concerns about leaving their friends, resist the temptation to tell them they'll make new ones. Instead, offer a sympathetic ear. Tell them you understand because you too feel upset about leaving good friends behind. Then, just as you will make provisions for staying in touch with your friends, help your children do the same:

- Arrange for your child and a special friend to spend a "good-bye day" together.
- Organize a cookout for a few close friends.
- Help your children exchange phone numbers and addresses with their friends, and keep them in a special address book.
- Set a firm date with old friends for a visit or long-distance phone call. Maintaining those ties for a while helps ease tensions after the move.

"Why?" "When?" "Where?"

Your children may have an endless list of questions about moving. But whatever they ask, try to keep your answers

- Direct
- Honest
- Reassuring
- Optimistic

After you've answered all your children's questions, be prepared to answer them again, and then again. Repeated questions don't mean that your children don't understand, or that they want you to change your answers. Most often, the repetition of questions and answers helps children gradually adjust to change. So, with patience, repeat your answers as often as your children ask their questions.

How to Address Problem Behaviors

Despite your best efforts, some children will not immediately adjust to the idea of moving. The following are typical problem behaviors that indicate children's fear, reluctance, or confusion.

Children Aged Three to Seven

• *Whining and clinging.* Young children can't always express their fears with words, but they certainly can with these attention-demanding actions.

• *Temper tantrums.* Even children who are usually mild mannered may tell you they're upset by reacting to even the smallest problem with a temper tantrum.

• *Babyish behavior.* When children feel insecure it's very common for them to revert to a babylike state. Your children may take up thumb-sucking again, or they may revert to bed-wetting, or they may even start soiling their underpants again.

• *Fearfulness.* When the family starts to prepare for a move, it's not at all unusual for young children to show their insecurity through fear. Fears like fear of the dark, nightmares, and renewed separation anxieties are common reactions to the idea of moving.

If your children show these outward signs of distress, encourage them to talk to you about their feelings. Playacting games are a wonderful way to "talk" with young children who have trouble expressing their feelings. Using dolls, stuffed animals, and doll houses (even if just made out of boxes), act out scenes about moving. Play out a scene in which one little person is unhappy about the move and then let your child talk for that character. If you play the game often, you'll give your children lots of opportunities to share their feelings.

Children Aged Eight to Twelve

Older children may show their feelings in subtle ways. If your child is upset about the move, you can expect one or all of these reactions:

• *Lethargy.* Your children may begin to mope and sulk. If you ask "What's wrong?" he or she will say (in a very sad and forlorn voice) "Oh, nothing."

• *Irritability.* Children who are too old for temper tantrums will show their anger in other ways. They may argue with everything you say. They may treat you rudely and answer you abruptly. If you ask "What's wrong?" they may angrily retort "Get off my case."

• *Withdrawal.* Some children will draw away from you. They will ignore you, kill you with silence, and hide from social interaction.

• *Passive aggression.* Your children may show their resistance to the idea of moving by acting out in passive ways. They might, for example, become very forgetful. They may practice the art of incessant dawdling or procrastinating. They may pretend they can't hear you tell them to come to dinner or do their chores. This kind of noncompliant behavior can become maddening after a while, but keep in mind that it's really just a way of expressing feelings.

These are all common responses that your older children may use to show you how they feel. Try to be patient. If you argue about their attitude, or tell them to "cheer up," you'll affirm their belief that you don't really understand how they feel. If you completely ignore their attempt to communicate, they may never be able to tell you about their worries.

The best approach to these negative behaviors is to keep your own attitude positive and occasionally find a quiet time to talk to your children. Take the initiative in talking about moving by sharing your own feelings. Say something like, "Ya know, sometimes I get nervous about moving to a new home. I feel badly about leaving my friends here and I worry that maybe I won't like anyone in the new neighborhood. Do you ever worry about that?"

Don't push too hard for a completely truthful confession, and don't bring up the negative behaviors you've noticed. Just leave the door open and frequently make time for talking. If repeatedly given the opportunity, most children will eventually open up.

After the Move

When you're all settled in your new home, you can expect still more questions and occasional behavior problems. Adjustment to a new environment takes time, so the need for frequent and honest communication will continue.

After about one month in your new home, take some time to sit back and reflect. By that time, you'll probably be able to see that moving with a child also has a positive side. Moving can help children develop pride in having mastered a difficult situation. It can also teach the importance and value of adaptability and self-reliance. You may even find that the experience of moving has fostered a strong sense of family togetherness.

Suggested Reading

For Parents

Dickinson, Jan. *Jan Dickinson's Complete Guide to Family Relocation*. Lake Oswego, Oreg.: Wheatherstone Press, 1983.

Friedrich, Barbara. *Did Somebody Pack the Baby? The Family Moving Book.* Englewood Cliffs, N.J.: Prentice-Hall, 1978.

Hayes, Nan DeVincentis. *Move It! A Guide To Relocating Family, Flora, and Fauna.* New York: Dembner Books, 1988.

For Children Aged Four to Seven

Berenstain, Stan, and Jan Berenstain. *The Berenstain Bears' Moving Day.* New York: Random Books for Young Readers, 1981.

Calstrom, Nancy White. *I'm Not Moving, Mama!* New York: Macmillan, 1990.

Cassedy, Sylvia. *The Best Cat Suit of All.* New York: Dial Books for Young Readers, 1991.

Hest, Amy. *The Best-Ever Good-Bye Party.* New York: Morrow, 1989.

Rogers, Fred. *Moving.* New York: Putnam, 1987.

Waber, Bernard. *Ira Says Goodbye.* Boston: Houghton Mifflin, 1988.

For Children Aged Eight to Twelve

Giff, Patricia Reilly. *Matthew Jackson Meets the Wall.* New York: Delacorte Press, 1990.

Hendry, Diana. *The Not-Anywhere House.* New York: Lothrop, Lee & Shepard Books, 1991.

New Baby in the Family

When you talk to your children about a new baby in the family, keep the following analogy in mind. It will help you understand why "brotherly love" is often an acquired feeling.

Imagine your reaction if your spouse were to bring home a new marriage partner and announce that all three of you are going to live together and it's going to be fun. After assuring you that you both will be loved equally and you both are important members of the family, your spouse asks you to love the new family member, share your things, and accept not getting as much attention as you used to because you can take care of yourself now.

How would you feel? If you say these same things to your children when you bring home a new baby, they'll feel the same way.

When Should You Tell Your Kids About the New Baby?

As you already know, nine months can be a long time to wait—to a young child, this is an inconceivable period of time. You can relieve the anxiety of extended anticipation by putting off the announcement at least until the pregnancy becomes noticeable. (This also guards against the possibility of having to explain a miscarriage, which is more likely to happen within the first three months.)

However, it's also best that your children hear about the upcoming arrival directly from you. If you intend to tell many people about the pregnancy and talk about it in front of your children, then tell them right away. Resentment can start early if your children think that everyone is trying to keep a secret from them.

Exactly when you tell your children about the expected family member is a personal choice. But once you break the news, it's time to pay attention to how you talk to your children about this change in the family structure.

How Should You Break the News?

Make your announcement simple. In a pleasant voice, tell your children, "We're going to have a new baby in the family." Resist any initial desire to assure your children that the baby will never take their place or take your love away from them. That sort of comment at this point will introduce ideas your children haven't thought of yet.

After you make your announcement, present a positive attitude no matter what reaction your children may have. Answer their questions honestly and assure them that you'll be happy to talk to them about the baby any time they like. (See the chapter entitled "Sex and Reproduction" for ideas on how to answer the question "Where do babies come from?")

You can ease the fears and apprehensions of older children (ages eight to eleven) by involving them in the pregnancy. Talk about the stages of fetal development; if you have picture books showing the growing fetus in the womb, share them. Let your children accompany you on your doctor visits, hear the baby's heartbeat, and see the sonogram, if possible. Try to arrange for your children to be nearby during your delivery so they will be "on the scene" for this important family event.

What to Say If Your Child Is Jealous

Children of all ages show jealousy in three fairly common ways:

1. They might get angry at you and act out by becoming exceptionally disobedient and demanding, or tearful and clinging, or withdrawn.
2. They might get angry at the baby and make the baby cry by hitting, shaking, squeezing, or in some other way inflicting pain or discomfort on the baby.
3. They might regress to babyish or selfish behavior.

What to Say When Your Kids Get Angry at You

If your children seem angry at you, try to keep in mind that they act with only one purpose in mind: to get your attention away from the baby and back on them, where they feel it belongs. In these cases, there's no use scolding; it is negative attention, and as such reinforces the child's belief that disobedience or whining will force you to turn away from the baby. Instead, assure the child that you understand how he or she feels and offer your continued love, as in the following examples:

If your children express their feelings through disobedience by saying something like "No, I won't go to bed and you can't make me," you can respond by ignoring their defiance and calmly, but firmly, escorting them to bed. Say to them, "I understand you don't want to go to bed, but it's time now. Let's go."

If your young children express their upset by being excessively tearful or clingy, you can say, "I see you're feeling sad. Would you like to sit by me for a little special attention?"

If your children choose to show you how they feel by withdrawing from family life, tell them, "I know you'd like to be alone, but I miss spending time with you. Can you spend some special time with me right now?"

You can encourage more positive behavior throughout the day by giving your children your attention when you catch them doing something good:

• Don't just count your blessings when your child plays quietly while the baby is napping; at that moment, give your child a hug and a smile and tell him, "Thank you for playing quietly while the baby sleeps."

• When you tell your child to do something and she does it, compliment her: "You're a big help to me when you do what I ask you. Thank you."

• If your withdrawn child begins to play with the baby and even offers a laugh, comment on this saying, "Your little brother likes to see you smile."

• When your child begins to cry or demand attention when you're busy with the baby, try to keep your temper and offer your child an alternate positive reaction. You might say, "I'm busy doing something else right now, but I promise I'll give you my full attention in five minutes."

A fun and effective way to make sure this promise is kept, is to set a kitchen timer to remind you and your child when it's time to switch the focus of your attention. When children learn that the timer will ring and you *will* turn your attention away from the baby at that time, they can better control their demanding behavior.

What to Say If Your Kids
Get Angry at the Baby

You know it would be hard to "be nice" to your spouse's new marriage partner. You can also imagine that being scolded by your spouse would not make you show more kindness toward the new family member. So keep this in mind when you ask your older child to "be nice."

Whether intentional or not, it's not uncommon for siblings to harm newborns physically. So, obviously, they should not be left together unsupervised. You should also establish firm rules, appropriate to your child's age, about handling the baby. Once that's done, you can feel free to let your children verbally express their angry feelings.

"I hate that baby. Send him back!" yelled five-year-old Alicia quite unexpectedly one morning.

Alicia's mom was shocked by the meanness of her daughter's statement. "Don't you dare say that about your baby brother. He hasn't done anything to you. You're the big sister now and you're supposed to love and care for him. Say you're sorry or go to your room."

Alicia ran to her room, slammed the door, and cried herself to sleep.

As difficult as it is to hear your children scream hateful epithets at your new baby, try to be patient. If you insist that your older child say only nice things about the baby, you may establish an implied restriction on voicing true feelings. Then you'll find, as in all life situations, that pent-up emotions eventually do find their way out—but often in destructive ways. Give your children permission to say unkind things.

When your children voice negative feelings about the baby, don't act shocked. Instead, show understanding and acceptance by saying something like, "Sounds like you're mad at the baby, maybe because he's been crying a lot and needing so much of my time. I know how you feel."

What to Say If Your Kids Show Signs of Regression

Your children will quickly realize that babies get priority attention because they're virtually helpless and must have everything done for them. Simple logic might convince your children that to get your attention they should act helpless or even infantile. It's not at all uncommon for young children to revert to baby talk, crawling, or sucking their thumb; they may cry to be carried or even relapse in their toileting skills.

Older children, too, may also regress in their behavior. We recently heard a story about a mother who stumbled into the house carrying her pocketbook, a box of laundered shirts, a bag of groceries, and a baby bundled in a snowsuit. As she fumbled to balance her packages and get the keys out of the door lock, her ten-year-old son stood and watched, making no effort to help. Then, this previously self-sufficient boy asked with annoyance, "When are you gonna make me lunch?" Yes, it takes a lot of patience to handle regression.

Generally, the best thing to do when a child regresses to babyish or selfish behaviors is to tolerate it without comment. You might calmly comment, "I've noticed you're doing some babyish things lately, but I'm sure it won't be long before you're feeling like your old self again." If you can avoid scolding or arguing when regressive behavior appears, you'll find that this stage will subside on its own. When you can, indulge your child's need for attention by offering extra doses of comfort and love.

Some General Do's and Don'ts

Do's

When you bring home a new baby, *do* say:

- "If you ever feel left out, come and tell me right away. I'll give you extra loving so you'll feel good again."
- "I need your help to give the baby his bath. Can you put soap on his legs?"
- "Let's get a sitter for the baby tomorrow afternoon so you and I can be together without being interrupted."
- "There are going to be times when this baby is going to bother us or even make us mad. Please let me know if you start feeling bothered."

Don'ts

When you bring home a new baby, *don't* say:

- "I'm sure you'll love and be proud of the baby."
- "Your baby sister doesn't cry as much as you."
- "You're the [big brother/big sister] now, so you can take care of yourself."
- "You have to give up your baby toys now that we have a new baby."

Sibling rivalry is an age-old occurrence. But the degree of anger and jealousy your children may feel when you bring home a new baby can often be reduced with sensitive parenting. There's no doubt that the entire family will experience some degree of stress when the baby arrives, and quite predictably, you won't have much time or energy to focus intently on your older children. But if you give your children comfort, understanding, and the freedom to talk honestly about their feelings, you'll set a good foundation for the growth of genuine brotherly love.

Suggested Reading

For Parents

England, Marjorie. *Color Atlas of Life Before Birth: Normal Fetal Development.* Chicago: Year Book Medical Publishers, 1983.

Rugh, Robert, and Landrum Shettles. *From Conception to Birth: The Drama of Life's Beginnings.* New York: Harper & Row, 1971.

For Children Aged Two to Seven

Aliki. *Welcome, Little Baby.* New York: Greenwillow Books, 1987.

Anholt, Catherine. *Aren't You Lucky!* Boston: Joy Street Books, 1991.

Berenstain, Stan, and Jan Berenstain. *The Berenstain Bears' New Baby.* New York: Random Books for Young Readers, 1985.

Birdseye, Tom. *Waiting for Baby.* New York: Holiday House, 1991.

Gliori, Debi. *New Big Sister.* New York: Bradbury Press, 1991.

Rogers, Fred. *The New Baby.* New York: Putnam, 1985.

For Children Aged Eight to Twelve

Adler, C. S. *One Sister Too Many.* New York: Macmillan, 1989.

Auch, Mary Jane. *Pick of the Litter.* New York: Holiday House, 1988.

Galbraith, Kathryn Osebold. *Waiting for Jennifer.* New York: M. K. McElderry Books, 1987.

Galbraith, Kathryn Osebold. *Roommates and Rachel.* New York: M. K. McElderry Books, 1991.

Remarriage and Stepparenting

May had been divorced for four years when she met Mark. During the two years they dated, May's children, five-year-old Virginia and nine-year-old Ryan, developed a warm and caring relationship with Mark. When the big day arrived, Virginia and Ryan were joyful members of the wedding party and afterward they all settled in as one big happy family.

"Then I started to notice a cold, resentful attitude creeping into Ryan's conversations with Mark," says May. "Ryan was becoming very disrespectful and sometimes downright rude. Pretty soon the little one picked up on Ryan's tone and attitude, and the whole atmosphere of our home became tense, and even hostile."

"I was so surprised the first time Ryan boldly told me, 'Mind your own business,'" remembers Mark. "We had a good relationship and I knew I hadn't done anything to offend him or change his feelings toward me. I still don't know what happened."

What happened in this household is very common in stepfamilies. Emotions and attitudes run the gamut from loving one day to resentful the next. Kids and stepparents often have no clearcut understanding of why they act the way they do in their blended family, but it's certain that what's needed to ease the tension and confusion is open, honest communication.

The problems encountered by stepfamilies affect millions of adults and children. The latest federal census figures indicate that one of two marriages ends in divorce and that two-thirds of the divorced population marry again within three years. This means that, nationally, half a million adults become stepparents each year and that more than fifteen million children under the age of eighteen are living in stepfamilies.

This chapter is written both for stepparents and for parents who have remarried and now need to talk to their biological children about the new family structure. These parents and children all face some degree of the emotional and psychological upheaval that are part of the package deal for blended families.

The advice we offer here is generally appropriate for children of any age. However, keep in mind that very young children (under age four) have little concept of "marriage" and therefore primarily need repeated and honest assurances of continued parental love. Older children adjust better to the new family when they are prepared in advance with the facts: how family holidays and traditions may be affected; how family rules may change; what role the stepparent will take in school, community, and family functions; what name the stepparent will be called by; and the like. But whether four or fourteen years old, all children need someone to talk to about the changes their parents' remarriage brings to their lives.

Kids' Problems That Affect Communication

When you talk to your kids about their new family it's important to keep in mind the fears and concerns they are bringing to the conversation. Whether they voice them aloud or not, these concerns generally include:

- Fear that they will lose the bond unique to children and their single parents;
- Fear that children born to the newly remarried parent might supplant them;
- Disappointment at the demise of hopes for reconciliation between their biological parents;
- Confusion over a conflict of loyalty between the absent parent and stepparent.

Stepparents' Problems That Affect Communication

Among the factors that influence communication about remarriage and stepparenting are the ambivalent feelings that stepparents may bring to the new family and the guilt the ambivalence causes. It's not at all unusual for the "new" parent to feel love, anger, resentment, and jealousy all at the same time—yet it's hard to admit these feelings, never mind talk about them.

To give yourself a fair chance to adjust to your new role as stepparent, allow yourself the freedom to feel many contradictory and yet equally intense emotions. When you can get over your guilt for occasionally feeling "unloving," you'll have a much better chance of talking openly and listening to your stepchildren about their own ambivalent feelings.

Also, if you, as a new stepparent, have children of your own from a previous marriage, it's inevitable that you will, at first, love your biological children more than your stepchildren. Although inevitable, the unrealistic expectation to love all children equally causes much unspoken guilt and interferes with the possibility of growing closer to the stepchildren as you get to know each other better. Be tolerant with yourself, and allow yourself time to build a loving relationship.

Why Talk to Stepchildren?

The story of a young newlywed in my neighborhood who cried throughout her first day as a stepparent offers a good illustration of why parents, stepparents, and children need to talk.

Rebecca's ten-year-old stepson, Dan, arrived on Saturday morning expecting the usual routine during his weekend visit: a trip to the park with his dad to throw a baseball around, an afternoon in front of the home-video screen, a quick pizza dinner, and then back home to his mom. But, on this special weekend (her first as a stepparent), Rebecca thought it would be fun to do new things together as a family. She carefully planned a day that included a picnic in the park, a trip to the zoo, and dinner at her parents' home. When Dan heard the plans, he turned to his dad and complained, "I don't want her to come with us. She's not part of my family."

The remarriage of a parent can threaten children's basic needs for predictability and unconditional love from the biological parent—hence the common negative reactions. Unfortunately, without help, most children can't verbalize their feelings of loss, so they often find undesirable ways of "talking" about their needs. Younger children may regress to babyish actions like thumb-sucking, whining, or clinging; older ones may choose negative behaviors like being uncooperative, demanding, rude, or disobedient.

Acting out negative feelings is typical for children in stepfamilies, but when you're alert to these pleas for help, you can keep this communication tactic from turning into a stepfamily fiasco. To head off trouble, don't wait for your children to come to you with their concerns. Whether you're the parent or the stepparent, encourage them to bring their feelings out into the open right away.

How to Talk About Remarriage and Stepparenting

How you talk about sensitive topics is often as important as *what* you say. Such is the case when talking to a stepchild or when talking to your child about a new stepparent.

Use a Positive Approach. Ordering kids to be happy is generally an ineffective parenting strategy. Still, you may find yourself on the verge of yelling something like, "I want you to stop this sulking right now. I've had enough of your cry-baby attitude." Although your patience may be stretched to the near-breaking point, try to use a positive approach with an open and tolerant attitude when you talk to your kids.

Whenever you can, as a parent or stepparent, respond to negative actions or remarks with comments like these:

"This must be a very hard time for you. Do you want to talk about it?"

"I know you must be feeling a little uncertain of what life will be like around here. I feel the same way myself sometimes."

"Why don't you tell me what you're feeling right now?"

Find Private Moments to Talk. Sometimes the most convenient time to talk to kids is not the best time. For example:

At the family dinner table, Jack asked his seven-year-old daughter, "So Kate, how are you getting along with your stepmom?"

While driving her three stepchildren to school, Jane tossed out the questions, "Hey guys, is everything okay with us? Am I a good mother so far?"

As the noncustodial dad drops off his four-year-old son at his mom's, she asked, "Jake, how did you like your new stepmother?"

Certainly these children have been invited to talk about their feelings, but how and when they were asked destroys any chance of honest communication.

When you invite your children to talk about their feelings, give them some privacy. Make some quiet time when the two of you can talk one-on-one and out of earshot of other family members. Your conversations don't necessarily need to revolve around the new family situation; talk about anything in general. It's these casual, quiet times that help children relax and express their thoughts most freely.

What to Say If You're a Stepparent

It's quite likely that there will be times when your stepchildren will shoot out remarks that hurt, confuse, or insult you. The following four retorts are classic in stepfamilies. Thinking about them in advance may help you resist the temptation to match wits with your stepchildren when they make these remarks.

"You're not my real mother [father]."

This refrain is certainly a classic—so expect it. But don't let it rule the tone of your relationship with your stepchildren. The best approach to dealing with the fact that you're not your stepchildren's "real" parent is to avoid setting yourself up for attack.

If your stepchildren seem resentful of your presence in their family, talk to your spouse about your title. It's best if you are not

introduced to anyone as "my children's new mother (or father)."
This instantly ignites resentment and fuels the feelings of guilt
connected with disloyalty to the biological parent.

Don't force stepchildren to call you "Mom" or "Dad" unless they
feel comfortable with these terms. Using these names too soon
implies that your relationship is close before it has had a chance
to develop. Instead, ask them (or have your spouse ask them) what
they'd like to call you; you might suggest that they call you by your
first name.

Discuss with your stepchildren the role you now play in their
lives. You might say, "Your mother [father] will always be your
mother [father], but as your stepparent, I'll also be taking care of
you at times. I'm not asking you to love me. I just want to have
a good relationship with you so that we can both like and trust
each other."

Children who reject a stepparent often perceive a threat to
the loyalty they feel for their biological parent who is not present.
When your stepchildren shout, "You're not my real mother," you
have an opportunity to lessen this conflict of divided loyalty. Say
clearly and more than once, "I'm not trying to be your mother
[father] because I know you already have [or 'have had' if the parent is deceased] a mother [father]. I am a grownup who can become your friend."

"My father knows more about everything than you do."

This little zinger is bound to boil some blood. But try count-
ing to ten before you give in to the temptation to respond, "Oh,
yeah? Well does he know about thermal nuclear waste and its effects
on the environment?"

Instead, use this circumstance to let the children know that you respect their absent parent and understand how much they love and miss that parent. Say firmly, without hint of hurt or insult, "I'm sure your father does know a great deal, but I'm not competing with your father and I have no desire to replace him. I do want to be a good friend to you, though, and share with you whatever I know."

"I don't have to do what you say."

This is a time-honored test of your authority as a disciplinarian. While you're feeling your way into the family system, it's best to leave major disciplinary decisions to the child's natural parent. Be sure your spouse knows that you do not wish to take on full parental responsibility immediately.

At some point, however, you will need to discipline your stepchildren and you should expect resistance. But don't back down. With great confidence in your authority, say, "As your stepparent, I have a responsibility to enforce the rules of this household. I understand how angry you are about this, but you *do* have to do what I say."

If the children continue to disregard your rules or instructions, you'll need to talk with your spouse about the rules of the house and appropriate punishment for disobedience. Then, together, tell the children, "These are household rules. They will be enforced by both parent and stepparent, and when they are broken, these are the consequences."

This firm and nonnegotiable approach to discipline lets children know what you expect from them. This alone will help ease the tension of stepparenting because kids need to know their boundaries. And, believe it or not, they do feel better when an adult cares enough to define and enforce the rules.

"I hate you. I wish my father [mother] never married you."

This line is generally yelled in anger as the child rushes from the room before the stepparent can respond. After the child has cooled off and returned, you might say something like, "I understand you were very angry at me before. And you're entitled to your thoughts and feelings. But it's important for us to get along better and I'd like to talk with you about what just happened." In your discussion, focus on the issue at hand and not on the child's emotional reaction.

Your stepchildren will find many other things to say to you that may hurt and confuse you. If they don't yell them out loud, they may be feeling them inside, adding to their own hurt and confusion. Whatever is said or felt, the general rules of communication remain stable:

- Be positive in your response.
- Be understanding of the fear behind the anger.
- Offer promise of warmth, friendship, and a special relationship that will not replace the absent parent.
- Be responsive to the times your stepchildren want to talk or play with you.
- Go slowly in forming the relationship.
- Don't worry if the first encounters don't go well.
- Don't reject the children even if they initially reject you.

What to Say If You're the Biological Parent

As the biological parent in your blended family, you, too, have an important role to play in talking to your kids about your remarriage and their new stepparent. Undoubtedly, there will be times when you find yourself in the awkward middle position between your spouse and your children.

What should Dan's father have said when Dan complained about his father's new wife, "I don't want her to come with us. She's not part of our family"? On the spot like this, Dan's dad was in a no-win situation. If he had agreed to leave his wife home, she would be upset. If he had insisted she come along, Dan would have been angry all day. The best medicine is preventive: parent and stepparent need to talk about how to handle these kinds of situations as a team *before* the problem arises.

It's very important that you show a willingness to cooperate with and support your spouse in all efforts to communicate with your children. Read over the retorts listed in "What to Say If You're a Stepparent"; the responses suggested for stepparents will have greater positive impact if they're echoed by you, too. If, for example, your child says, "I don't have to do what she says," you can respond, "I understand how angry you are about this, but you *do* have to do what your stepmother says."

Don't let your children divide and conquer. Work to present a unified attitude of understanding, love, and above all, patience.

Suggested Resources

Stepfamily Association of America
215 Centennial Mall South
Suite 212
Lincoln, NE 68508
402-477-7837

Suggested Reading

For Parents

Prilik, Pearl. *Stepmothering: Another Kind of Love: A Caring, Commonsense Guide to Stepfamily.* New York: Berkley Books, 1990.

Visher, Emily, and John Visher. *How to Win As a Stepfamily.* New York: Brunner-Mazel, 1991.

For Children Aged Four to Seven

Banks, Ann. *Me and My Stepfamily: A Kids' Journal.* New York: Penguin Books, 1990.

Berry, Joy Wilt. *Good Answers to Tough Questions About Stepfamilies.* Chicago: Childrens Press, 1990.

Boyd, Lizi. *Sam Is My Half-Brother.* New York: Viking, 1990.

For Children Aged Eight to Twelve

Danziger, Paula. *It's An Aardvark-Eat-Turtle World.* New York: Delacorte Press, 1985.

Glassman, Bruce. *Everything You Need to Know About Stepfamilies.* New York: Rosen Publishing Group, 1988.

Hathorn, Elizabeth. *Thunderwith.* Boston: Little, Brown, 1991.

Rosenberg, Maxine. *Talking About Stepfamilies.* New York: Bradbury Press, 1990.

Repeating a Grade

Ten-year-old Danielle is in a school system that requires all fourth graders who do not achieve grade-level scores on standardized achievement tests to repeat the grade. Unfortunately, because of this requirement Danielle will be in fourth grade again next year.

José suffers severe asthma. Excessive absenteeism caused him to miss a great deal of school work this year. Next year, he will repeat the third grade.

Second-grader Susan has trouble keeping up with her classmates in reading skills. Her supplemental reading teacher has recommended that Susan repeat the second grade.

Timmy is one of the youngest children in his kindergarten class. His teacher says that, although he's quite smart, he seems to be developmentally immature because he doesn't follow directions, pay attention, or sit still for very long. She has recommended that Timmy spend another year in kindergarten.

These four children sit in the center of a maelstrom of controversy. The debate over whether to make children repeat a grade continues to produce reams of research studies. For every expert in education and child development who condemns grade retention there is another who supports it. We cannot settle this dispute in this chapter, nor is there reason to try. Our goal is to help you talk to your children who, for whatever reason, must repeat a grade.

Whether good or bad, the practice of retaining children in school is a common occurrence. *The New York Times* has reported that America's public schools hold back 2.4 million children every year. The Center for Policy Research in Education at Rutgers University has estimated that by the time of high school graduation, one of every two American students has been held back at least once.

Sometimes retention is the result of parental request, sometimes it's a school mandate, sometimes it's a joint decision of teacher, parents, and child. However the decision to have a child repeat a grade is made, these astonishing numbers give us an idea of how many parents across the country have the difficult task each year of talking to their children about this sensitive issue.

Getting the Facts

As soon as it's certain that your child will repeat a grade, arrange for a face-to-face meeting with the teacher. Come prepared to ask lots of questions; you'll need to be absolutely clear on the reasons why retention is the best option for your child—so that when your child cries "Why?" you'll have the answers. Before you talk to your child, know the answers to these questions:

• *Is the problem developmental or academic?* Some children simply are not developmentally mature enough to do well in school. Although they may be quite intelligent, developmentally immature children lag behind their classmates emotionally and/or socially. Other children fall behind in their academic studies (especially in later grades) and need time to catch up before moving ahead. If your child has a specific academic deficiency, ask the teacher to show you test scores and isolate the problem areas.

• *What is the educational plan for the following year?* Find out if the school will have your child repeat the same curriculum program, or offer a different program with tutorial help. Ask if he or she will have the same teacher or a different one.

• *Is there anything your child can do at home to improve his or her chances of future school success?* Sometimes children who become more actively involved in their own education feel a sense of accomplishment that eases the blow of being left back. Are there games or projects your child can do to enhance readiness? Are there specific subject areas that need more attention than others? Would a tutor be helpful? Are there supplemental resources the school can lend you?

Talking to Your Child

Once you're sure grade retention is the best or only option for your child, there's one more thing you should do before you talk to him or her: put on a positive attitude. Your child's acceptance of grade retention will depend, to a large extent, on how you break the news. No matter what the cause or who's to blame, there's no point in adding your own upset or anger to the burden your child will already be asked to bear.

Be sure you've fully accepted the retention before talking to your children so you won't blurt out painful accusations like this collection of angry retorts: "It's your own fault!" "If you had paid attention and tried you would be going ahead with your class." "I told you that if you didn't calm down and behave you wouldn't be allowed to go to the next grade." "Well, maybe now you'll learn that if you don't study, you don't pass."

Whether the reason for grade retention is developmental or academic, and whether your child is in kindergarten or fourth grade, there is no easy way to break the news. Your goal in this initial discussion is to give the facts in a calm and nonjudgmental way.

After you've gathered the facts from the teacher, find an unhurried time, away from other children, to give the news. Start off being empathic and then present your decision as a positive thing by saying something like this:

"I know you've been finding school very hard this year. Well, your teacher and I have come up with a plan that will help you do well in school next year. Rather than go into the next grade, you're going to stay in the grade you're in now. This will make you one of the oldest, happiest, and possibly smartest children in the class."

Responding to Your Child's Feelings

After the news is out, what you say to your child will depend on his or her reaction. The child may respond with forceful feelings immediately, or may ponder the idea during the school break and voice feelings later. Whenever the child chooses to respond, she or he probably will not be happy about the idea—but don't let your child's negative feelings affect your decision. If retention is the only option, state it clearly, and then help your child accept it. If you show uncertainty or anger, you'll make the situation more difficult for your child.

Make it clear that you understand your child's negative feelings. Let the child yell, cry, moan, and plead. Offer a sympathetic shoulder, but then return to the fact and add a positive view. The following are some negative reactions your child might experience and the kind of responses you can use to defuse those feelings.

Anger and Obstinacy

"I won't go back to school!"

- Mirror the child's feelings: "I can see you're really angry about this."
- Offer your understanding: "I understand why you feel this way right now, and I don't blame you."
- Look to the positive: "But I also know you feel angry when your school work is hard and it takes you a long time to finish it."
- Offer continued support: "Anytime you think about your class next year, you can come to me to talk about it. I'm here for you, and together we'll make next year your best school year ever."

Embarrassment

"The kids will laugh at me!"

- Mirror the child's feelings: "You feel embarrassed and you're worried about what other kids will say."
- Look to the positive: "But this decision can also make you feel proud. Next year you'll do better work because you'll be familiar with what your teacher expects you to do. The other kids won't know about the hard time you had this past year, and you won't feel embarrassed in your classroom anymore."
- Offer coping strategies: "If kids from your old class laugh at you, ignore them. They're probably the same kids who laugh when someone makes a mistake or does poorly in school. Now you have a chance to make new friends."

Blaming

"It's your fault. You shouldn't have let this happen!"

- Mirror the child's feelings: "I know you're angry at me right now for putting you in this class before you were ready."
- Assume some responsibility, if appropriate: "We should have realized that we started you in school before you were ready. We made a big mistake and I'm sorry."
- Look to the positive: "But now that we understand the problems you've been having, we're sure this is the best decision for you."

Self-pity

"I'm so stupid!"

- Mirror the child's feelings: "You feel that you're being left back because you're not smart."
- Explain the facts positively: "The truth is, we know you are smart, but you just haven't had a chance to show us yet."
- Remind the child of commonality: "Lots of children repeat a grade in school, and it has nothing to do with being 'stupid.' Did you know that almost two and a half *million* children will be repeating a grade just like you?"
- Look to the positive: "Struggling to keep up with your classmates this past year probably did make you feel as if you weren't as smart as everyone else. But by repeating the grade, next year you'll be the one everyone tries to keep up with!"

Moralism

"It's not fair."

- Mirror the child's feelings and offer understanding: "I understand why you feel this decision isn't fair to you."
- Look to the positive: "But it's also not fair to make you struggle to keep up with classmates." Here you might use the analogy of a race. Ask your child if it would be fair to have to run a race against children who were bigger and stronger. Then explain that your child wasn't ready for first (or second, or whatever) grade, that the others were in a way "bigger and stronger," and so your child is being given a chance to run the race again, competing against children who are more evenly matched.
- Offer support: "Now that I know you had such trouble, I'm going to be right next to you this time, coaching and encouraging you so that this time, you'll come out a winner."

If you can convince your child that grade retention can be a good thing, that he or she is not being punished, that the child did not "fail," that nobody is mad at or disappointed in the child, then the hardest part of dealing with this sensitive issue will have been mastered.

Then be sure to continue this encouraging and positive attitude as your child enters the next school year. Your unwavering support will ease the difficulties and occasional uncomfortable moments that are bound to occur.

Suggested Reading

For Parents

Ilg, Frances, L., and others. *School Readiness.* Rev. ed. New York: Harper & Row, 1978.

For Children

Hobby, Janice Hale. *Staying Back.* Gainesville, Fla.: Triad, 1982. (Presents the true stories of seven elementary school children who shared the difficult experience of repeating a grade.)

Sleep-Away Camp

Monday

    Dear Mom and Dad,

    The food is awful
    The counselor is mean.
    I hate the kids here.
    I want to come home.

            Love,
            Jeffrey

Wednesday

    Dear Mom and Dad,

    Me and my bunkmate found a frog and put it in the girls'
      cabin—it was great!
    We roasted marshmallows on a real campfire last night.
    My counselor says he's gonna teach us how to shoot a bow
      and arrow.
    Can I stay an extra week?

            Love,
            Jeffrey

The dramatic change in the tone of these letters is not at all unusual for kids who stay at any of the United States' 5,500 resident camps each summer. Even the gung-ho kids who sleep in their camp shirts the entire week before camp begins will probably feel a bit homesick at first. The degree of homesickness, however, can be reduced by the way you prepare your kids for camp and by the way you respond to their pleas for mercy once they get there.

Take Time to Prepare

In the following typical dialogue, the parent is setting herself up for trouble:

"Okay Katherine, you're all set. This July while Dad and I visit Grandma after her operation, we're sending you to Camp Sleepover. We'll miss you terribly, but we talked to the camp director and he says you're gonna love it there."

"But Mom, what's the camp like?"

"Oh, honey. I wouldn't send you to any camp that wasn't just wonderful. Now don't you worry about a thing. You'll have a great time."

"Can I come home if I want to?"

"Sure you can. You just call me at Grandma's and I'll come get you."

If Katherine is going to be happy at sleep-away camp, she'll need to be better prepared for the experience before she packs her bags, and she'll need more encouragement to stick it out.

As you set about selecting a camp, involve your children, if possible. Explore the details together. These are some of the things you and your kids need to know:

How many kids in a cabin?

Are there cots? Bunkbeds? Sleeping bags?

What's the daily schedule?

What's the menu?

Who are the counselors?

Where do kids go if they're injured or sick?

What do they do on a rainy day?

When you've talked about all the information you have, ask your kids what else they'd like to know. Help them keep a running list of their questions, and when you think they've got their queries in order, call or write the camp director to get the answers. The more information your kids have before they arrive, the more easily they will adjust to the new environment and routine.

You can also help prepare your children by talking about camp in ways that build self-confidence. You should, for example, talk about camp as a privilege, not a punishment. Tell them, "You're allowed to go to camp this summer," rather than, "I'm sending you to camp." Continue this positive approach by talking about the excitement of camp and playing down the "I'll-miss-you" part.

Say to your children, "We love you and we think you're going to have a good time at camp." If you went to camp yourself, share specific good memories and joys. You might say something like, "I remember the day it rained and we watched movies, ate popcorn, and laughed all day long."

Lastly, before your children go off to camp, discuss the common occurrence called homesickness. Some degree of homesickness is bound to affect many campers, especially during the first three days. Assure your children that this happens all the time to lots of kids. Tell them, "It's nothing to be embarrassed about— it's okay to feel a little lonely and miss home."

Then express confidence in their ability to get over this feeling if it should happen. Say, "Like lots of kids, you might miss home at first. But after a few days that feeling usually starts to go away and you'll enjoy your stay at camp more and more."

What to Do About Cold Feet

For the last three years, ten-year-old Jason has gone to day camp. This year he's excited because his parents have agreed to let him go to a sleep-away camp.

"Only two months and twenty-four days," he announced the morning after his parents gave him the okay. The countdown continued until the morning when only eight days were left to go, and Jason changed his mind. "I'd rather go to the day camp," he declared and walked slowly out of the room.

His parents had no real reason to make Jason go to a sleep-over camp if he didn't want to, but because he had been so anxious to go, they knew their son would be disappointed in himself if he didn't give it a try. So before canceling his reservation, Jason's parents tried a few tactics that you might use if your children wake up one morning with "cold feet."

Help Uncover the Reason. Don't jump on this sign of hesitation as proof that your kid isn't ready for camp. Try to find out what your camper is apprehensive about—meeting new friends? Learning to swim? Having to shower with bunkmates? Having to shower instead of bathe? Fear of wolves? Who knows what has popped into your child's mind. Express your interest in helping by saying something like, "I know you want to go to camp, so let's see if together we can uncover what it is that's making you a little worried." Then try to draw out the problem and deal with that directly.

Stage a Rehearsal.   Here are a couple of ways you can rehearse sleep-over camp. First, you might arrange for your child to sleep over at a relative's or friend's house. If your child is unaccustomed to being away from you, this will help ease fears of separation.

Also, you can "camp" right at home. A tent in the backyard, or a cot on the porch, or a blanket thrown over the kitchen table can all make the idea of "roughing it" sound like fun.

Talk with Confidence.   If your child starts to feel anxious about going away to camp, talk about past experiences that called for similar bravery. You might say, for example, "Remember that time when you were worried about being in the school play, and you even said you didn't want to go on opening night? Remember how much fun it was once you got there?" There are probably a number of occasions you can think of when your child was apprehensive about something, but then went ahead and succeeded. Now is a good time to talk about them.

As you work to build your child's confidence, be careful not to offer an easy out. Saying "If you still don't like camp by Sunday, I'll come and get you" sets the stage for failure. Once you set such a deadline, your child has no reason to try to adjust. Be supportive, optimistic, and unrelenting in your belief: "I think you'll adjust to camp life and have a good time."

Curing Homesickness

Long-distance sobbing over the telephone can demoralize even the most seasoned parents. What can you say to distressful pleas like "Please come get me. I hate it here. I miss you!"?

Well, the worst thing you can say is, "I'll be right there." Given some time and understanding, the vast majority of homesick campers end up staying and having a good time.

If you receive a "help" call, the first thing you should do is *listen.* Give your children freedom to talk about their worries, fears, and gripes. Without acknowledging right or wrong, focus on the problem by saying, "I can tell you're feeling lonely."

Then express confidence in your child's ability to solve the problem: "Once you get involved in all the activities scheduled for this week, I know you'll feel good about being there."

Try steering the conversation to positive things by asking questions you're pretty sure will lead to talk about the good side of camp. You might ask,

"Have you gone swimming yet?"

"Did you get a chance to ride in a canoe?"

"Are you building campfires at night?"

"Have you met anyone else who also likes baseball?"

These kinds of questions will help get your child thinking about the new and interesting things going on.

If you feel your child is emotionally ready to be separated from you, don't rush to the rescue. Lend a sympathetic ear and encouragement, and then wait. Camp counselors agree that children who are given the opportunity to find their niche, end up enjoying their stay and feeling proud of themselves for facing and solving a problem.

The following Do's and Don'ts will help you handle a homesick camper.

Do's

- Pack a comfort item such as a favorite stuffed animal or a family photo.
- Send a letter a few days before your child leaves for

camp so your words of encouragement will arrive when they're most needed—in the first day or two.

- Send frequent postcards that chat about routine stuff and convey the message that the child isn't really missing anything special.
- Expect some complaints and bouts of homesickness.

Don'ts

- Don't panic or get angry.
- Don't write strong "I miss you" letters that describe how everyone, including the dog, is sad.
- Don't discuss worrisome family problems, like a divorce, illness, a new baby, or an upcoming move.
- Don't describe exciting and fun-filled activities at home that your child will regret missing.

Calling It Quits

If you become concerned that your child is suffering from more than the usual transient homesickness, call the camp director before you discuss the possibility of coming home with your child. Try to find out if there is anything that can be done to encourage the camper to stay: perhaps a change to another cabin, a new counselor, or a little more attention to activities favored by your child. But if you feel the problem is not going to be solved because your child simply wasn't ready for camp, then follow your heart and bring him or her home.

If you decide that coming home is best, it will be very important to keep your child from feeling like a failure.

Be careful not to show anger at having paid a lot of money for nothing, or for believing your child was more mature than he or she is, or for wasting your travel time.

Also, watch out for other more subtle put-downs: don't compare your child to the hundreds of other campers who do stick it out. And don't imply that your child will never be able to stay away from home or rule out the possibility of trying a sleep-away some other year.

Even as you drive away from the camp with your child, continue to be positive and supportive. Praise your child for trying and say, "Maybe next year you'll want to stay longer." And do try again next year, because when children master their fear of separation the benefits of summer camp are many.

Camp provides youngsters with a unique opportunity for emotional, educational, and social growth. This kind of group living experience offers a child a chance to learn how to cooperate with others and to tolerate individual differences. The routines of camp give children a sense of order and predictability. Within this secure setting, children's autonomy and individualization can increase. Children also develop confidence in their ability to handle real-life experiences on their own.

Suggested Reading

For Children Aged Four to Eight

Berenstain, Stan, and Jan Berenstain. *The Berenstain Bears Go to Camp.* New York: Random Books for Young Readers, 1989.

Part II

Concerns of Youth

Many of our children's concerns focus on sensitive topics such as sexuality, violence, drugs, and war. Unfortunately, these are often the topics that we feel most uncomfortable talking about, and so we put off informative discussions until the proverbial "tomorrow." Ironically, these are the very issues about which children need more, not less, information and parental guidance.

The following chapters will help you break through the barriers of embarrassment, lack of information, ignorance, and fear. They will help you give your children the knowledge they need to understand complex issues relevant to their lives in these modern times.

Knowledge is power—power to anticipate events and to prepare for them. With this information and your loving attitude your children can better understand and cope with confusing, sometimes frightening topics such as pornography, strangers, prejudice, birth, and death.

Death

The sun seemed especially bright that spring morning and a nostalgic smell of new flowers and fresh earth hung in the air. Duane remembers the details of the day because they stood in such stark contrast to the question on his daughter's mind.

"We were walking to the corner store for the newspaper," Duane recalls, "when my five-year-old, Jannette, looked up at me and asked, 'Daddy, what does *dead* mean?' I don't remember exactly what I said (I think I mumbled something about death being what happens to everybody eventually), but I do remember very clearly how surprised I was that on such a beautiful day, Jannette would ask such a sad question."

Questions about death are a very natural part of a child's continuous search for life's meaning. They don't imply any deep-seated problems or morbid personality traits. They are asked with the same innocence and curiosity that moves a child to ask "Why was I born?"

Because Duane was taken off-guard by a question about death, he lost an opportunity to talk with his daughter at an early age about this important subject. Unemotional and exploratory discussions about death at moments like these can serve two valuable purposes: (1) they help children learn to view death as natural, not mysterious or frightening, and (2) they help children prepare for inevitable death experiences such as the loss of a pet or relative.

Questions about death are bound to come up, so it's a good idea to think ahead about what you'll say.

Consider Your Child's Level of Understanding

Children's concerns about death vary according to their age. Try to remember this and tailor the details you offer to reflect your child's level of understanding.

Toddlers

Before the age of three, children are unable to comprehend death. Obviously, it isn't at all necessary to discuss this subject with such young children. At each level of development after this, however, children's ability to grasp the concept of mortality gradually increases with every life/death experience they witness.

Children Aged Three to Five

- A preschooler knows death is somehow connected with sadness.
- Most preschoolers regard life and death as related to mobility: moving means life; lack of movement means death.
- Death is not perceived as a final event, but as a temporary and reversible happening. (Watching cartoon characters rise up again after being completely crushed tends to reinforce this notion.)
- Preschoolers often ask questions like "What do dead people eat?" "What if the dead person is afraid of the dark?" "Can dead people see underground?"
- The fear of death at this age centers on separation from parents; death may be perceived as abandonment.

Children Aged Six to Eight

- Six- to eight-year-olds are beginning to realize the finality of death.
- They tend to associate death with a skeleton, a monster, or a ghostlike figure such as the grim reaper. (This often leads to nightmares and fear of the dark.)
- The child this age often does not comprehend the inevitability of his own death.
- When a loved one dies, children may feel it is a punishment for their own bad thoughts or behaviors.

Children Aged Nine to Twelve

- From nine or ten through adolescence, children begin to realize fully that death is irreversible, universal, and inevitable.
- After age eight children come to understand that all living things die, and that they, too, will die someday.
- They know death happens to people according to certain physical laws: for example, sometimes the body wears out just like an old car and can't run any longer.
- Children in this age group realize that the body can be fatally injured by accidents.

How Not to Talk to Children About Death

Once you have an idea of your child's level of understanding, you're almost ready to respond to that inevitable question "Why do people die?" But first, consider the following tips that outline how *not* to talk to your kids about death.

- *Don't equate death with sleep.* Avoid using metaphors such as "someone went to sleep" or "to eternal rest." If your children confuse death with sleep, they may become afraid of going to bed or taking naps, since they may fear they won't wake up.

• *Don't say someone who died "went away" or on a "long long trip."* Children may feel deserted or wonder why the person did not say good-bye. Also children may fear that other adults who go away, for a vacation or another simple reason, may not return either.

• *Don't tell young children that someone died because he or she got "sick."* Preschoolers cannot tell the difference between temporary and terminal illness. With young children it's best to explain that only a *very* serious sickness can cause death, and that although we all get a little sick at times, we quickly recover from these minor ailments.

• *Don't say, "Only old people die."* Children will soon discover that young people die, too. It's better to say something like: "Most people live a long time, but some don't. I expect you and I will live a very long time."

• *Don't avoid the subject.* If your child asks you a question about death, avoid the temptation to say, "Oh, that's not something you have to worry about now." Let your child see by your willingness to openly discuss the subject that death isn't an unspeakable topic.

How to Talk to Children About Death

What you say to your children about death will depend on many things, including your own beliefs and your children's level of understanding. There are, however, some guidelines that will help you give sound, meaningful answers to children's questions about death.

Be Comfortable Talking About Death. Each of us must accept and make our peace with death. When you can accept death, intellectually and emotionally, you can help your children learn to feel comfortable talking about it. Death should not be considered a frightening or morbid topic of conversation, so try to accept a child's questions about death with an attitude of "I won't know all the answers, but it's okay to ask." Let your children feel that you are as willing to talk about death as about birth.

Introduce Children to the Idea of Death at an Early Age. Learning about the meaning of death should be a gradual process and a part of everyday experiences. The simplest way to introduce children to the concept of death—even if they're too young to fully comprehend—is to talk openly about the natural life cycles of flowers, insects, and animals. Give your children opportunities to be responsible for the care of pets and plants. Encourage them to observe the natural stages of the birth, growth, reproduction, and death of these living things. Explain that all living things age continuously from birth and eventually die. In this way, the fact that living things—including people—die will be as natural as the fact that they are born.

Take Time to Understand Exactly What Your Child Is Asking. To avoid overwhelming your child, answer specific questions without adding information that the child has not requested. Here are some examples of limited responses to children's questions.

"Will I die when I grow up?"
"Everyone dies someday."

"Are you going to die too?"
Reassure the child by saying, "Yes, but I expect to go on living for a long time."

"Why is [a specific person in mourning] crying?"

You might say something like, "Aunt Ethel is crying because she is sad that Uncle Joe has died. She misses him very much. We all feel sad when someone we care about dies."

Make Concrete Statements. Since children under the age of nine have difficulty understanding abstract concepts, be simple and direct. Explain death to young children by relating your answers to a child's own experiences.

You might help a child define death in terms of the absence of life: a dead person does *not* breathe, talk, feel, sleep, or need food; a dead dog does *not* bark or run anymore.

When Jannette asked, "What is dead?" Duane might have responded, "Dead means not to be alive anymore. It's like these flowers—they're alive now, but in the winter their color fades and they wilt and die. The body, too, doesn't work anymore when it's dead. It doesn't move, or hear, or breathe, or feel, or even sleep. It just stops."

Introduce Ideas Gradually Over Time. Don't try to explain death in one discussion. Remember that children learn through repetition, so it's okay if they ask the same question over and over again. As they grow older and more mature, children will ask for even more clarification and elaboration—and that's good.

Duane missed his first chance to talk to his daughter about death, but he needn't worry—the subject will certainly come up again because kids are unceasingly curious and because examples of life and death are all around us.

Suggested Reading

For Parents

Grollman, Earl A. *Talking About Death: A Dialogue Between Parent and Child.* Boston: Beacon Press, 1987.

Kübler-Ross, Elisabeth. *On Death and Dying.* New York: Macmillan, 1969.

Lonetto, Richard. *Children's Conception of Death.* New York: Springer, 1980.

Stein, S. B. *About Dying.* New York: Walker, 1974.

Children Aged Four to Seven

Brown, Margaret Wise. *The Dead Bird.* Reading, Mass.: Addison-Wesley, Young Scott Books, 1965.

Stein, Sara B. *About Dying.* New York: Walker, 1974.

White, E. B. *Charlotte's Web.* New York: HarperCollins Child Books, 1952.

Children Aged Eight to Twelve

Cohen, Barbara. *Thank You, Jackie Robinson.* New York: Lothrop, 1974.

Zim, Herbert, and Sonia Bleeker. *Life and Death.* New York: Morrow, 1970.

Drug Abuse

"Look what I have."

"Where'd you get beer?"

"Never mind where I got it—let's drink it."

"I don't know—won't we get in trouble?"

"Don't be such a baby. How we gonna get in trouble if nobody knows. Come on. Let's see if you can drink a whole can in one gulp."

"But what about cheerleading practice?"

"We'll make it on time. And besides, beer loosens you up and makes it easier to do splits and stuff. It'll be great."

"Well, okay, if you're sure it's okay."

This dialogue between two eight-year-old girls is fictional, but you'd better believe that real-life conversations just like it occur in thousands of homes and schools all over this country. The majority of our children will be engaged in this kind of discussion at one time or another. Before that happens—it's time to talk.

Drug abuse is not something that happens only to other people's kids or only in big cities. We all know stories about good kids from good families whose lives were ruined by drugs. It's also not something that just randomly happens; research studies repeatedly show that a child's family has a strong influence over his or her likelihood of abusing drugs. Parental love, guidance, and support help children develop self-esteem, self-confidence, personal values, and goals—all of which contribute to the making of drug-free kids.

This chapter will look at a small piece of this big family picture: the role of family communication in preventing drug abuse.

When Should You Talk to Your Kids About Drug Abuse?

The best time to talk to children about drug abuse is obviously before they become drug abusers. For the most part, children ages 4 to 12 are non-users and still willing to listen to your beliefs and advice about this problem which affects too many of our young children.

According to a survey by the National Institute on Drug Abuse (NIDA), more than 1.6 million children, aged 12 to 17, use illicit drugs. Moreover, just under five million alcohol users are children under age 17. The NIDA survey also found that the average age at which a child initially takes alcohol is age eleven; for marijuana use, the starting age is 12. That's why now—TODAY—is the best time to begin a dialogue with your children about drug use and abuse.

How Should You Talk to Your Kids About Drug Abuse?

Drug use and abuse are very effectively "discussed" through example. Children can inadvertently learn from their parents to view drugs as a panacea for pain and tension. Too frequently, a parent may pass comments like, "I need a cigarette." Or, "Boy, I earned this drink today." Or, simply, "Jimmy, get me my tranquilizers. What a day I've had." These remarks convey the idea that daily tensions are routinely relieved with drugs.

On the other hand, your moderate use of over-the-counter medication and alcohol can be used to help children identify with responsible drug use. Because drug education is commonly taught in school, viewed in public-service ads, and even preached in religious education classes, it should not surprise you if your young child suddenly recoils in horror as you pour yourself a glass of wine at dinner.

"Mommy!" she might yell. "My teacher said liquor is a drug and you shouldn't take drugs!"

Or, your son might caution you, "Daddy, you shouldn't buy things at the *drug* store."

These kinds of situations offer you a chance to explain your personal use of drugs and how that differs from drug abuse.

Begin with Family Rules.   Kids need limits and rules, and they need to know what you expect of them. Set firm, clear standards that say unequivocally "In our house we care about our health and we do not abuse any drugs."

Explain Laws About Drugs.   Explain that some drugs are legal and using them sensibly is not necessarily bad. It is not unhealthy or against the law for adults to drink wine. It *is* against the law and unhealthy for young people to drink any kind of alcohol, and it's very unhealthy for adults to drink too much alcohol. But moderate use of legal drugs is not necessarily bad.

In the same way, use prescription and over-the-counter drugs with caution and explanation. Try to avoid taking any medications in front of your children and when you must, talk about the reason. You might say, "I'm taking this cold medicine because a drug like this can be helpful if I don't take too much or use it too often." Let your children know that drugs have positive medicinal purposes when taken in the proper way.

Critique Ads for Drugs with Your Kids. Information about the good and bad sides of legal drugs is often conveyed through advertisements for medications, alcohol, and cigarettes. Television, radio, and print ads promise that life's physical and social problems can be instantly cured with a pill, a cigarette, or a drink. Kids see adults buying remedies for everything that ails them.

The message that chemical substances can cure all our ills and promote beauty, success, and fun is a dangerous one. It doesn't include the physical consequences of drug-taking, such as hangovers, vomiting, and addiction. And it implies that realities such as daily stress and people's personal characteristics can be altered simply. To help your children see through ads, ask them questions such as these:

"Do you think it's really the cigarette that makes that woman feel happy?"

"What will happen if that man quickly drinks that whole bottle of liquor?"

"Can you think of something besides that sleeping pill that might help the lady fall asleep?"

"If all those spicy foods make that man's stomach hurt, how could he stop having stomach aches without taking that medicine?"

These kinds of questions help children become critical of the idea that happiness can be found in chemical substances.

Use the Media to Give Your Children a Balanced Picture of Drug Use. Scan the daily papers and circle articles related to drug use. Some will show the devastating effects of drug abuse in alcohol-related car accidents, drug-war murders, and lung cancer deaths. Others will highlight beneficial and even life-saving medicines. These stories can give you opportunities to teach your children the difference between responsible use and life-threatening abuse.

Talking About Drugs with Children in Kindergarten through Grade Three

Young children cannot fully understand the negative effects of drug abuse. But they can understand that people can stay healthy by putting good things like fruits and vegetables into their bodies, and become very ill by putting bad things like junk food, pollutants, and "bad" drugs into their bodies. Although it might not yet be time to discuss the details of drug abuse, this is a good time to instill positive concepts of good health and personal choice.

Talk About Your Family Attitudes and Rules. Drug-abuse prevention begins at home with the establishment of moral attitudes and clear cut rules. Talk to your children from a very early age about what is right and wrong, and let them know that your family has certain rules that must be followed. When a moral situation arises, take the time to talk about the "whys" of your actions and beliefs. Here are some examples:

- "You cannot take that gum from the store without paying because taking something that doesn't belong to you is wrong."
- "We will give this food to the poor because we like to share what we have with people who don't have as much."
- "Even if your friends use that word, the people in our family don't, and I don't want to hear you talk like that."

- "Don't laugh or yell at that child who doesn't know how to play the game as well as you do because that hurts his feelings. Instead, help him practice to become better."
- "In this family we don't abuse drugs or use illegal drugs. We use only drugs that are legal and that our doctor says will help a medical problem."

Such ongoing explanations of "good and bad" help young children establish their own value systems, which will later enable them to decide for themselves that abusing drugs is bad.

Talk About the Importance of Good Health.   Young children can gradually come to understand that what they put into their bodies has a direct effect on how well their body works. The next time you tell your children to cut out the junk food or to eat their vegetables, take an extra minute to explain *why*. Here are some things you might say:

- "Your body likes it when you feed it good foods like that apple, because that kind of food gives your body the energy it needs to grow and feel good."
- "If you fill yourself with food like that candy, your body doesn't get what it needs to build muscle and bones and keep you feeling healthy."
- "Cigarettes, too much alcohol, and some drugs are not good because they can make the body sick."
- "Don't ever taste anything that you find on the street. It could be something that would hurt your body and make you sick."

These kinds of comments teach and reinforce the important drug-prevention concept that putting harmful substances into the body is a bad idea.

Talk About Good and Bad Drugs.   Young children are quite concrete and literal in their thinking. If their teacher says, "Say *no* to drugs," your child will lump all drugs into the "bad" category. You can help your child begin to understand drug *abuse* by offering your own observations when a family situation presents an opportunity. When your child is ill and the doctor prescribes a medication, for example, you can use that circumstance to comment on the useful properties of some drugs. At the same time you can explain why the doctor tells you exactly how much medicine to use and when to use it: this helps you use the drug properly and avoid making the child sicker by over-using medication.

Or, if you're in the room with a drunk friend or relative, you can say to your children, "She can't control the way she talks or acts because she drank too much alcohol. She'll probably feel very sick in a little while." You can also note that the people who drink just a little do not lose control or feel sick.

Talk About Saying No.   Young children eagerly agree to say no should anyone offer them "bad" drugs. Unfortunately, research has found that today's kids need more than a slogan to help them when the real situation arises. You can give your kids the self-empowerment to say no to drugs by teaching them how to resist peer pressure while they're still young.

Role playing through the What-If game is a tried-and-true way to teach resistance skills. Start out with casual inquiries like, "What if Jamie asked you to ride your bike to the park without asking me first. What would you say to him?" Or, "What if Marianne told you it was okay to go swimming with no grown-ups around? What would you say to her?"

You can extend the game to help develop good responses to peer pressure. Here's an example:

"What if Jake told you to steal candy from the store? What would you say to him?"

"I'd tell him no."

"What if he said you were a scaredy-cat if you didn't take the candy?"

"I'd tell him I am not."

"What if Jake said he'd tell all the kids at school that you were a baby if you didn't take the candy?"

"I don't know what I'd say."

This kind of "game" teaches children that their friends may not give up just because they say no once. Help them practice saying no in these make-believe scenes until they feel pride in their ability to say no over and over again.

Talking About Drugs with Children in Grades Four to Six

The White House Drug Abuse Policy Office has stated that children feel pressure to use drugs and drink alcohol by the fourth grade. At this age, the pressure comes mainly from their peers. Children in grades four to six begin moving away from their parents' influence and look for acceptance and approval from children their own age.

This need to conform can weaken your child's belief in the family rules and standards you've established over the years. Thus, in the elementary school years, it's crucial to have an ongoing dialogue with your children about drug use and abuse.

Remember: at this age, if your kids aren't getting their information about drugs from you, they're certainly getting it from someone else.

Talk About Up-to-Date Facts.   The U.S. Department of Education's booklet, *Growing Up Drug Free: A Parent's Guide to Prevention*, says that children in grades four to six should know the following information:

- Ways to identify specific drugs, including alcohol, tobacco, marijuana, inhalants, and cocaine in their various forms
- The long- and short-term effects and consequences of use
- The effects of drugs on different parts of the body, and the reasons drugs are especially dangerous for growing bodies
- The consequences of alcohol and other illegal drug use to the family, society, and the user

To discuss this information effectively with your children, you need the most up-to-date facts. You can't convince your children that you know what you're talking about if you use old, outdated terms or information. So, now is the time to study up on illicit drugs, learn the facts, and keep up on the lingo. We can't begin to detail all these facts here, but the resources listed at the end of this chapter will help you find the information you need.

Share Information as You Find It.   As you begin your discussions about drug abuse, you don't have to hide the fact that you don't know everything about illicit drugs. When you obtain material you want to study, share it with your child; explore it together. State clearly that because you love your child very much you want to learn all about the drug abuse problem that affects so many young people.

You might look up from your reading and ask questions like these:

"Did you know that sniffing glue, nail polish remover, or type-writer correction fluid can cause irreversible brain damage?"

"It says here that some children are starting to use crack in elementary school. Why do you think they do that?"

"It's illegal to smoke marijuana. Do you know why?"

As you search for the facts, find out if drug education is a part of your school's curriculum. If it is, ask your children's teachers to tell you when the topic will be discussed and exactly what is in the lesson. Use this information to further explore the subject at home. Ask your kids, "What did you learn in class today about drugs?" Then take some time to combine this information with your family's values, beliefs, and feelings.

Be Honest About Your Own Experience. When you open the floor to discussions about drugs, don't be surprised if your kids want to know if you ever smoked pot, used other illegal drugs, or engaged in underage drinking. Given that the media has broad-cast the experimental marijuana use by even President Clinton, the casual drug abuse of the sixties and seventies is bound to come back to haunt many parents.

If you did smoke pot, pop pills, drop acid, use other illegal drugs, or abuse alcohol, truthfulness with clarification is the best way to respond to your kids' questions. If you lie or are evasive, you'll lose credibility in your kids' eyes when they probe relatives and old friends and find out the real story. Here are some things you might say:

- "Yes, I made a mistake, and if I had to do it over again I wouldn't."
- Point out your personal knowledge of the adverse effects and dangers of your use: "I remember driving while I was high and putting myself and everyone in the car in great danger. It was a stupid thing to do."
- Without implying justification, explain the social climate of the times: "Drugs were a part of the youth culture. They were often as freely available at parties as potato chips are today. Also, all the facts about the dangers and long-term effects of drug use weren't known yet."
- Caution your kids that the dangers of drug use then were, indeed, less than today. Barbara McCrady, professor of psychology and the clinical director for the Center of Alcohol Studies at Rutgers University has found, "the marijuana around now is much, much stronger. Drug clinics today are even reporting withdrawal symptoms from it, which was unheard of years ago. The potential for danger from drugs that were once pretty innocuous is far higher."

Talk About Saying No.   Saying no to drugs is a skill of self-assertion. Children who can resist peer pressure gain confidence and develop a positive self-image that helps them say no again and again in the future. But the effectiveness of this strategy is weak unless your children have opportunities to think about *how* they will say no.

The following "Say No Tips" are adapted from a list suggested by drug prevention experts of the National Institute on Drug Abuse.

Talk to your children about these six ways to say no. Let them pick out the ones that feel most comfortable to use, and then role play situations in which these responses might be useful.

- *Give a reason.* If kids know the facts they won't be fooled if someone tells them that it feels good to be stoned. Tell your kids they can say something like, "No, I know it's bad for me. I feel fine right now."
- *Have something else to do.* Kids should know they can say no and then leave. Help them practice saying, "No thanks. I'm going to get something to eat."
- *Make it simple.* Tell your kids that they don't have to explain why they don't want to use drugs if they don't want to. They can just say "No." If that doesn't work, help them practice saying "No" again, or even stronger, "No way."
- *Avoid the situation.* If your kids see or know of places where people often use drugs, impress on them the importance of staying away from those places. If they hear that people will be using drugs at a party, remind them of your family rule against partying with drugs and let them use you as an excuse. Encourage them to say, "My parents won't let me go."
- *Change the subject.* Help your children be prepared with a statement that will quickly change the subject. Tell them, for example, that if someone says, "Let's try some pot," they can say, "No, I was on my way to the store. Do you want to come along?"
- *Hang out with friends who don't use drugs.* This is an ideal way to avoid peer pressure. Stay involved with your kids, meet their friends and encourage activities that put them in contact with other kids who are involved in school, community, or religious activities.

In addition, talk to your children about the qualities of true friendship. Tell them, "Real friends won't get mad when you say no. Real friends won't ridicule or threaten you for standing up for what you believe in."

Talking with your children about drug use and abuse is not a one-time thing. It's an ongoing dialogue that will change in depth and information as your children grow—so keep the conversation going. Use teachable moments offered by television, commercials, MTV, newspapers, and your children's own life experiences to let your children know that you're informed and concerned and always available to talk about this important topic.

Suggested Resources

American Council for Drug Education
204 Monroe Street
Suite 110
Rockville, MD 20850
301-294-0600

National Clearinghouse for Alcohol and Drug Information
P.O. Box 2345
Rockville, MD 20852
301-468-2600

PRIDE (National Parents' Resource Institute for Drug Education)
50 Hurt Plaza, Suite 210
Atlanta, GA 30303
404-577-4500

Suggested Reading

For Parents

Baron, Jason D. *Kids & Drugs: A Parent's Handbook of Drug Abuse, Prevention and Treatment.* New York: Perigee Books, 1984.

DeStefano, Susan. *Drugs and the Family.* Frederick, Md.: Twenty-First Century Books, 1991.

Growing Up Drug Free: A Parent's Guide to Prevention. Washington, D.C.: U.S. Dept. of Education, 1990.

The Fact Is . . . You Can Prevent Alcohol and Other Drug Problems Among Elementary School Children. Rockville, Md.: National Clearinghouse for Alcohol and Drug Information, 1988.

For Children Aged Five to Seven

Berenstain, Stan, and Jan Berenstain. *The Berenstain Bears & the Drug Free Zone.* New York: Random Books for Young Readers, 1993.

Seixas, Judith S. *Drugs: What They Are, What They Do.* New York: Greenwillow Books, 1987.

Super, Gretchen. *What Are Drugs?* Frederick, Md.: Twenty-First Century Books, 1990.

Super, Gretchen. *You Can Say "No" To Drugs!* Frederick, Md.: Twenty-First Century Books, 1990.

Vigna, Judith. *My Big Sister Takes Drugs.* Niles, Ill.: Whitman, 1990.

For Children Aged Eight to Twelve

Berger, Gilda. *Meg's Story: Get Real! Straight Talk About Drugs.* Brookfield, Conn.: Millbrook Press, 1992.

Berry, Joy Wilt. *Good Answers to Tough Questions About Substance Abuse.* Chicago: Childrens Press, 1990.

Friedman, David P. *Focus on Drugs and the Brain.* Frederick, Md.: Twenty-First Century Books, 1990.

Woods, Geraldine. *Drug Use and Drug Abuse.* 2nd ed. New York: F. Watts, 1986.

HIV/AIDS

A group of young children in the school yard were running away from a small boy yelling, "Don't let him touch you! He has AIDS!" The children squealed and laughed and circled the cowering child. This poor boy certainly did not have AIDS; he had what, in days past, we might have called "cooties." Remember that feared and completely nondefinable condition that afflicted unpopular souls and warranted isolation and ridicule?

This playground scene gives a very clear picture of how HIV/ AIDS is understood by many children in elementary school—they know AIDS is something terrible that is contagious, but they have no concept of what it really is.

Young children need to know the facts about AIDS because, unfortunately, it's a part of their world. In 1992, over four thousand children under the age of thirteen had been infected with the AIDS virus. As parents, we have a responsibility to talk openly to our kids about this epidemic of our time so they can live their lives in good health and without undue fear.

When you talk to your kids about HIV, you should strive to meet two goals:

1. Dispel myths and give the facts.
2. Teach compassion for those infected.

The information you give your kids will vary according to their age, level of maturity, background experiences, and knowledge.

With this in mind, this chapter is broken into three sections. The first gives general information that will help you talk about the subject of HIV/AIDS with all children aged four to twelve. The second section offers dialogue suggestions for children from four to seven, and the third section will help you discuss this subject with children aged eight to twelve.

When Should You Bring Up the Subject of HIV/AIDS?

Our children cannot, and should not, be shielded from facts about the HIV/AIDS epidemic. News of its spread is all around us—in the classroom, on TV sitcoms and news shows, at booths at community fairs, and in magazines and newspapers. HIV/AIDS will be a major world event in our children's lives and someone they know will probably become infected.

Media Reports

The facts of HIV/AIDS are best discussed during what we call "teachable" moments. The media, for starters, give you ample opportunities to discuss the facts. If, for example, it's reported on the news that some well-known personality has died of an HIV-related illness, you can point this out to your children and open the door for an exchange of ideas.

You might ask younger children, "Do you know what AIDS is?" Older children may be able to verbalize what they've picked up about the syndrome if you ask, "Do you know how this person could have gotten HIV?" Or, you can simply comment, "What a shame there's no known cure for AIDS." Your children will likely want to know more about what's going on.

If you calmly and naturally use such teachable moments to

open the subject of HIV/AIDS, they'll learn that you are someone they can bring their questions to.

School Programs

Many schools have begun to introduce the subject of HIV/ AIDS in the elementary grades. Call your child's school and find out if HIV/AIDS is in the curriculum. If it is, find out exactly when it will be discussed in the classroom. This gives you the perfect opening to ask, "What did your teacher tell you about HIV or AIDS today?" "Do you understand what that means?" "Do you have any questions about that information?"

When your children do ask questions, answer as honestly as possible, giving the amount of information you feel appropriate for their age and experiences.

If you are unsure of the answer, don't hesitate to say so; the facts about AIDS are new to all of us. But don't say, "Gee, I don't know," and then drop it. If the answer is not included in this chapter, ask your doctor or use your public library or one of the free resources listed at the end of this chapter. Find out. You and your children will both benefit from this kind of inquisitive research.

How to Talk About HIV/AIDS?

Don't lecture. A discussion about HIV/AIDS should not be a studied and rehearsed presentation. Make it a conversation, an exchange of information and ideas, a give-and-take of feelings and facts. Your discussion of AIDS should also be an ongoing one, not a one-shot deal. Children are receptive to different information at different times of their lives. So as your children mature, you should keep talking and listening and let them know that you are always open to questions.

Children Aged Four to Seven: Common Questions and Suggested Answers

Children aged four to seven usually don't require too much specific information about the methods of HIV transmission or the effects of the virus on the body. However, at this stage, it is important to give children general information that will keep them from being frightened or misled by the rumors they may hear around the neighborhood or in school. It's also a good time to lay the groundwork for open communication in later years, when they'll need more detailed information.

"What is AIDS?"

"AIDS is a group of diseases that are caused by a virus called HIV. This virus can cause people to die because it affects the immune system, which is needed to keep people healthy."

"How do you get AIDS?"

"You get the AIDS-related diseases from HIV. People with HIV get it from other people who already have it."

"Will I get HIV?"

"You will not get HIV because it's very difficult to get it from other people. The virus must go directly into your blood from another person's blood, and that's very hard to do."

Young children live in the here-and-now. Don't try to explain what might happen if they practice risky behaviors when they get older.

"Why do some children have AIDS?"

"Some children get HIV when they are born. If a mother has HIV, she can pass it into her child's bloodstream during pregnancy or at birth. This didn't happen to you because I'm not infected with HIV.

"Some other children have gotten the AIDS virus when they were sick and needed some extra blood. A long time ago, some of the blood that doctors gave to their patients had the AIDS virus in it, and so the virus went into the people along with this blood. This rarely happens now because doctors only give people blood that is tested for HIV, so only blood that is free of the virus is used."

"Will I get HIV from a kid in my school who has it?"

"No, you will not. HIV and AIDS are not passed to other people who live or play with infected people. You can play with infected children, swim in the same pool, use the same toilet and water fountain, share the same toys, and you won't get HIV."

"Do people who have AIDS get better?"

"Right now, there is no cure for AIDS. But new medicines and treatments are helping people with HIV stay healthy for many years. Most people with HIV stay healthy for at least ten years."

Children Aged Eight to Twelve: Common Questions and Suggested Answers

Children aged eight to twelve understand a bit more about contagious illnesses and many are also aware that AIDS has something to do with sex and drugs. Your answers therefore need to be tailored to each child's individual level of maturity. The following question-

and-answer examples will give you an idea of how much information most children this age should have.

"What is AIDS?"

"The letters *A,I,D,* and *S* stand for *Acquired Immune Deficiency Syndrome.* This is a medical term for certain illnesses caused by the human immunodeficiency virus—HIV. This virus stops the body's natural ability to protect itself against infections. People with HIV often get serious illnesses that other people don't usually get, like rare cancers, infections, or pneumonia, which eventually cause them to die."

"Do only gay people get AIDS?"

"No. When AIDS first hit the news in the early 1980s, it seemed to be confined to the gay community. So, many nonhomosexual people thought they weren't in danger of becoming infected. But that isn't true. Now we know that anyone—men, women, children, husbands, wives, grandfathers, ministers, teachers—anyone can become infected with HIV."

"How do you get AIDS?"

"AIDS is caused by a virus that passes from an infected person to another person. But it's a different kind of virus than the cold or flu viruses that people give each other when they sneeze or cough or hold hands. HIV passes from one person to another only when blood or other body fluids infected with HIV go from the infected person directly into the blood or body of another person.

"If young children get HIV, they usually are infected in one of two ways: One way is that children can become infected with HIV during pregnancy or at birth if their mothers were already infected with HIV and the virus passed into the bloodstream of the newborn child. Rarely, HIV can be passed to an infant from an infected mother through breastfeeding.

"Some children also became infected with HIV from medical blood transfusions that were given before 1985, when the blood supply wasn't yet treated for HIV like it is today.

"Older people can get the AIDS virus in two other ways. One way is by sharing HIV–infected needles used to inject drugs into their bodies. When a person with HIV uses a needle or syringe to shoot drugs and then lets another person use it, the infected blood that is still on the needle or syringe can be injected into the second person. Then that second person may develop HIV, too.

"Another way is through unprotected sexual intercourse with a person who is infected with HIV."

"How can I tell if someone has HIV?"

"You cannot tell by looking at someone if he or she has HIV. In fact, people who have the virus may not know it themselves because they have no symptoms yet. People with AIDS only look sick when they develop cancers or infections that result from HIV infection."

"Can I get HIV from a kid in my school who has it?"

"No. No one has ever gotten HIV from another person through casual contact. HIV cannot go from one person to another like a cold, the flu, or the chicken pox can—through coughing, sneezing, touching, or playing. HIV is not 'catching' that way, so you can't get it by sharing toilets, pencils, desks, secrets, telephones, food, or doorknobs. In fact, children with HIV/AIDS can play, eat, sleep, kiss, and fight with their brothers and sisters and their parents. There has never been a case of HIV/AIDS transmission from this kind of day-to-day contact.

"However, it's the HIV-infected child who may endanger his or her health by playing with you. Because HIV weakens the body's ability to fight off illnesses, the child with HIV might easily catch your cold or flu virus and become very ill because that child's immune system is not as strong as it needs to be.

"You have nothing to worry about. You will not get HIV from the infected child in your school."

As your children mature, they will need more information about exactly how sexual intercourse spreads HIV and how they can protect themselves from infection. But for children aged four to twelve, the most important message is one of reassurance. To be sure your children understand you, tell them plainly, "You cannot get HIV from playing with children who have the virus." And show your children the need for compassion in this world by frequently reminding them that "children with HIV need our love and friendship, not our ridicule or fear."

Suggested Resources

National AIDS Network
1012 14th Street NW
Suite 601
Washington, DC 20005
202-293-2437

National AIDS Clearinghouse
Rockville, MD
800-458-5231

How to Talk to Your Children About AIDS
(free booklet)
Send self-addressed stamped envelope to
Dept. of Health Education
SIECUS/New York University
Dept. BHG
32 Washington Place
New York, NY 10003
212-819-9770
AIDS Hotline:
800-342-AIDS
This hotline gives a free four-minute recorded message about the
facts of AIDS. It also gives a second toll-free number you can call
to talk to experts who can answer your questions.
This service is available in Spanish at 800-344-SIDA, and for the
hearing impaired: 800-AIDS-TTY

Suggested Reading

For Parents

Hausherr, Rosmarie. *Children and the AIDS Virus: A Book for Children, Parents, and Teachers.* New York: Clarion Books, 1989.

For Children Aged Four to Seven

Girard, Linda Walvoord. *Alex, The Kid with AIDS.* Niles, Ill.: A. Whitman, 1991.
Jordan, Mary Kate. *Losing Uncle Tim.* Niles, Ill.: A. Whitman, 1989.
Merrifield, Margaret. *Come Sit By Me.* Toronto, Canada: Woman's Press, 1990.

For Children Aged Eight to Twelve

Bevan, Nicholas. *AIDS and Drugs.* New York: F. Watts, 1988.

Greenberg, Lorna. *AIDS: How It Works in the Body*. New York: F. Watts, 1992.

Hyde, Margaret O. *Know About AIDS*. New York: Walker, 1987.

Lerner, Ethan A. *Understanding AIDS*. Minneapolis: Lerner Publications, 1987.

Turck, Mary. *AIDS*. Mankato, Minn.: Crestwood House, 1988.

White, Ryan. *Ryan White, My Own Story*. New York: Dial Books, 1991.

Homosexuality

Do you remember when or how you first learned about homosexuality? Most of us don't recall the exact moment, but Alfred Martin sure remembers the day his eight-year-old son learned the facts.

"I brought Rick and his friend to a nearby park to roller skate one Saturday morning," remembers Alfred. "Nothing out of the ordinary happened until Rick saw two men holding hands. I saw Rick elbow his friend and point to the men. What happened next shocked me. These eight-year-olds started yelling out names like 'fag,' 'queer,' and 'homo' to two perfect strangers who hadn't done anything to bother them. I was so angry, I grabbed my son's arm and demanded to know how he could publicly ridicule people like that."

"They're not people," Rick laughed.

"They're homos," finished his friend.

"I couldn't believe what I was hearing. How could a son of mine talk like that? I told the boys to take off their skates and meet me in the car. It was time for a talk."

The National Gay and Lesbian Task Force reports that in five major urban areas where such records are kept, there were 1898 cases of violence against homosexuals in 1992. If children as young as Alfred's son act as if homosexuals are "nonpeople," this shocking statistic can be expected to increase in the coming years.

And, as is true with any form of prejudice, this bias will erode the quality of life for everyone. Our children will live, work, and associate with male and female homosexuals throughout their lives; some will grow to discover their own homosexual orientation.

Clearly, their adult years will be more peaceful and productive if we pass on the facts about homosexuality in ways that counter the negative emotions and prejudices that litter our world today.

Examine Your Own Attitudes

If you are a straight parent with negative opinions about homosexuality, it's very important that you make an effort to think about your feelings on this subject before you talk with your children. It's not the intent of this chapter to change your beliefs, but it is my hope that I can encourage you to allow your children a more tolerant attitude.

If you feel strongly against homosexuals, take a moment to consider why you feel this way. Many of the old beliefs that may have influenced you are changing. In 1973, for example, the American Psychiatric Association removed homosexuality from its list of psychological disorders, and in 1975 the American Psychological Association began an aggressive campaign to remove the label of mental illness from homosexuality. So it is not, as you might have been taught, a psychological illness. Also, most religions are currently changing their traditional policy of condemning homosexuality, instead now defining homosexuals as "persons of sacred worth." Perhaps your views of homosexuality as deviant or immoral behavior have not kept up with these changes. Whatever your feelings, it is to your child's benefit to convey a tolerant, unemotional, and matter-of-fact view of homosexuality.

If you are a straight parent who has an unprejudiced out-look, you surely will be able to talk to your children about homosexuality without intentional bias. However, you too should check your attitude before you speak. Many well-intentioned straight people express pity for the sexual orientation itself, rather than outrage for the prejudice it attracts. For example, it's important not to present homosexuality as a "problem" some people have. You also want to be careful not to emphasize the societal difficulties experienced by the "poor" homosexual. Homosexuals don't want anyone's pity; they need matter-of-fact acceptance as human beings.

You can also unintentionally convey negative messages about homosexuality in the way you stereotype boys and girls. When your son is learning to throw a baseball, for instance, don't say, "You're throwing like a sissy. Put some power behind it." And when your daughter wants to climb trees or build a fort, don't encourage her to play with dolls instead. If you don't make disparaging comments about "gay" behaviors, and if you respect your children's unique personality traits, you'll set down a good base for teaching them to respect all human beings.

If you are a gay parent, you most certainly have a need to talk directly with your children about homosexuality. However, you'll find that because most parents and therefore most of our readers are not gay, the information offered here may not address your circumstance exactly. Still, you surely will find some words that will help you answer the inevitable questions your children will ask.

Consider Your Child's Age

Discussions of sexual identity begin as soon as children learn to talk. "Are you a boy or a girl?" we'd ask my one-year-old daughter.

"Boy!" she'd yell with delight because she couldn't yet pronounce "girl."

As we explained, "No, you're a girl," we began our lessons in sexual identification and function that now continue to expand in detail as she grows.

Your discussions of homosexuality, however, are bound to be different in frequency and focus. Unless your child is living with a homosexual couple, the subject will come up only occasionally and the information will be focused on others. Also different is the fact that, although you need to discuss the anatomical details of reproductive sex with your young and preteen children, there's no reason to offer explicit functional details of homosexuality. Instead, your talk should focus more on the fact that homosexuals are "different" from some other people (not deviant or immoral) because they fall in love with people of the same sex.

Children aged four to seven are certainly able to understand the concepts of love and affection. Use this knowledge to explain homosexuality in a simple way. You might say, "Many men and women fall in love, just like Mommy and Daddy. But some men fall in love with other men and some women fall in love with other women. This has always been the case, since the beginning of time. Grown people who love people of the same sex are called homosexuals, or sometimes 'gay.'"

Children between the ages of eight and twelve may want more information. If they seem curious or ask questions, give them the specific information they ask for.

Look for Teachable Moments

Like reproductive sexuality, homosexuality is not a subject that lends itself to long lectures out of the blue. It is best discussed during teachable moments. Alfred's experience in the park with his son, is a perfect example of a moment that gives a parent the opportunity to talk about homosexuality. These boys had an expressed reason to listen and learn.

Use the Media

Other teachable moments occur all the time. The television, radio, and newspapers, for instance, often focus on the issue of homosexuality. In the early 1990s, the presence of gays in the military and the debate over their right to be there has been big news.

Use this kind of media event by asking your children, for example, "Do you know why gay people have not been allowed in the armed services?"

Then you can offer a factual explanation such as, "Well, gay men and women are what's called homosexual. That means that they consistently prefer to develop emotional and sexual relationships with people of the same sex. There are some people who believe that if a man in the army fell in love with another man in the army they wouldn't be able to be good soldiers. Not everyone agrees that being a homosexual has anything to do with being a good soldier, and that's why there's so much arguing about the subject."

After you present basic background information about the media report, follow your children's lead. If they want more information at this time, they'll ask questions, which you should answer as fully as possible. If they have no further comments or questions, let the subject drop knowing you've opened the door for further discussion at another time.

Use Everyday Experiences

There is great debate over the actual number of homosexuals in America. Depending on whose statistics you read they represent somewhere between 2.3 and 10 percent of the population. Whatever the exact number, it's quite likely that your children will see homosexual couples at some time. When this happens, don't turn their attention to something else or admonish them for being curious with comments like, "Don't stare!" Instead, use the opportunity to talk about what they see.

You might say, "Those two women are holding hands because they're homosexual. Just like some men and women like to hold hands to show affection, sometimes two women or two men will want to show affection to each other in the same way. It's nothing to stare at. There are many people like those two who prefer to love someone of the same sex. Who someone chooses to love is really none of our business."

Use Kids' Own Comments and Questions

Other teachable moments are often presented by children themselves. Listen to your children. Do they use words like "fag" or "queer" when they put down their friends? If they do, that's an opportunity for you to ask, "Do you know what 'fag' means?" Then explain, "*Fag* is a hurtful name used to talk about homosexuals. Do you know what a homosexual is?" Then take your discussion from there, based on your child's response.

And of course, it is always opportune to talk to your kids about homosexuality when they ask questions about it. The following questions and answers will give you an idea of how you might respond to some of the things children frequently wonder about.

If your children should ask questions not mentioned here, remember the fundamental guideline: answer in an unemotional and matter-of-fact way that conveys tolerance and acceptance for the differences among all people.

Common Questions and Suggested Answers

Children between the ages of eight and twelve are curious about human sexuality and certainly may ask you questions about homosexuality. This is your opportunity to show your children that you'll give them factual and matter-of-fact answers to questions they themselves may feel uncomfortable or embarrassed about asking.

"What is a homosexual?"

"Homosexuals are men and women who consistently prefer to develop emotional and sexual relationships with people of the same sex. *Gay* is a word that (usually) means 'homosexual.' *Lesbian* is a word that means 'homosexual women.'"

"Why do gay men like other men?"

"No one really knows why some adults are homosexual. Most researchers today believe they are born that way. But some think it has more to do with the things they experience as they're growing up. It's like trying to figure out why a man and a woman become attracted to each other—there are a lot of reasons, and it's hard to sort them all out."

"I'm a girl and I like other girls. Does that mean I'm gay?"

"No. All women like other women, and all men like other men. There's nothing homosexual about those feelings. Homosexuality involves very intense feelings of love, affection, and physical attraction that adults may have toward someone of the same sex. Homosexuality is not evident in children of your age, so it's not something you have to think about now. If, when you are a teenager, you have any worries or concerns about your feelings toward other girls, we'll talk about this again."

(In rare instances, children may know they are homosexual at a very young age. But the majority are still too young to know for sure if their attraction to peers of the same sex is rooted in homosexuality or simple friendship. Therefore, it's best to postpone a discussion about personal sexual tendencies until the teen years.)

"Why do gay people get AIDS?"

"AIDS is not a disease that affects only gay people. Both gay and straight people can become infected by the virus that causes AIDS."

"How do gay people have sex?"

"There are lots of ways people can show love for each other. Like anyone else they hug, kiss, and touch each other affectionately."

(It's not necessary to give explicit details of homosexual activities to children under the age of twelve unless you are specifically asked.)

The complexity of homosexuality may well be the subject of many discussions with your children as they grow. Right now, the most important thing you can pass on to them when you discuss this topic is an accepting and tolerant attitude.

Let your children know that homosexuality isn't a good or bad thing—it's a sexual orientation that has nothing to do with the person's value as a human being. This attitude prepares your chil-

198 Concerns of Youth

dren to live peacefully with all different kinds of people in this world. It also lets your children know that if they feel homosexual tendencies as they grow in their own sexuality, they can talk to you about it without fear of losing your love.

Suggested Resources

Federation of Parents and Friends of Lesbians and Gays
P.O. Box 27605
Washington, DC 20038

National Gay and Lesbian Task Force Policy Institute
1734 Fourteenth Street, NW
Washington, DC 20005

Suggested Reading

For Parents

Blumenfeld, Warren J., and Diane Raymond. *Looking at Gay and Lesbian Life*. Boston: Beacon Press, 1989.

Bozett, Frederick W., ed. *Gay and Lesbian Parents*. New York: Praeger, 1987.

Whitney, Catherine. *Uncommon Lives: Gay Men & Straight Women*. New York: New American Library, 1990.

For Children Aged Four to Seven

Willhoite, Michael. *Daddy's Roommate*. Boston: Alyson Publications, 1991.

Willhoite, Michael. *Families: A Coloring Book*. Boston: Alyson Publications, 1991.

For Children Aged Eight to Twelve

Jennes, Aylette. *Families: A Celebration of Diversity, Commitment, and Love*. Boston: Houghton Mifflin, 1990.

Newman, Leslea. *Heather Has Two Mommies*. Boston: Alyson Publications, 1989.

Money and Work

Denise and Brad have made up a household budget that helps them curtail their spending while they save money to buy a house. But once in a while, the budgeted money runs out before the week does, and so Denise will stop at the bank to make a withdrawal.

"I know," says Denise, "that I've often made a comment in front of my daughter like, 'Oh, I'm out of money. I've got to stop at the bank and get more before we can go food shopping.' But I never thought about how a five-year-old would interpret that until just the other day. I told her that I just didn't have money to spend on toys right now, and without missing a beat she answered, 'Well, just go to the bank. They always give you money when you need it.' It was obviously time for a lesson in finance."

This five-year-old's observation of where money comes from is very typical of young children. Unfortunately, too many children grow to be teen and adult consumers who still don't have a sound idea of how money is earned, saved, or spent. That's why the use and misuse of money is a subject that should be discussed with children of all ages.

Certainly, your kids will learn about American currency from their teachers in school. But you're the one who will teach them the value of money. For the most part, your personal attitude toward money and the example you offer in the use of money will teach the most memorable lessons.

How Your Attitude Shapes
Your Kids' Values

For good or bad, your attitude toward money will rub off on your kids. So before you *tell* your kids that it's important to learn how to earn, save, and spend money, take some time to think about what they see you *do* with money.

Do you have a budget? Does your budget include money for savings? Do you pay bills on time? Do you overuse your credit cards? Do you comparison shop? Do you regularly give money to your church or charitable organization? The answers to these kinds of questions will tell you what you're already teaching your kids about the value of money.

If you have some money habits you'd like to change, now would be a good time to work on them and to talk aloud about your decision to do so. You might admit to your children, "I would really like to buy this bicycle for myself, but I've been spending too much money lately. I think I'll pass it up for today and put the money in the bank to pay some of my overdue bills." It's personal examples like this that teach money attitudes.

A routine shopping trip offers a perfect opportunity to teach value economics to kids of any age. If you clip coupons, let your children help you cut them out and explain how coupons save you money. Once you're in the store, you probably read price tags and compare brands and sizes when you select one item over another. So, the next time, tell your kids what you're thinking. When you choose one pair of shoes instead of another because the quality appears the same but the price is lower, say so. If you decide to buy a large box of cereal rather than the small snack-size boxes because the unit price is much lower, explain your reason to your kids. When you pay for your items, show your children the total so they get an idea of how much it costs to live.

What to Say About Family Finances

How you discuss your family finances with your children is a personal matter. Some families are very open about exactly how much the parents earn and how much their monthly bills cost. Other families don't share this information with the children. Whatever your personal preference, you can use your own financial situation to help your kids understand money priorities.

Making Money Decisions

Find Opportunities That Allow Your Children Some Financial Control. We all have to make money choices. Should I remodel the kitchen or save to buy a new car? Should I save money for the kids' college education or pay for a private elementary school education now? Children aged eight to eleven should be actively involved in making some financial decisions for your family.

You might ask, "Do you want to buy two pairs of these shorts or one pair of this more expensive style?"

"Do you want to buy two boxes of store-brand cookies or one box of name-brand cookies?"

Include Children in Deciding on Large Family Expenditures. Once in a while, you might involve your children in a decision such as how to spend your vacation money. For example, you could say, "Would you like to spend one week in a beach house by the ocean or would you rather spend one week taking day trips to places like the zoo and amusement parks? We can't afford to do both, but we can afford and would enjoy either one. What do you think?" This kind of decision making opportunity gives kids a concrete feel for financial responsibility.

What to Say When You're Unemployed

If you or your spouse is laid off from your job, the financial side of the situation is a matter that you should talk to your kids about. There's no reason to hide it from your kids. In fact, they can benefit from the situation. If your kids are always sheltered from bad news, they'll never learn that families are for sharing the good and the bad in life.

Give Your Children Age-Appropriate Information. Young children may need to know only that "Mommy doesn't have a job right now, but she's looking for a new one." Then a hug and honest assurances that you still have enough money to live on is all that is required.

Older children can understand more detailed explanations such as, "My company didn't make enough money last year to pay all their employees, so they've laid off one hundred workers and I'm one of them."

Prepare Your Children for the Changes to Come. When you tell your children that you're out of work, be sure to explain the financial consequences of unemployment. For example, *before* birthdays and holidays roll around, explain, "While I'm out of work, I'm afraid I won't be able to buy you the big presents I used to. But how about we find a new way to make the day special?" If you simply buy a token gift assuming that your children will understand because last month you told them you're short on money, you'll see long faces when the gift is unwrapped.

You might also have to establish new family traditions. These might include changes such as: "We won't be eating out every Friday night anymore, but we can learn how to make pizza and eat at home instead." Or, "We won't be going to the movies much right now, but we'll cook up a batch of popcorn and rent movies on video."

Be Honest About Why You're Cutting Back. Tell your kids when you're worried about spending money. Giving them the facts helps assure them that the changes in your spending habits have nothing to do with your feelings toward them.

One family I know learned this lesson the hard way. After the children were in bed, Michelle and Ted began to argue over the kind of cake they should buy for their son's upcoming birthday party. Michelle wanted to buy a sheet cake from the bakery, but Ted wanted her to save money by making a cake at home. The argument went back and forth until their son appeared in the doorway.

"Stop fighting," he said. "I don't want any cake for my birthday."

Of course the argument had nothing to do with their feelings toward their son, but he didn't know that. If you're financially strapped, don't pull in the purse strings without an explanation.

How to Handle Allowance and Savings

Modeling a healthy attitude toward money and talking to your kids about your family finances are good ways to start teaching them the value of a dollar. But to really influence the way they save and spend money, kids need to have money of their own.

At What Age?

As you map out your allowance plans keep these age considerations in mind:

Most preschoolers have no real concept of what money is or how saving it in a piggy bank can sometimes be better than spending it all at once. If you give your preschoolers an allowance, let them enjoy the fun of "pay day," but don't expect much in terms of financial accountability.

Children aged five to seven are ready to grasp the concept of money. They're able to understand that high-priced items must be saved for, that some items are very expensive but of little value, and that earning money comes before spending it. This is a good age to offer an allowance.

Kids aged eight to eleven can grasp more of the complexities of money. They are developing decision-making skills that will help them decide whether to save or spend. They have more patience to save for something they really want and they can understand the way the banking system works. This is a good time to help your children open their own savings accounts with the bank.

Money for Chores?

Many families give children an allowance as a reward for doing chores. This common practice has fallen out of favor in recent years for a number of reasons. This use of money can sabotage another important family lesson: we all do chores because we belong to this family and we help each other because we *should*— not because we get paid.

Another reason not to connect allowance to chores is to avoid setting up a reward and punishment system based on money. If the allowance depends on the child taking out the garbage every day, for example, it follows then that, "if you don't take out the garbage, you won't get your allowance." This twists money into a disciplinary tool, and chores are done solely for the monetary gain.

Helen and Bob had always paid their two sons an allowance for doing daily chores. This arrangement worked fine until Helen went back to work full-time. When she explained that this change in her schedule meant she would need the boys to pitch in and do more things around the house, they balked and loudly insisted on an increase in their allowance.

"We're not gonna do extra work and not get paid for it," the oldest announced. This sounds selfish, but to these boys it was only reasonable. They had been taught to associate chores with money— not personal or family responsibility.

Overall, it's best to give your children an allowance with no strings attached. Just as they do chores because they are contributing family members, they get money because as family members you recognize their financial needs.

You can and should, however, offer extra money for extra work. If you want the garage cleaned out, for example, and this task isn't one of your child's regular chores, it's appropriate to pay for the job to help your child earn extra money.

How Much?

The amount of your child's allowance is a personal family decision. But before you set the amount, consider how the money will be used.

Allowance Should Cover Fixed Weekly Expenses. If, for example, you routinely pay for school lunches, let your children pay for it with money from their allowance. This teaches them that the money for lunch comes from somewhere and that necessities like this deplete the store of cash available for more "fun" stuff.

Add Some Money for Spending and Saving.   It's this dis-
cretionary cash that will teach your kids how to handle money.

You might start with fifty cents a week for children aged four
and five, one dollar for six-, seven- and eight-year-olds; and two
to three dollars for kids aged eight to eleven. Young kids don't need
too much money each week; more than five dollars will defeat the
purpose of helping them realize the value of a dollar and of forgo-
ing small purchases to save for the higher-priced items.

To Spend or Save?

Do you tell your kids to save their pocket money, or do you
encourage them to spend it on something for themselves? Your
personal philosophy on saving and spending will determine how
you answer this question. It will also determine whether you pass
on the belief that sometimes money is more than just money. Some
people, for example, hoard money because they see it as a source
of security; others spend it freely because they've tied their self-
esteem to material possessions. Somewhere in between is the middle
ground you want your kids to find. If you find it for them by dic-
tating how they must save or spend their money, you take away
a valuable learning opportunity.

***Encourage Your Children to Save Some and Spend Some
Every Week.***   Give your kids sound financial advice, but leave
the final decision of what to do with their money to them. As
your kids begin to explore their financial powers, they'll soon realize on their own that spending is the easy part, and saving takes
more effort.

Set Short-Term Savings Goals.   Once children are of school
age, they can understand the benefits of saving money—but only

to a certain point. Children best understand and benefit from saving for short-term goals, like a small toy. But they won't learn anything about the value of saving if they reach for long-term saving goals like college.

Give your children only as much allowance as you feel they should spend each week, but then help them see the value of saving some also. If, for example, your children want a pair of fifty-dollar roller skates, you might say, "I'll pay forty dollars if you save the other ten." This joint effort shows kids that some purchases have to be postponed until enough money is saved and it gives them a personal reason to want to save money.

Make Saving Money Practical, Not Painful. If you feel it's very important for your children to put money away every week, add special "savings money" to their allowance. Explain that this designated amount is for savings only, but that the rest can be spent or saved as they wish. That way they still have money to spend and they also get in the habit of saving.

Bank accounts are a good idea for kids over the age of seven. To get the most out of banking, your kids should have their own passbook and go with you to the bank to make all transactions. This helps kids see that banks don't just give money away: first you deposit it, then you withdraw it.

Once again, to learn the value of banking let your children do both—deposit and withdraw. Saving gets a bad reputation from parents who insist that their kids' money be deposited and never withdrawn. Preteens are too young to appreciate the benefits of this kind of saving. All they learn is, "If I put my money in the bank, I'll never see it again."

Tell your kids, "When you want to save your money for a special or future purchase, we'll help you deposit it in the bank. Then when you want to buy something that costs more than you have at home, you can withdraw the money from the bank." (This doesn't mean that you have to allow your child to spend $150.00 on sneakers, just because the child has that much money in the bank. You still have the last word on what's an appropriate purchase and what's not.)

Talking to kids about money is an ongoing conversation. If you use your own spending and saving habits as an example, talk matter-of-factly about family finances, and set up an allowance system that gives your kids control over their own money, they will grow little by little into teen and adult consumers who know how to save and spend wisely.

Suggested Reading

For Parents

Drew, Bonnie. *Moneyskills: 101 Activities to Teach Your Child About Money.* Hawthorne, New Jersey: Career Press, 1992.

Weinstein, Grace. *Children and Money: A Parents' Guide.* Laguna Hills, Calif.: Charter House, 1975.

For Children Aged Four to Seven

Berenstain, Stan, and Jan Berenstain. *The Berenstain Bears' Trouble with Money.* New York: Random Books for Young Readers, 1983.

Elkin, Benjamin. *Money.* Chicago: Childrens Press, 1983.

Maestro, Betsy. *Dollars and Cents for Harriet.* New York: Crown, 1988.

For Children Aged Eight to Twelve

Barkin, Carol. *Jobs for Kids.* New York: Lothrop, Lee & Shepard Books, 1990.

Belliston, Larry. *Extra Cash for Kids*. Brentwood, Tenn.: Wolgemuth & Hyatt, 1989.

Danziger, Paula. *Not for a Billion Gazillion Dollars*. New York: Delacorte, 1992.

Wilkinson, Elizabeth. *Making Cents: Every Kids' Guide to Money*. Boston: Little, Brown, 1989.

Wyatt, Elaine. *The Money Book: A Smart Kid's Guide to Savvy Saving and Spending*. New York: Tambourine Books, 1991.

Pornography

Janette was flipping through the cable TV channels looking for something to entertain her four-year-old son when she came across something that shocked her. There on the screen was a pornographic display of several men and women engaging in an orgy. "The program was 'scrambled,' which is supposed to keep nonsubscribers from viewing the show," Janette explained. "But anyone could certainly make out what was going on. I quickly changed the station, but I'm sure there are many parents who have no idea that this junk is coming into their homes whether they want it or not. And I'm absolutely sure there is a whole bunch of young kids who do know all about it."

Indeed, our children do live in a world where there is easy access to sexually explicit material in magazines and books, as well as on television and in motion pictures. It's virtually impossible to shield children from all forms of pornography since it is as close as the nearest newsstand. But it is possible to be vigilant in our efforts to keep pornography out of our homes and to help our children understand its deviant and abnormal nature.

Young children under the age of eight who are carefully supervised in and out of the home should have little opportunity to view sexually explicit material. Therefore, in only the rare circumstance of early exposure do we need to talk about pornography with children in this age bracket. As our children grow, however, they naturally become more independent and have more and more unsupervised time. They may spend an afternoon with a friend in the park, they may be left alone at home while you work or run errands, or they may want to spend more "alone" time in their own rooms. Any of these circumstances leave children free to find and explore pornographic material.

When to Talk to Your Kids About Pornography

Talking about pornography with preteen children is a delicate task. It's certainly not appropriate to bring out samples and discuss them because this is still a topic these children are best shielded from at this time. But it's also a fact that it can be quite harmful to a child's developing sexuality if pornography is viewed without explanation.

First of all, it's important to understand the changing face of pornography. Explicit material is no longer limited to the girly magazines a fifteen-year-old might keep under his bed. Today the trend in pornography is toward portrayals of sexual violence, degradation, and humiliation rather than just nudity. Common themes include sadism, incest, child molestation, rape, and even murder.

These forms of pornography affect children's attitudes about sex in several ways. They show sex as depersonalized and reduced to a mechanistic function devoid of any feelings. They portray sex without dignity, respect, and love. Pornography glorifies hedonism and self-centeredness rather than love, tenderness, and commitment. It suggests that there is nothing out of the ordinary about sexually brutalizing other people, especially woman and children. Aggressive sex is portrayed as normal and exciting. These are not abstract values. Studies have shown a distinct correlation between the rise in both pornography sales and crimes of sexual violence between the early 1980s and the early 1990s.

Pornography is therefore a subject you need to discuss with your preteens in certain situations. Such circumstances would include finding pornographic material in your children's rooms, finding them watching X-rated shows, or believing that their friends are likely to expose them to sexually explicit material. This was the situation that made Maryann decide to talk to her eight-year-old son about this subject.

Maryann was searching the neighborhood one summer afternoon looking for her cat. When she peered behind an old shed, she found her thirteen-year-old neighbor, Shawn, sitting among a pile of pornographic magazines.

"I didn't think it was my place to scold or lecture the boy," Maryann says, "so I just asked him if he had seen my cat and then went on my way. But because my son often spends time with Shawn, I was very worried that on those afternoons I thought they were playing video games, they were really looking through that trash." Maryann had a reason to talk to her young son about pornography and tell him how she felt about it.

What to Say About Pornography

Whatever circumstance brings you to talk to your preteens about pornography, do it without anger. The root of their interest in this kind of material surely is curiosity, so offering straightforward information is a good way to start.

Nudity

If the material in question is photos of nude men or women alone, start your discussion with a positive comment about the human body. You might say, "Yes, the [female or male] body is very beautiful." Tell your children that the great art museums are filled with portraits and sculptures of nude bodies.

Then explain, "However, when the nudity is publicly presented only for sexual arousal—which is a private and personal matter—then it's called 'pornography.' Pornography is not meant for young people. In fact, it's against the law to sell pornographic material to minors, so I don't want you to read this kind of material again."

Heterosexual Intercourse

If the material that brings you to talk to your preteens about pornography involves actual intercourse between a man and a woman, your discussion should review (or introduce) the facts of life as outlined in the chapter entitled "Sex and Reproduction." Tell your children that although sexual intercourse is a perfectly normal act between a man and a woman, what these pictures (or movie scenes) depict is called pornography because they lack the most important elements of the human sex act. This kind of pornography suggests that intercourse is impersonal and devoid of love and compassion—it is not.

Your young children have no guidelines for judging what's right or wrong in this area, so teach them what you believe. Tell them, "Pornography takes something that is gentle and beautiful and turns it into something ugly and degrading. One of the things that separates us from the animals is that we don't have intercourse in public. The people who do this are not engaging in the kind of loving relationship that you will want to have when you grow up and fall in love."

Then let your children know that sex itself isn't an off-limits subject. Say, "I'd be glad to answer any questions you might have about sexual intercourse, or if you'd rather I can find you some well-written books on the subject. But it's very important that you understand that what's good and pleasurable about human sexuality is not what's portrayed in pornographic materials."

Homosexual Activities

If you find your children viewing pornography involving homosexual activities, they'll certainly need an explanation of what's going on. The chapter entitled "Homosexuality" will give you some guidelines about how to talk to your kids about homosexuality in general. Then, as you would explain heterosexual pornography, you'll need to explain the distorted nature of what they have seen. Remind your children that any sexual act is a private and personal occurrence that is cheapened through public display. Emphasize that pornography of any kind is not approved by you or allowed in your house.

Child Pornography, Bestiality, and Violent Sex

If your children get ahold of pornography that depicts what I'll call "normal" sexual acts, your goal is to explain that although men and women do have beautiful bodies and the act of intercourse is a very natural and universal activity, they should not be displayed for the entertainment of others. This message should be delivered without anger; it's a lesson that's intended to help young people put human sexuality in its appropriate perspective—not to heap on the guilt.

On the other hand, if your children find pornography that depicts "abnormal" acts, such as child pornography, bestiality, or violent sexual acts, they need to be told immediately and firmly that this is not what sex is all about.

This kind of pornography is especially dangerous to the developing morality of our children. It gives a false impression of the way normal, civilized men and women engage in sexual activity. It can also interfere with a child's ability to develop a healthy sexual attitude because it offers sexually sick people as models of behavior, and emphasizes perversity and cruelty as norms. If you find your children with this kind of pornographic material, they must be told in no uncertain terms that this is not normal and not acceptable.

Without anger or blame, but still with a no-nonsense demeanor, tell your children that this kind of pornography is pure trash. It is the work of very unbalanced people who enjoy hurting others. Tell your children, "This is not a healthy way to express sexual feelings. It is not the kind of sexual activity you will ever be a part of, so let's throw it out and promise not to spend time looking at such garbage again."

Then assure your children that you are not angry with them. Because you had never spoken about this subject before, you can't scold them for their curiosity (even though they certainly had an inkling this wasn't material you'd approve of). But let them know that if they spend time with pornographic material again in the future, you will be very angry and will indeed punish their disobedience.

Keeping Pornography Out of Your Home

You can take some control over the availability of pornographic material that comes into your home. You can start by purchasing a key for your cable television box. This key, which most cable companies rent for about one dollar a month, allows you to lock a cable station so no one can view it without your permission.

You can ensure that no one in your home uses telephone "dial-a-porn" services. Just call your business operator and request that outgoing 900 calls be blocked from your phone line.

You can also join the fight against mail-order pornography. Go to your post office and ask for Form 2201. Follow the instructions and record your name and the names of your children under the age of nineteen. They will be added to the Sexually Oriented Advertising (SOA) Prohibitory Reference List, which the Postal Service makes available to mailers.

If you or your children receive a sexually explicit advertisement thirty days or more after your name has been added to the SOA Prohibitory Reference List, take it to the post office for further action. For a first offense, the sender is liable for a fine of up to $5000, or up to five years in prison, or both. Subsequent offenses are punishable by a fine of up to $10,000, or up to ten years in prison, or both. The listing terminates five years after the date your name is placed on the list or if you move. If you wish to be kept on the list, you'll need to fill out a new application at that time.

The experience of viewing pornographic material without parental explanation can harm children both physically and emotionally. To protect our children from this experience, we should make a concerted effort to keep pornographic material out of our homes, and we should help children understand that pornography is an abnormal and deviant portrayal of human sexuality.

Prejudice

Ramine's fourth birthday party looked like a preschool version of a United Nations gathering. Friends from his multiethnic neighborhood mingled with his white school friends. His Iranian cousins partied with the African American, Spanish, and Korean children of his parents' friends. From a distance, the children seemed well integrated as they enjoyed the clown, balloons, and cake.

Of course, as is bound to happen when many small children gather in the same room, there were occasional disturbances, but many adults at the party were shocked by the racist remarks they heard coming from some of the children.

"I don't want to sit next to that black boy," said one little white child quite matter-of-factly.

"Look how squinty his eyes are," laughed one young boy, pointing to an Asian guest as his friends giggled in agreement.

"Why do you talk funny?" asked one little girl of a boy with a Spanish accent.

Would you say these children are prejudiced? I don't believe so. What they're doing is quite common at this stage of development: they are beginning to notice how they are alike and different from other kids. This helps them establish their identity as individuals and as members of ethnic, religious, and racial groups. What appears as a display of prejudice is really a sign of limited experience and immature ways of interpreting the differences among human beings.

217

However, without deliberate help from sensitive adults, these childish actions could grow to become the biases that fuel prejudice. These same circumstances at a tenth birthday party would indicate far more than an immature developmental stage. At that stage, they're established opinions about certain groups of people that are based on stereotypes and bias—and they can be called prejudice.

Our children will need to appreciate, rather than condemn, racial differences if they are to grow and flourish in the twenty-first century. It's predicted that early in this new century, minorities will become the majority in fifty cities, and the work force will be largely composed of members of today's minority groups. Prejudice will be especially destructive to the functioning of a multiethnic society brimming with African Americans, Native Americans, Latinos, and Asians.

Children are not born with prejudices. They learn them gradually from the society they live in. But from that same society they can learn to be appreciative and tolerant of differences if we, their parents, make a deliberate effort to nurture this attitude. Researchers have found that lessons in the acceptance of racial diversity are best begun around age three, when children begin to recognize the differences between groups of people. But children of any age can learn these lessons in a healthy, open, and trusting home environment.

Monitor Your Own Prejudices

You can best convey a nonbiased attitude to your children if you first take some time to tune into your own prejudices. In truth, we all are prejudiced to some degree. Deep down, do you believe that some ethnic groups are dumb, or smart, or naturally good at sports? Think about your own beliefs before you talk to your children.

Don't Identify People by Race. If your child wants to invite a friend over after school, but you're not sure which child she means, don't ask, "Is that the Chinese girl?" Look for another form of identification such as, "Is that the girl with the dark hair who played on your soccer team last year?"

Don't Focus Conversation on Racial Differences. When you talk about others whom you meet at work, in the community, or from your children's school, don't let your comments focus on racial differences. If you have a problem with a family in your neighborhood, for example, don't attribute your conflict to racial, ethnic, class, or religious factors. Talk about the problem you have with that individual—completely isolated from his or her ancestry.

Avoid Ethnic Jokes. Stereotypical ethnic humor is a traditional staple of comedy. However, your example in this matter is most important to your children. It will be very difficult for them to understand why it's okay to poke fun at "dumb" Polish people around the dinner table, but it's not acceptable to ridicule a Polish child on the playground for being "dumb."

Don't Stereotype People. Be careful how you explain why certain people have particular skills, talents, or habits. If, for example, a young friend is especially good at soccer, be careful not to attribute that fact to the child's race or nationality. Or, if your child wants to know why a family on your block often has such very large family gatherings, don't explain the occurrence based on your understanding of the family's ethnic origin.

Instead, always relate exceptional qualities or circumstances to the individual—not to the person's race.

Practice Impartiality. What you *do* speaks louder to your children than anything you can say, so teach your values by your actions.

- Do sit next to a family of a different race in the fast-food restaurant.
- Do invite children of different races from your child's class or neighborhood into your home.
- Do keep a pleasant tone of voice and manner when interacting with strangers of other races in the store, on the bus, or the like.
- Do show your children that the way you act toward people has nothing to do with the way they look.

Build Your Child's Self-Esteem

Low self-esteem plays an integral role in the development of prejudice in two ways: (1) children who have a poor self-image are prone to put down others in an attempt to bolster their own self-worth, and (2) minority children with low self-esteem have a weak psychological defense against prejudice. In either case, you can help your children grow to respect themselves and others by nurturing pride in their unique qualities.

Compliment Your Children Often. Let your children know that you're aware of the difficulties involved in managing their activities—in keeping up an organized baseball card collection, for example. Comment positively when they dress nicely. Stay attentive to their school work and activities, and compliment any and every attempt at responsible and independent work. Children who feel capable don't need to put down others to feel important.

The goal in building a child's self-esteem is to build pride in self—not to promote a sense of superiority. It would be counter-productive to the cause of teaching tolerance and acceptance if you say, "Don't let that white boy tell you what to do. Whites just want to keep you down."

Or, "If you study hard, you'll be even smarter than that Korean girl in your class."

Or, "You can play basketball as well as any black athlete—don't let them tell you you can't."

Instead, compliment and encourage your children on what they do as unique individuals—not what they do compared to people of other races.

Let Your Kids Know You Love Them. Only when a person's needs for affection and acceptance are met is he or she capable of caring about the needs of others.

Recognize and Discuss Differences

One popular strategy for imparting an attitude of racial equality involves not acknowledging differences among the various races. Although this approach is a well-intentioned effort to convey the message that all people are the same, it doesn't work. This "color-blind" idea doesn't satisfy children's curiosity or give them the facts they need to explain what they can see for themselves—in some ways, people of different races *are* different.

"When I was growing up," a friend recalls, "it was understood that racial differences just weren't discussed in my home. I remember one day my family was traveling by car through an Asian-Indian neighborhood when my youngest brother jumped up to the window pointing and shouting, 'Look! That man has a towel wrapped around his head and that lady has a dot on her forehead!' My parents were obviously mortified. My dad quickly rolled up the windows while my mother tried to hush up my brother by pushing him down to the floor of the car. We kind of giggled through our embarrassment. Then no one brought up the subject again."

This kind of reaction to a child's observation that people of different races sometimes look different does not teach the intended message: "Don't make fun of others." Instead, it implies that being of a different color or culture is a deviance from the norm and is best not discussed.

An effective technique that teaches children to accept and appreciate people of different races is simply to use opportunities presented in everyday life to talk about the facts. My friend's parents could have used the incident in the car to teach their young son about Indian culture. If they were unsure exactly why the man wears a turban or the woman a dot, the incident offered an opportunity to say, "When we go to the library, let's get a book that tells us more about that country. Let's find out where India is on the map and if the turban and the dot means anything specific in their culture."

Children can also learn prejudiced attitudes from television. It's not uncommon for TV shows to cast Latin Americans as drug dealers, African Americans as teenage hoods, and Native Americans as bloodthirsty savages. When you see these stereotypes on television, talk with your kids about them.

You might ask, "I wonder why they always cast the teenagers who commit crimes as black kids. Do you think all black teens act like that?" And then discuss your child's response.

Respond to Racial Slurs

A not-to-be-missed opportunity to talk about racial tolerance presents itself when you hear someone—perhaps even your own child—make a racial slur, joke, or comment. What would you say to your child if you heard these kinds of remarks shouted on the school yard:

"I don't want to play with Gordon. His eyes are squinty."

"Don't let the nigger play!"

"Get out of here. No white boys allowed."

There are lots of ways you might react, but remember this: don't get angry and don't ignore. Anger makes children defensive and closed to a learning opportunity; ignoring implies acceptance. Instead, keeping a calm tone, ask your children why they feel a person of a different race would not be a good playmate. Listen to the response.

Ask, "Does the color of skin change the way they act or feel?" Again, let your children try to verbalize their feelings.

Then admit: "There may be children you don't like to play with."

Then teach: "But the reason should have nothing to do with the way they look or the color of their skin."

Questions and Answers

Children are curious about the differences among races. When they ask you about these differences, try to offer the facts cushioned in just a bit of your own tolerant attitude. These are some questions your children might ask, and some ways you might answer them.

"Why is Zoya's skin black?"

Very young children can be told, "Zoya's skin is black because her mommy and daddy's skin is black." Older children can understand more: "Yes, Zoya's skin is very black and quite beautiful. The color of everybody's skin is caused by a chemical in our bodies called melanin. How much melanin you have in your body depends on how much your parents have. If you have a lot of melanin, your skin is dark. If you have only a little melanin, your skin is light. Do you and I have a lot of melanin or a little?"

"Why does Peresh's mother dress funny?"

"I think by 'funny' you really mean 'different.' What seems different to us is really quite ordinary in the country Peresh's mother comes from. She is wearing the clothes she wore when she lived in India. Instead of thinking of her clothes as 'funny,' I think of them as beautifully different."

"Why does Arthur Yamamoto talk weird?"

"Arthur doesn't talk weird. He talks with an accent that mixes his family's Japanese language with English. His parents speak to him in Japanese and his teachers and friends talk to him in English. It's wonderful that he can speak two languages at such a young age. Even though it's hard to understand him sometimes, you should remember how hard it must be for him to speak as clearly as his classmates. Maybe tomorrow you could help him learn some new American words."

Encourage Exposure to Different Cultures

If racial differences scare your children or make them feel uncomfortable, they are more likely to be intolerant. That's why they'll learn a powerful lesson about racial equality when they see differences accepted and welcomed by you. You can show this attitude by looking for opportunities to expose your children to cultures different from their own.

- When you choose books for your children, look for ones that use illustrations of children from different races.
- Look for dance performances, art shows, children's plays, festivals, and the like sponsored by ethnic groups. Exposure to other cultures in a "fun" atmosphere adds to the positive image you're trying to convey.
- Talk about the advances made in the last few decades to reduce prejudice in America. You'll find, for example, that kids are always fascinated by the story of baseball's first black player, Jackie Robinson. It's incredible to think that not too long ago, this man wasn't allowed to sleep in the same hotels as his white teammates. Absolutely amazing.

As you expose your children to the differences in cultures, be sure also to remind them of the overriding similarities: the human capacities for thought, love, and feelings are the same in all of us. The ways individuals act and feel are the ways we judge their worth—not by the color of their skin, the appearance of their face, or the clothing on their back.

What to Say to Children Who Are Victims of Prejudice

The tone of voice you use when discussing racism gives children more than the meaning of your words. A calm assertive tone tells children you have confidence in your own self-worth and your position in our society—your children need to pick up this confident attitude to combat prejudice. If your child complains, "The kids at school are laughing at me because they say I look funny," you may have to swallow your impulse to lash out at these children whom you may want to label "prejudiced, narrow-minded little fools."

Instead, stay calm and offer empathy and strength. Because you, too, may sometimes feel out of place, you can acknowledge that your child is upset for good reason. Then you'll have to calmly explain that, indeed, there are some mean people in this world who don't like anyone who's not just like them.

Next, you'll need to give your children "scripts" of things to say back to their taunters. This will help them feel less vulnerable at the thought of being teased, rejected, or stereotyped, and it will also help them confront the problem rather than run away from it. You might, for example, ask your child to rehearse saying "I don't like it when you talk like that" or "That's not true what you're saying, so stop it."

Finally, be sure you make a distinction between stereotyping and personal experience. If your children cry, "I hate white people. They call me names," point out the racist quality of their own words. Acknowledge that that particular group of children who are white did hurt your child's feelings, but emphasize that that one group doesn't represent the entire race of white people. It's important that our children learn to judge each instance in view of the individuals involved, not the cultural heritage of their forefathers.

If your children are learning prejudice from people who are biased against them, you can help. Use the information offered in this chapter to strengthen your children's spirits and soften their attitudes. All our children will enjoy the world they will live in in the twenty-first century if we adults can monitor our own prejudices, build our children's sense of self-esteem, recognize and discuss the problem of racism, and expose our children to the excitement and glory of other cultures.

Suggested Resources

Anti-Defamation League of B'nai-B'rith
823 United Nations Plaza
New York, NY 10017
212-490-2525

Council on Interracial Books for Children
1841 Broadway
New York, NY 10023
212-757-5339

National Association for the Advancement of Colored People
4805 Mt. Hope Drive
Baltimore, MD 21215
410-358-8900

National Institute Against Prejudice and Violence
31 South Greene Street
Baltimore, MD 21201
410-328-5170

Suggested Reading

For Parents

Aboud, Frances. *Children and Prejudice.* Cambridge, Mass.: Blackwell Publishers, 1988.

Clark, Kenneth B. *Prejudice and Your Child.* Hanover, N.H.: University Press of New England, 1988.

Children Aged Four to Seven

Berridge, Celia. *Going Swimming.* New York: Random House, 1987.

Johnson, Angela. *Tell Me A Story, Mama.* New York: Orchard Books, 1989.

Simon, Norma. *All Kinds of Families.* Niles, Ill.: A. Whitman, 1976.

Children Aged Eight to Twelve

Carlson, Natalie Savage. *The Empty Schoolhouse.* New York: Harper & Row, 1965.

Levine, Ellen. *I Hate English!* New York: Scholastic, 1989.

Mendez, Phil. *The Black Snowman.* New York: Scholastic, 1989.

Taylor, Mildred D. *The Friendship.* New York: Dial Books for Young Readers, 1987.

Taylor, Mildred D. *The Gold Cadillac.* New York: Dial Books for Young Readers, 1987.

Taylor, Mildred D. *Mississippi Bridge.* New York: Dial Books for Young Readers, 1989.

Puberty

Jill and Fred laughed themselves silly the afternoon they shared their "introduction to puberty" experiences. "I vividly remember the day I came home from seventh grade," laughs Jill, "and found blood on my underwear. I was sure I had some rare disease and was going to die. But even in my panic, I was horrified at the thought of telling my mother because I didn't want her to see my dirty underwear. That was just too embarrassing to imagine."

"I think I felt pretty much the same way the morning I woke up and found my sheets all wet and my underwear sticky," says Fred. "I was so confused and embarrassed. All I knew was that something 'weird' had happened and I didn't want anyone to know about it."

Although they laugh now at their naiveté, both Jill and Fred vow to handle their own kids differently. "I think I'll feel uncomfortable talking to our son about things like wet dreams," admits Fred, "but I'm going to tell him everything I know about the changes in his body during puberty because I don't ever want him to feel the shame and confusion I felt as a kid."

How did you learn about the bodily changes that occur during puberty? We can't say that there's one best way to give a child this information, but we do know that you—the child's parents—should be a primary source of information. Books, films, school lessons, and friends are all avenues of explanation, but to be most useful to your child, these sources should serve only as an adjunct to your own discussions.

What Exactly Is Puberty?

Puberty is a period of time in which a child reaches sexual maturity and becomes able to reproduce. The onset of puberty is not dictated by a specific age, but rather by certain physical and emotional changes that can occur over the course of several years. The process is unique in each child. The first physical sign of puberty in girls usually appears sometime between the ages of nine and thirteen. In boys, it usually appears sometime between age ten and age fourteen. But no one can say, for example, that all girls should have underarm hair by age fifteen, or that boys should have beards at seventeen. Some teens develop all their sex characteristics early and quickly; others mature later and more slowly. Either course (and everything in between) is perfectly normal.

Because you can't be sure when your child will enter puberty, it's very tempting to put off talking about it. Unfortunately, if you wait until you see physical signals of change, you may be too late to help your child avoid the fear and embarrassment caused by surprises like Jill's and Fred's. So aim to discuss puberty before it occurs—at about age nine. Remember: you're talking about the way the human body grows—it's a universal fact of life. So don't shy away from this topic.

How to Talk About Puberty

Although puberty is as natural and inevitable as the sunrise, you might want to think ahead about how you'll present the subject to your kids.

Know the Facts.   You don't need a college degree in human sexuality to talk to kids about puberty, but you do want to know the basic facts about the physical and emotional changes that it causes. When you're clear about what happens, you can better re-lay the information in simple, easy-to-understand language, and you can answer the questions your children will probably have. The books suggested at the end of this chapter will help you brush up on the subject of puberty.

Stay Upbeat and Matter-of-Fact. You would not stand alone if you perceived the female menstrual cycle to be a "curse" or the male's involuntary erection as an embarrassing inconveni-ence. When you talk to your kids about these occurrences, how-ever, it's important to keep your attitude positive. Your children need to hear from you that the changes brought on by puberty are signs of normal, healthy development.

A young teen's self-image and sense of self-esteem can be-come very closely connected to his or her ability to accept the bodily changes that signal growing sexuality. You can promote a strong self-image by conveying the message that the bodily changes your child will experience are a part of the exciting process of growing up.

Use Teachable Moments to Open Discussions. Like the "birds and the bees," puberty is not a subject well suited to a one-time discussion. Your kids will need different information at differ-ent times during puberty. They'll forget what you said the first time, and they'll need reassurances that their experiences throughout puberty are normal.

To have discussions about puberty that make an impact on your children, try to tie your talks into other things going on in their lives.

232 Concerns of Youth

- If your son or daughter finds a box of sanitary pads in the bathroom cabinet and asks what it is, use this as an opportunity to talk about menstruation. (Whatever their sex, your children should know about both the male and female body.)
- If you're in the park and you see a dog with an erection, use this experience to talk about human erections.
- If you see a woman breastfeeding, talk about the growth and function of the female breast.

These are all teachable moments that open the door to parent-child discussions.

Discuss Information Offered at School. In addition to teachable moments, you might be able to tie your talks about puberty into your child's classroom lessons. Call your child's school and ask for an outline of their health program (or family life course, or sex education, or whatever name your district uses). Look to see if and when the physical and emotional changes of puberty are part of these lessons. If the school does cover this information, use the classroom lesson as your launch pad. Ask your child or the teacher to tell you when puberty is being covered and then let your child direct the discussion at that time.

You might ask:

"What does your book say happens to boys and girls when they reach puberty?"

"Do you understand what your teacher said about ejaculation?"

"Have you noticed any of these changes happening in your body?"

Show by your casual tone and matter-of-fact attitude that you're open to talking about puberty and assure your kids that if they have any questions at any time, they should feel comfortable asking you for answers.

All About Girls

Although the female's reproductive organs are primarily hidden inside the body, there are some outer physical changes your daughters will observe during puberty:

First the hips begin to broaden and the breasts begin to develop. (Tell your daughters that it's normal for one breast to grow more quickly than the other.)

Then hair will appear under the armpits and in the genital area.

Body height increases as much as three inches, and hands and feet may seem disproportionately large because they grow faster than the rest of the body. (This is when your daughters may give up bowling so they don't have to advertise their shoe size. They may also begin to slump over to camouflage the fact that they're taller than the boys.)

Skin becomes thicker, more oily, and sometimes pimply, and perspiration increases. (This is a good time to put renewed emphasis on personal hygiene.)

Finally, about two to two and a half years after breast development begins, your daughter will begin menstruation.

Talking About Menstruation

Before your daughter menstruates, let her know what happens in a woman's body each month and why. Unless your daughter's friends are already talking about menstruation, young girls don't usually ask for this information. So you have to bring up the subject

at a time when the two of you are alone and have some uninter-
rupted time. This is not a time for a lecture, but rather a time to
open the door to frequent and factual discussions.

The key to establishing a positive, accepting attitude toward
menstruation is in the way you prepare your daughter in advance.
Shortly after you notice hip and breast development, it's time to
talk about the inevitable monthly period.

Rather than begin your talk with an explanation of ovaries and
eggs, it's best to begin with the part of menstruation that most overtly
affects your daughter—monthly bleeding. Some girls already know
about monthly periods from their friends or school lessons, but still
you'll want to make sure that your child has her facts straight.

Show your daughter your own tampons and sanitary pads and
explain: "These are products that absorb the blood that passes out
of a woman's uterus and through the vagina every month. This
monthly bleeding is called menstruation. Because you're getting
older, soon you'll start menstruating and I don't want you to be
frightened when you see blood. I want you to know it's perfectly
normal and a good sign that you're becoming a healthy woman."

Use yourself as a model (if you're a dad, talk about women in
general). "Every month, I bleed through my vagina for about four
or five days. I put a tampon into my vagina to absorb the blood
and I put a pad in my underwear to catch any blood that seeps
out. I change my tampon every few hours."

At this point, your daughters will either ask you why this happens or they'll tell you they already know about periods. In either
case, continue:

"Because you will be getting your monthly period sometime
in the next year or two, I think it's important for you to know why
women bleed like this."

At this time, give your daughter the facts. You might want to refer to one of the books suggested at the end of this chapter or you can give your own knowledgeable explanation. In brief, remember to mention these points:

Females are born with a supply of eggs in their ovaries. Beginning during pubescence, one egg at a time is released approximately every twenty-eight days by one of the ovaries. This egg travels through tubes from the ovary to the uterus. The uterus prepares to receive it by creating a lining composed of blood and other fluids and substances. If the egg is fertilized as a result of sexual intercourse, the egg becomes embedded in this lining and a baby develops. If the egg is not fertilized, the lining dissolves and is released as menstrual flow through the vagina.

Most importantly, tell your daughter what to do when she first begins menstruating. Assure her that when she first sees a bit of blood, she need not worry. If she is away from home, she should go to the school nurse or nearest bathroom for a sanitary pad or a wad of toilet tissue.

Emphasize the normal aspect of menstruation and encourage your daughter to let you know if she should see any blood or even brown stains on her underwear or on the toilet tissue when she wipes herself after urination.

Here are a few questions you can expect and suggested answers:

"How much blood comes out?"

"The menstrual discharge is heaviest during the first few days. The total menstrual discharge amounts to about half a cup, but there are only four to six tablespoons of blood. The rest is made up mostly of extra uterine lining, which explains why the discharge is often brownish in color."

"Will I still be able to go to gym class and play outside?"

"Menstruation is a normal part of every woman's life and there's no reason to change any part of your daily schedule at this time. You can shower, dance, run, exercise, swim, and play without worrying."

"Will I feel sick?"

"Most women feel perfectly fine throughout their period. Some do experience some abdominal cramps, but light exercise or a heating pad usually relieves the discomfort. Others feel a little moody or tense just before their period begins. The reason for this is simple: the female hormones—estrogen and progesterone—that cause the lining of the uterus to thicken usually make you feel especially well. Just before menstruation begins, the production of these hormones is reduced, resulting in a let-down feeling. This feeling is strictly temporary and disappears as menstruation starts."

"Will I have a period for the rest of my life?"

"Women do not menstruate during pregnancy, but otherwise, they generally have periods every month until they are about fifty years old. The end of menstruation, called menopause, usually occurs between forty-five and fifty-five years of age.

"There are a few factors, such as extreme stress or excessive dieting or exercising, that can interrupt the normal menstrual cycle. If you ever skip a period, be sure to let me know so I can help you find out why."

All About Boys

Boys' introduction to puberty begins with slow but sure physical changes that affect their size and appearance. You should first talk to your son about the changes he'll be most acutely aware of. These are the main ones:

- *Skin.* During puberty, pimples may begin to appear on the face and often on the back. In approximately seventy percent of teenagers (especially boys) acne will become a problem.
- *Chest.* A boy's breasts may get slightly larger and feel tender temporarily. Assure your son that if this happens to him, it is perfectly normal and will soon pass.
- *Voice.* The male voice gets deeper during puberty, but while in transition it may crack or squeak occasionally. Let your son know that this is to be expected and he should not feel embarrassed when it happens.
- *Body hair.* Alert your son to the fact that he will soon begin growing hair in his genital area, under his arms, on his chest, and eventually on his face.
- *Sweat glands.* This is the time to emphasize good hygiene and introduce deodorant because boys will now begin to perspire more.
- *Size.* As your boy grows rapidly in size and weight during puberty, he may find that he temporarily loses some physical coordination and may feel clumsy at times. He should also know that some boys grow early and quickly, others grow later and slowly, and both are perfectly normal.
- *Genitals.* As the male body develops in sexuality, first the scrotum and testicles begin to enlarge. Later the penis itself increases in size.

About one year after the beginning of these changes, boys usually acquire the capacity to produce and ejaculate sperm. This typically occurs during masturbation or a wet dream. A boy's first ejaculation often occurs as a surprise or as confirmation of locker-room talk. Your son will accept the bodily changes of puberty in a positive way if you tell him *beforehand* that soon he will be capable of producing and ejaculating sperm.

Your son may be somewhat embarrassed by a discussion of ejaculation, but he will also be relieved to know that he can talk to you about *anything* during this time of change. Here are some questions you might expect and some suggested answers:

"How does an erection happen?"

"Erections happen when the penis becomes enlarged and firm and stands erect. Like yawning, erections are very normal and often involuntary. They're a natural part of being male. During the teen years, the penis becomes more sensitive, and erections occur more frequently, sometimes for no apparent reason. Although this may be embarrassing, it's normal. Generally erections occur in three ways:

"When a male is sexually aroused, blood fills the spongelike tissues in the penis, which causes it to become enlarged.

"While he is asleep, a male may experience a buildup of semen that will give him an erection.

"A bladder full of urine can put pressure on the reproductive organs and cause the penis to become erect. That's why males from infancy through adulthood often wake in the morning with an erection."

"What does it mean to 'come'?"

"When a man is sexually aroused, he can reach a peak of excitement that can end with an orgasm. Having an orgasm is called 'coming.' When a man has an orgasm, his penis muscles contract and relax while a whitish sticky fluid called semen shoots out of the tip in short spurts. This is called an ejaculation. Ejaculation can result from sexual stimulation such as masturbation or sexual intercourse. After ejaculation, the penis returns to its normal size."

"Why do some guys have large penises
and others have small ones?"

"There is no such thing as a 'normal' penis. The size and appearance of external sexual organs are different in every person. Size and shape have nothing to do with sexual pleasure or masculinity."

"If I don't come when I have an erection,
will I get sick or hurt my penis?"

"No. If the erection lasts for a long time, you may experience a dull, sensitive, swollen feeling, especially in the testes, when the penis returns to its soft state. This feeling is short-lived, is not harmful, and will not make you sick or injure your penis."

"What's a wet dream?"

"Wet dreams happen when you ejaculate while you're sleeping. They are one way that a man's body gets rid of extra sperm, and they are very normal. If you wake in the morning and find you've had a wet dream, just take your sheets off the bed and put them with your pajamas in the laundry (or on the washing machine, or whatever). Don't feel embarrrassed. Your mom and I expect that this will happen because you're growing up now."

The Emotional Side of Puberty

There is one aspect of puberty that affects both boys and girls in much the same way. Along with the changing body parts and the physiology of sexual development, puberty brings with it a whole new set of emotions, feelings, and worries. Your young adults will worry excessively about their appearance (just at a time when they are feeling most unattractive), they will ceaselessly compare their physical development to that of their friends (which is usually behind or ahead of their own), and they will experience new and sometimes frightening sexual feelings that they aren't yet ready to act upon.

Be patient with your kids. Growing into an adult body is an exciting process, but it can also cause tension and insecurities that only these young people can fully understand.

The most valuable gift you can give your children during this time of their lives is self-esteem. Assure them repeatedly of their attractive qualities. Let them know they're not alone in their confused feelings. And assure them over and over that you are ready to listen to their concerns and answer their questions.

Suggested Reading

For Parents

Boston Woman's Health Book Collective Staff. *Our Bodies, Ourselves*. New York: Simon & Schuster, 1976.

Flowers, John V. *Raising Your Child to Be a Sexually Healthy Adult*. Englewood Cliffs, N.J.: Prentice-Hall, 1982.

Lewis, Howard R. *Sex Education Begins at Home: How to Raise Sexually Healthy Children*. E. Norwalk, Conn.: Appleton-Century-Crofts, 1983.

For Children Entering Puberty

Baldwin, Dorothy. *How You Grow and Change*. New York: Bookwright Press, 1984.

Ball, Jacqueline A. *Puberty*. Vero Beach, Fla.: Rourke Publications, 1988.

Calderone, Mary, and Eric Johnson. *The Family Book About Sexuality.* New York: Harper & Row, 1981.

Glassman, Bruce. *Everything You Need to Know About Growing Up Male.* New York: Rosen Publishing Group, 1991.

Johnson, Eric W. *Love And Sex And Growing Up.* New York: Bantam Books, 1990.

Kahaner, Ellen. *Everything You Need to Know About Growing Up Female.* New York: Rosen Publishing Group, 1991.

McCoy, Kathy. *Growing and Changing: A Handbook for Preteens.* New York: Perigee Books, 1986.

Madaras, Lynda, and Area Madaras. *What's Happening to My Body? A Book for Girls: A Growing Up Guide for Parents and Daughters.* New York: Newmarket Press, 1987.

Madaras, Lynda, and Dane Saavedra. *What's Happening to My Body? A Book for Boys: A Growing Up Guide for Parents and Sons.* New York: Newmarket Press, 1991.

Mayle, Peter. *What's Happening To Me? The Answers to Some of the World's Most Embarrassing Questions.* New York: Carol Publishing Group, 1975.

Risk Taking and Failure

When my son was three months old, I left him overnight with my parents while my spouse and I snuck off for a weekend alone. This was the first time I teetered on that fine line between being sensibly cautious and being overprotective. I worried about my baby's comfort in the "strange" environment, about his feelings at being separated from me, about his schedule being disrupted, and about a hundred other things. But, finally, I took the risk and said good-bye, with my fingers crossed for luck. Despite my fears, that weekend turned out to be a good experience for all of us.

Seventeen years later I found myself teetering on that same line. In his junior year of high school, my son was elected to represent his school at a special gathering of teens in Washington, D.C. Although I was proud of his accomplishments, it seemed awfully risky to put this boy on an airplane by himself and send him off to spend a week with strangers. If he stayed at home, he'd be safe and would avoid the chance of getting hurt or lost, or of feeling lonely. But I knew he'd also miss out on opportunities for adventure, knowledge, and growth. So I decided to encourage him to take the risk and again said good-bye and crossed my fingers.

In between these two events there have been countless risk-taking experiences that I've hesitantly encouraged my children to try: learning to walk, riding a bike, climbing trees, skateboarding, ice skating, playing football, performing in the school play, and asking girls for dates. With each adventure, I wonder: how far do we go to protect our children and how much should we encourage them to explore new things? The answer is difficult to pinpoint because, paradoxically, part of our job as parents is to keep our children physically and emotionally safe, and yet another part is to allow them the freedom to venture into places and situations where they might get hurt.

When our children are very young, we can evaluate the degree of hazard and decide for them how far they should venture into risky territory. (The greatest obstacle at this time is often our own fears.) But what does a parent say to an eleven-year-old who wants to bungee jump at the amusement park, or to an eight-year-old who won't join the baseball team because he's afraid he'll strike out? Well, over the years I've learned that before you talk to kids about taking chances, you need to determine if the quest is what I call a "reasonable risk."

Taking Reasonable Risks

A reasonable risk exists when the possible benefits outweigh the potential loss. You can teach children between the ages of five and eleven to be reasonabe risk takers by talking to them about demanding new activities and circumstances as they come up in their lives. If your children are considering a decision involving an element of risk, ask them these questions and then help them work out the answers:

- "What are your chances of succeeding at this?"
- "What is the risk involved?"
- "What are the benefits you'll gain?"
- "Do the good things you'll gain justify the risk?"

There's a story told about Charles Lindbergh that illustrates this approach to risk taking. It seems that Lindbergh's boys once asked his permission to climb an awesomely tall tree. He responded, "How are you going up?"

Scott, the twelve-year-old, pointed and said, "First this limb, then that."

"You're going to get stuck after that aren't you?" Lindbergh prodded.

The boys sadly agreed. Only when they had calculated their chances on various routes up the tree did their father give his consent. Then, to a watching friend, he said, "They must learn to take calculated risks, as long as they figure out everything ahead of time and just don't go off half-cocked."

Children who are reckless risk takers benefit most from dialogues that help them learn to think about risk. Reckless risk takers seem to fear nothing. From the moment they become mobile, they dangle out windows, climb to high places, and jump before looking. These daredevils habitually take unreasonable risks that put them in dangerous situations where nothing positive can be gained. In these situations, when the risk poses certain danger, of course you'll need to take a firm stand against the activity. But other times when the risk is manageable, use the questions above to help your children practice thinking about the risks involved before they jump into something. Once they get into the habit of thinking first, you'll find they'll begin to distinguish for themselves reckless risk taking from reasonable risk taking.

Encouraging Risk Taking

Some children are overly cautious and avoid all risky situations completely. Rather than take chances, these children prefer to stay in the "comfort zone"—a safe and secure environment—even when it means mediocrity and boredom.

If your children are overly cautious, you need to talk to them about the situations they're avoiding even though the experiences would contribute to their emotional and/or physical development. This might be in the classroom, where your children won't raise their hands to risk offering an answer; or in a sports program, where they won't even try; or in music lessons, where they won't play for an audience.

When you see this pattern of avoidance developing, talk about the risks involved, the possible consequences (good and bad), and the ways of enjoying the good and coping with the bad. Ask your children:

"What do you worry will happen if you do this?"

"How would you feel if you gave it a try and did very well?"

"How would you feel if you gave it a try and did poorly?"

"How will you feel if you don't try at all?"

Letting your children verbalize their feelings about avoiding risk may help them see that they are missing out on fun things out of fear rather than lack of interest.

Jack Henderson gave this a try with his ten-year-old daughter. All winter, Myrna had been looking forward to her first year on a softball team and talked excitedly about her plans and aspirations. But as opening day drew near, Myrna started backing out.

"I was very surprised," remembers Jack, "because I knew Myrna wanted to play. My first inclination was to let her make her own decision and not push her into something she wasn't sure she wanted. Then I remembered how much she really had wanted to play and decided to try to get her to talk about her reasons for changing her mind."

Jack asked Myrna how she would feel about playing if she knew for certain that she would be a starting shortstop. Then he asked her how she would feel if she had to sit on the bench a few innings each game. He continued asking questions about her fears and feelings to help her see that if she didn't risk sitting on the bench, she had no chance of ever enjoying the feeling of being a starting shortstop. It turned out that once Myrna voiced her fears aloud, she felt more confident in her ability to take the risk and deal with the consequences.

Reasonable risk taking gives children two valuable life lessons: (1) by risking and winning, children learn to trust themselves and they gain confidence in their abilities; (2) by risking and losing, they learn to face failure and deal with its frustration. It's this second lesson that's the hardest to learn.

Facing Failure

Fear of making mistakes and of being humiliated interferes with a person's willingness to take reasonable risks. Yet, ironically, it's failure that teaches the most valuable lessons about success. That's why it's part of our job to teach our children that failures are an inevitable and useful part of life.

Talk About Failure. When your children talk about their failures and mistakes, listen for a tendency to blame others or give up too quickly. If your children aren't doing well in school, do they blame the teacher or say "What's the use"? If their building blocks fall down, do they blame the blocks or stop trying? If they lose the game, do they blame their teammates or decide they're just no good? If your kids are making comments like these, they may believe that failing at one or two things makes them a failure. Perfectionists, especially, feel their self-worth depends on external factors such as being successful at everything they do. These children need to learn about the positive side of failure.

Mistakes are a part of everyone's daily life, so it's not difficult to find opportunities to talk about this subject. When your child brings home a school paper with a mistake, for example, don't focus on the grade alone; talk about the error itself. Tell your child, "Making mistakes is one of the ways we learn things. So, let's see what you can learn from this mistake." Then help your child find the correct answer. Or, if your child tries to build a castle with building blocks, but the castle falls down before it's finished, encourage him or her to use this event constructively. Ask the child, "Why do you think it fell down?" "What can you do differently the next time?" "Let's see you give it another try."

Talk About Your Own Failures. It's a good feeling when our children think we're perfect and can do anything in the world—but it's also unrealistic and offers an impossible model for them to live up to. You can encourage your children to risk failure by talking about your own experience with risk taking and by admitting your mistakes and failures. You might talk to your kids about the time you ran for class president and lost, or tried out for a team and didn't make it, or tried to build a model airplane by yourself but found that you needed help.

Demonstrate Resilience. You can model the attitude toward failure that you want your children to develop.

If you try a new recipe for dinner and it tastes awful, don't curse the cookbook. Admit your frustration with this meal and vow to try something new another night.

If you attempt to fix a broken window and fail, don't throw away your tools and blame the age of the wood. Admit your difficulty aloud and talk about ways to improve your approach.

If you're afraid to take a new job or take on a difficult project, talk out loud about your feelings and fears. This demonstrates to your kids that risk taking and the possibility of failure go hand-in-hand throughout life.

Help Your Children Practice Failure.　Children need to learn and accept the fact that no one can be the best at everything, that no one can win all the time, and that it's possible to enjoy a game even when you don't win. In short, it's human to fail and make mistakes, and this imperfection does not diminish our self-worth or reduce our chances of succeeding in the future.

One way to teach this lesson is to arrange situations in which you occasionally let your children fail. When you play card or board games, for example, don't always let your children win. When your kids run races, don't always insist that the little one be given a head start. If you play tennis or basketball, don't consistently give your children the advantage. Let them experience the disappointment of losing in a protected environment, with you in your home. Then encourage them to try again. It's these little lessons that give our children the confidence and perseverance they'll need to master difficult tasks and pursue challenging goals in their lives.

All kids need opportunities to take risks in order to develop courage, confidence, and self-esteem. So give them the freedom to try, and the encouragement they need to try again. As you do this, your goal should be to help them develop an attitude like the one that prompted Thomas Edison to say, "Failure? Not really. I've just learned ten thousand ways not to invent a light bulb."

Suggested Reading

For Children Aged Four to Seven

Berenstain, Stan, and Jan Berenstain. *The Berenstain Bears' Soccer Star.* New York: Random Books for Young Readers, 1983.

Berenstain, Stan, and Jan Berenstain. *The Berenstain Bears Get Stage Fright.* New York: Random Books for Young Readers, 1986.

Berenstain, Stan, and Jan Berenstain. *The Berenstain Bears and the Big Road Race.* New York: Random Books for Young Readers, 1987.

Berenstain, Stan, and Jan Berenstain. *The Berenstain Bears Go Out for the Team.* New York: Random Books for Young Readers, 1987.

Santa Claus

"Ho! Ho! Ho! What do you want for Christmas, little boy?"

With a wail of protest, another baby became part of the Christmas ritual—a visit with Santa Claus.

Why, I wondered, was this young mother happily handing over her crying son to a complete stranger with a red suit and white beard? Why were all these parents willing to stand in long, slow-moving lines with these fearful, anxious, and hopeful children? Why do these parents encourage their children to believe in this all-knowing, all-loving, and all-giving mythical man?

Considering my own presence in the shopping mall, I also wondered why we all battle crowds of shoppers to spend more money than we can afford. And to top it off, we do this to give glory and credit to someone else—someone who steals into our homes in the dark of night and magically makes all our children's dreams come true.

Why do we do this?

Some parents who celebrate Christmas have asked me if it wouldn't be better to tell their children right from infancy that there is no Santa Claus at all. Plenty of parents object that sometimes Santa Claus commercializes a religious holiday and turns kids' holy thoughts to greed. But before you debunk the myth, keep in mind that child-development experts have long encouraged parents to allow their children to enjoy the fantastical world of Santa Claus.

Santa embodies all the wonderful characteristics of a living fantasy. He's a mysterious man who lives very far away and yet sees everything we do. He has a workshop full of toys made by little elves. He has flying reindeer who defy the laws of science. And he delivers toys to boys and girls who have tried to be good, even if they've failed.

Christmas is Christ's birthday, and Santa can help your children experience the joy of this birth in the gifts he gives to celebrate. In fact, rather than taking away from the religious spirit of the season, Santa can enhance it. Santa Claus tells children that it's okay to believe with all your heart in something you've never seen. (Isn't this same kind of blind faith the foundation of religion?) Look closely at small faces squished up against cold window panes on Christmas Eve; you'll see a devout faith and hope.

Kids grow up too quickly. Our society often pushes them into a world of adult problems before they even have a full set of permanent teeth. Belief in Santa makes the short days of youth all that more special because he gives children license to be children.

We can't stop our children from growing up, but we can savor this time of innocence. We can cherish every squeal of delight and hushed whisper of suspense. We can use our children's Christmas passion to help us remember that this is not just a season of headaches and traffic jams.

Because of your belief in what Santa *embodies*—goodness and generosity—you can sincerely say to your young children, "Yes, there is a Santa Claus."

Once you decide to pass on the story of Santa, you can prepare yourself for that inevitable day when your children are somewhere between the ages of four and ten, and they ask you if Santa Claus is real.

Hank Korolak, a neighborhood dad, told us about his recent response to this question. "To be honest," he said, "I always thought the answer to this question would be picked up from siblings and friends—passed down from older kids in hushed tones and never laid directly at my feet. Then one day my own eight-year-old boldly asked, 'Do you buy all the presents and put them under the tree, or does Santa Claus do it?'"

Hank knew many of his son's friends were already professing the "truth," and he didn't want to persist in the fantasy if it would make him the brunt of ridicule. But he remembers feeling a sense of loss at that moment. "I didn't want him to lose the wide-eyed wonder and excitement that pure belief brings to Christmas," says Hank. "So I hesitated and grappled for an answer. I didn't know what to say."

One recent study of middle-class children from Christian families revealed that at age four, about eighty-five percent of children believe in Santa. At age eight, only about a quarter of them still really believe, a little more than half of them are torn between belief and nonbelief, and about twenty percent of them do not believe at all. My son was, at that moment, among the uncertain.

So, how should you answer that inevitable question, "Is there really a Santa Claus?"

First listen carefully to figure out what your children are really asking. Start by turning the question back to them. Ask them, "Well, what do you think?"

An answer like "I still kinda believe in him but he didn't eat the cookies we left him last year," suggests that your child isn't ready for the truth but wants to know that it's okay to keep believing. In this case, feel free to offer assurance that you believe in him also and that he probably just wasn't hungry last year.

However, as children learn more about the world they live in and their vision of the line between fantasy and reality becomes more clearly defined, their questions about obvious contradictions in the Santa story may reveal a serious doubt and a desire to know the truth. Children soon realize that by the laws of science, a man cannot visit all the world's houses in one night and cannot possibly carry toys for all the world's children in one sled. In this case, it's time for honesty tempered with spiritualism.

You could tell your children, "Actually, Santa Claus *is* a pretend person. But in many ways, the things you believed about Santa are true. Santa is the spirit of Christmas. He helps young children understand the idea of giving and loving and enjoying the birth of Christ. Now that you're older, you can see that spirit lives in God. It's really God who can see when you're good and when you're bad, and it's God who is loving and caring and who gives us the most precious gift of family and love."

Hank's son did not take the news well at first. He asked, "Why did you lie to me all these years?" Hank turned the question back to him, "When you grow and become a parent, will you encourage your children to believe in Santa Claus? I'll bet you will because he's a joyful part of our holiday tradition. I don't think you would have wanted me to deprive you of all that fun. And I still hope that your memories of those years will warm all your Christmases yet to come."

(This technique of turning the question back to your children to uncover how much they really want the truth is an effective strategy for handling questions about the tooth fairy and Easter Bunny as well.)

The importance lies in what Santa Claus represents. Discussing the spirit behind Santa can defuse children's questions about whether or not you actually misled them, and it can help them better understand the role of fantasy in childhood.

Sex and Reproduction

We had gathered with family and friends in a large restaurant to celebrate a very special birthday. As we were waiting for the main course, my five-year-old yelled across the table, "What's sex?" It seemed to me that every diner in the room had turned toward us to listen for the answer.

There was a long pause before my spouse turned to me pleading, "Why don't you handle this one." This wasn't the time or the place to discuss human sexuality, so I employed a time-honored parenting technique—distraction.

"That's something I'll talk to you about later, honey," I said. "But right now, why don't you tell me what you're going to have for dessert."

"Chocolate cake," my daughter answered, and the crisis was over. We went on with our celebration and I made a mental note to answer her question when we returned home.

All children learn about the birds and bees eventually, but what they learn and how they learn differs greatly from one child to another. That's why talking about human sexuality with our children is so important—if we don't, someone else will.

The goal in talking to children about the subject of sex is really quite simple: as parents we want to ensure that as our children grow, and their questions and concerns about this subject become more complex and sensitive, they'll turn to us for honest answers. That's really what this chapter is all about.

When Should You Talk to Your Child About Sex?

As soon as children are old enough to ask questions about sex, they are old enough for honest answers. This can be as early as two years.

If your children don't ask questions or don't seem interested in talking about sex and reproduction by the age of seven, they've probably gotten the impression that sex is a forbidden or embarrassing subject.

If you feel that your child is past the age when he or she should be asking questions, you should bring up the subject during "teachable moments." These are occasions when your children are most likely to be open to sexual information and guidance. It's awkward to announce suddenly one day, "Johnny, today I want to tell you what happens when a man and a woman have sex." But you might easily glide into this discussion by remarking about something the two of you see on television; even prime-time shows openly discuss sexual relationships and situations.

If a male character is teased by his friend for being a virgin, for example, you can casually explain to young children, "That means he has never made love to a woman." To older children explain, "That means he has never had sexual intercourse before." As your children learn that you're open to frank discussions, they'll soon join in the conversation and ask for more details.

You might also make observations about animal behavior. If your children see a male dog with an erection, don't always divert their attention away from the scene. You can use the opportunity to discuss male anatomy or sexual response (depending on your child's age and background knowledge).

You might say something as simple as, "Look, that dog must

be a boy because he has a penis." Or as factual as, "That dog knows the other dog across the park is a female and that makes his penis become erect."

During teachable moments, show your children that you're not afraid or embarrassed to talk about sex. This is how they'll learn that they don't need to be afraid or embarrassed to talk to you about this sensitive subject.

How Should You Talk to Your Child About Sex?

An important aspect of sex education is conveying family values, standards, and attitudes. So, before you begin to teach your children about sex, examine your own feelings. It's okay to feel uncomfortable about talking to your children about sex, as long as you don't let it paralyze you. You can keep your own discomfort from interfering with the way you talk to your children in two simple ways:

• *Start early.* Begin talking to your children about their own sexuality when they are very young. Then when they get older and need more detailed information you'll feel more comfortable having set the stage early.

• *Be open about your feelings.* Don't be ashamed to admit to your older children that you feel awkward discussing sex. You might say, "This isn't an easy subject for me to talk about. When I was young, sex wasn't discussed in the home. But I believe this is an important topic and I want to discuss it with you." Your children will respect you for your honesty.

If human sexuality arouses in you feelings of guilt, disgust, or shame, you're likely to pass on this attitude to your children. If this is the case, you might be able to develop a healthier attitude for yourself through readings; human sexuality courses; open discussions with your spouse, a trusted friend, or a minister, rabbi, or priest; or you might consider professional therapy and counseling. In the meantime, it might be easiest for you to convey a healthy attitude about sex to your children by using some of the books suggested at the end of this chapter, or by asking a trusted adult to talk to your children about their sexuality.

Answer the Question Asked. Try to avoid the common mistake of telling too much too soon. Listen carefully to what your child is asking and answer only that question. If the question's not clear, try to find out the meaning by asking "In what way?" or "What do you mean?"

When answering your children's questions, keep in mind the old story of the little boy who asked his father, "Where did I come from?" After listening to a long discourse on reproduction, the child replied, "Oh. Well the boy next door came from Chicago. I just wondered where I came from."

Use Correct Terms. Just as you teach your children the proper names of body parts such as fingers, toes, and elbows, teach them the proper names of their reproductive anatomy. The term "pee-pee" for a boy's penis, for example, sounds cute when the child is very young, but the term makes it difficult to talk seriously about human sexuality when he's older.

The following words are not too difficult for young children to say and should be the ones you use when talking to your children about their body parts and sexuality: *penis, vulva, vagina, testicles, buttocks, anus, breasts, sexual intercourse, clitoris, nipples, semen, sperm, erection, ejaculation,* and *masturbation.*

Use these words naturally and freely when you talk to your children about sex. They help make the subject less confusing, mysterious, and difficult to discuss.

Don't Laugh.   Children need to feel that their ideas and concerns about sex and their sexual development are worth listening to—not funny, ignorant, or trite. Yet sometimes the impulse to laugh at our children's budding sexual awareness is hard to resist.

One day Debbie entered her five-year-old's bedroom to find Jennifer sitting on her bed, naked from the waist up, pinching her nipples and pulling them out from her body. "Why won't these things get big like yours?" she asked greatly perplexed. Laughter would be an understandable reaction, but this is one of these teachable moments that would be lost if answered with humor.

Instead, Debbie might say, "Isn't it wonderful to be a girl and know that when you get to be about twelve or thirteen years old, your breasts will grow big like mine?"

"But I want them big now," Jennifer might complain.

Then Debbie could introduce her daughter to the purpose and function of the female breast by saying something like, "Right now you don't need large breasts because you're not ready to have a baby. Mothers need breasts to store milk for their babies. That's why the dark area is called a nipple. Babies can get milk by sucking on the nipple of a bottle or they can get milk by sucking on their mothers' nipples."

Jennifer may continue to pull on her nipples, but she'll also know more about the female breast than she did before.

Where Do Babies Come From?

By the time children are in kindergarten, they should know where babies come from and the facts about obvious anatomical differences between boys and girls. The following dialogues are examples of the questions children ask on these topics and ways to answer them.

A Discussion with a Preschooler

"Where do babies come from?"

"Babies grow inside their mommies until they are ready to be born."

"Where does a baby grow inside the mommy?"

"In a special place just for babies, called a uterus."

"How does a baby get inside the mommy?"

"A small sperm from a daddy's body enters the mommy's body and meets a tiny egg from the mommy. They join together and the baby grows from that. When it's big enough, the baby is born."

"How does the baby get out?"

"From a special opening in the mommy's body for the baby to come through."

A Discussion with a School-Age Child

"How do you have sex?"

"A man and a woman lie close together and feel loving toward each other. The man's penis fits into the woman's vagina. That's called sexual intercourse."

"Does the man go to the bathroom inside the woman?"

"No. The penis does carry a man's urine, but it also can carry what's called semen and that's what comes out of the penis and goes into the woman's vagina during sexual intercourse."

"How does the baby get out of the mother?"

"A special hole opens up in her body between her legs. The skin and muscles stretch and there is enough room for the baby to squeeze through, usually with the head coming first."

Basic Guidelines for Talking About Sex

Whether you talk to your children about sex and reproduction when they ask you questions or whether you use teachable moments, the lessons will be most effective if you remember these basic guidelines:

Be Matter-of-Fact. Treat the topic of sex as you would any other subject. If children are given facts about sex in a straightforward manner, they'll accept them as the factual matters that they are.

Be Brief. Steer away from lectures. A long speech will either confuse your children or turn them off. Informal, spontaneous exchanges are best. Be brief and leave the door open for further discussion. When your young children ask you a question about sex, a good rule of thumb is to give a minimal answer and then wait to see whether they are satisfied. If they want more, they'll ask.

Be Honest. Don't let embarrassment distort the truth. Stories about the stork may be enshrined in tradition, but they're confusing to children who live in these progressive and media-controlled times. Giving special powers of creation to doctors and hospitals also skirts the issue. Give your kids honest information.

Give Immediate Feedback. Be prepared to handle questions as they come up. If you postpone your response, your children are likely to have forgotten what they wanted to know by the time you're ready to discuss it. The teachable moment will be gone and your children will be without information they asked for. If circumstances make it impossible to respond immediately, be sure to find an opportunity to return to the question as soon as possible.

Be Prepared to Repeat Yourself. Children learn about sex and reproduction slowly, as they gradually mature. As the same questions come up over the years, keep the dialogue going by offering more elaborate and graphic details. Like moral education, sex education is a continuous process that begins early and continues throughout one's life.

Know What's Being Taught in School. If your school offers a family life curriculum, you can use the guidelines offered in this chapter to support the information your children learn in school. If you ask questions about what's being taught, school lessons can give you many teachable moments. Discussions about school lessons also give you not-to-be-missed opportunities to put the facts of human sexuality into the framework of your own family's standards and values.

Remember, if you talk to your young children honestly about their sexuality, you'll find that as they get older and need more explicit information, they'll feel comfortable getting that information from you.

Suggested Reading

For Parents

Calderone, Mary Steichen. *Talking with Your Children About Sex: Questions and Answers for Children from Birth to Puberty*. New York: Ballantine, 1983.

Flowers, John V. *Raising Your Child to Be a Sexually Healthy Adult*. Englewood Cliffs, N.J.: Prentice-Hall, 1982.

Goldman, Ronald. *Show Me Yours: Understanding Children's Sexuality*. New York: Penguin Books, 1988.

Lewis, Howard R. *Sex Education Begins at Home: How to Raise Sexually Healthy Children*. E. Norwalk, Conn.: Appleton-Century-Crofts, 1983.

For Children Aged Four to Seven

Girard, Linda Walvoord. *You Were Born on Your Very First Birthday*. Niles, Ill.: A. Whitman, 1983.

Ziefert, Harriet. *Getting Ready for New Baby*. New York: Harper & Row, 1990.

For Children Aged Eight to Twelve

Baldwin, Dorothy. *How You Grow and Change*. New York: Bookwright Press, 1984.

Gordon, Sol. *Did the Sun Shine Before You Were Born? A Sex Education Primer*. Fayetteville, N.Y.: Education University Press, 1982.

Johnson, Eric W. *Love and Sex and Growing Up*. New York: Bantam Books, 1990.

Marsh, Carole. *AIDS to Zits: A "Sextionary" for Kids*. Decatur, Ga.: Gallopade, 1992.

Meredith, Susan. *Where Do Babies Come From?* Tulsa, Okla.: EDC Publishing, 1991.

Sex Play and Masturbation

Kevin opened the closet door and then stood there completely dumbfounded. There on the floor, stark naked, were his six-year-old daughter, Kim, and her seven-year-old friend, Jeffrey.

"I didn't know what to say or do," says Kevin. "I don't think I'd have been more shocked if they were both seventeen and I found them in bed together. It was just an awful feeling that I couldn't shake for a long time."

After a few seconds, Kevin scooped up his daughter and told Jeffrey to get dressed and go home. In stony silence, Kevin carried Kim off to the bedroom where he quickly dressed her and abruptly left her alone.

"I guess I didn't handle that so well," admits Kevin, "but if I'd said anything at that time, I would have blurted out some very angry words."

Kevin was smart to hold his tongue. But surely his daughter had no doubt that he was furiously upset. Many parents in similar situations find it hard to remember that childhood sex play as well as masturbation are universal activities and normal aspects of self-exploration for both boys and girls. There is nothing fundamentally wrong with either activity. Still, it's understandable why parents might react with alarm, anger, or embarrassment.

If we react to their sexual exploration with shock, we may lose their trust and confidence. This can make it difficult to talk about human sexuality with an open attitude at a later time. Passing on feelings of guilt, shame, or anxiety can affect children's views of themselves and their sexuality. That's why you'll find that a more effective way to respond to sex play or masturbation is with a parent-to-child talk that is simple, direct, and unemotional.

Sex Play

"Let's play doctor. Take off your clothes."

"Okay. You show me yours and I'll show you mine."

This brief exchange of ideas is probably not what you want to hear coming out of your children's playroom. But it is quite commonly heard among children aged six to ten, who have a natural need to satisfy their curiosity. If you hear your children talking about their body parts or find them looking at or touching each other's genital areas, you may naturally feel some immediate discomfort, but don't show your distress. Remember, it's quite easy to unintentionally attach guilt to perfectly normal, healthy urges.

So what should you do?

If you walk in on children in the act of sex play, you should casually interrupt them. Don't, at that moment, discuss their actions, because you may not be able to control your emotions, and they may feel embarrassed or defensive. Instead, direct their attention to another activity.

When he opened the closet door, for example, Kevin might have stated, "This isn't a good game to play. Come on, get dressed both of you, and I'll meet you in the kitchen for some finger painting." This would have ended the activity that upset him and it would have given him time to calm his strong feelings and approach the situation in a constructive way.

Then what?

Well, later, when some time has calmed your immediate reaction to the sex play activity and your child is less emotionally involved in the situation, it's important to talk about your views on this kind of play. In the same way, if you hear your children making plans for body exploration, you can join their discussion at that time, and clearly state your feelings about their idea.

When you do talk to your children about sex play, you'll want to meet two goals: (1) satisfy the curiosity that led them to the situation to begin with, and (2) help them develop acceptable sexual boundaries for themselves.

Help Your Children Satisfy Their Curiosity. After a sex play incident, find a quiet peaceful time to invite your children to sit down and talk with you about the "game" they played. In a very matter-of-fact way, discuss the human body. Invite your children to talk about the differences between boys and girls. Answer their questions as best you can. (See the chapter entitled "Sex" for helpful hints on age-appropriate approaches.) Then schedule a trip to the library to find books that show the naked human body they're so curious to see.

Follow your child's lead in deciding how much information to offer. Most sex play is motivated by curiosity about how human genitals *look*, not how they function. Your discussions and your readings don't necessarily need to focus on sexual intercourse and reproduction unless your child's questions lead you to these topics.

Help Your Children Set Appropriate Sexual Boundaries. Talking about sex play offers you a good opportunity to help your children develop sound sexual boundaries for themselves. Without making your children feel they are "bad" or have done an "evil" act, you can use this circumstance to explain your view on recreational sexual activity. In a firm tone of voice, you might say, for example, "Our bodies are private and special. We don't use them to play games."

This is also a good time to remind your children of the "good touch" and "bad touch" lessons outlined in the chapter entitled "Sexual Abuse." Reinforce the fact that even among their friends, they have an absolute right to say no to any touching that makes them feel uncomfortable.

The day after the sex play incident, Kim and her father talked about it. She told her father that Jeffrey had dared her to take off her clothes and called her a baby when she didn't want to. This gave Kevin an ideal opportunity to talk directly about the issues of personal rights and how to say no. In this way, the incident that had been so upsetting to Kevin ended up giving him a chance to teach a vital lesson in self-confidence and assertiveness.

Masturbation

By eighteen months of age, all children have discovered their genitals and many masturbate. We should not, however, associate this action with the sexual behavior and feelings experienced by adults. Children masturbate and fondle their genitals for two primary reasons: (1) they are learning that their sex organs are a source of sensual (not sexual) pleasure, and (2) like thumb-sucking, the act gives comfort and relieves tension.

If your children masturbate, you should not feel the need to talk to them about this activity because you think it's abnormal or harmful. If you find that they masturbate occasionally in your home, ignore it and say nothing. But, if they masturbate or fondle themselves excessively, or if they do these things in public, then you need to talk to them about this practice.

Like sex play, there's nothing "wrong" with masturbating, so you will not want to associate it with words like *bad* or *harmful.* To do so can pass on feelings of guilt and shame. The following guidelines, adapted from our book *Good Kids/Bad Habits,* will help you handle this sensitive issue of childhood masturbation.

Find Ways to Reduce the Time Your Child Spends Masturbating. If your child masturbates more than twice a day, your first goal will be to reduce the time he or she spends in this activity. The less the child masturbates, the weaker the habit will become, and eventually the pattern will break.

When you see your child masturbating, don't overreact: don't scold, don't call attention to the act, and don't abruptly change the child's position. Instead, calmly draw the child's attention away from his or her body to some other activity. Quite matter-of-factly, invite the child to play a game of checkers, color a picture, or squeeze some clay. If the child resists your invitation, gently direct his or her attention by physically guiding the child toward something else. Make no comment about what the child is doing. Without saying a word, this will reduce the time spent masturbating.

In addition to these preventative strategies, you might try to identify any underlying cause for excessively frequent masturbation. Here are some possible causes to consider:

1. *Boredom.* A more active and stimulating schedule (away from the television) might be the solution.
2. *Tension.* Because masturbation relieves tension, frequent masturbation may be an attempt to cope with stress. If you can reduce the stress your child is experiencing, you will also reduce the urge to masturbate.
3. *Low self-esteem.* Children who suffer low self-esteem will

look to other sources, like masturbation, for pleasure and comfort. Look for activities that offer your children opportunities for success. Offer your attention and praise for even simple activities like jumping rope, riding a bike, or coloring. Let your children know you think they're special.

4. *Sexual abuse.* Children who are being sexually abused may begin to show signs of adult sexual behaviors. During what should be a latency period, these children will use masturbation for sexual arousal. They will also talk about sex acts and engage in frequent sex play activities. If you suspect this cause, be sure to read over the chapter entitled "Sexual Abuse" for guidelines on how to handle this situation.

Help Your Child Become More Self-Aware. Children may have no awareness of when, where, or how often they masturbate, so you'll need to help your child become more conscious of what he or she is doing. Approach your child in the act when the two of you are alone in the house. Explain in an understanding way what you want the child to do in the future. You might say something like, "I know you like to rub yourself in this way, but this is something people do when they're alone, not in front of others. So from now on, why don't you do it only when you're alone in your room." End your discussion with a hug and a smile.

Offer Your Child a Competing Response. You can help your child break a pattern of behavior by providing something to do in place of the undesirable behavior. This is what is meant by "a competing response."

If you know where and when your child is most likely to masturbate, you can reduce the frequency of the behavior if you provide other activities in those circumstances. If you know your child often masturbates while riding in the car or watching television, for example, put small games, books, and puzzles in those locations to give the child something else to do.

Let your children know that you would like them to keep their hands busy while sitting around. You might say, "I bought a new pad of paper for you today. Why don't you draw me a picture of what you're watching on television."

If your little boy is in the habit of holding his penis wherever he goes, a competing response may help. Ask him to hold your bags at the store. Give him a ball to squeeze or your spare keys to jingle. Give him a rabbit's foot or a tennis ball to carry for "good luck" whenever he goes out in public. Keep his hands busy and you won't have to deal with the "problem."

Childhood masturbation and self-touching are certainly more embarrassing for you than for your children. Unless they are displaying symptoms of tension, low self-esteem, or sexual abuse, most children are innocently following natural urges, so don't give in to the temptation to shout "Will you stop that!"

"Stopping" should not be your goal. Rather, you want to direct these behaviors into a more acceptable environment and convey to your children a sense of privacy about the human body and about self-stimulation.

Suggested Reading

For Parents

Leight, L. *The Parent's Guide to Raising Sexually Healthy Children.* New York: Rawson Associates, 1988.

Schaefer, Charles, and Theresa F. DiGeronimo. *Good Kids/Bad Habits.* New York: Crown, 1993.

Wattleton, Fay. *How to Talk with Your Child About Sexuality.* New York: Doubleday, 1986.

Sexual Abuse

The shrill ring of the phone broke the morning silence. It was an old friend calling in panic.

"I've just picked up the newspaper," the voice on the other end blurted out, "and I read that a man on the other side of our neighborhood has been arrested for sexually molesting young girls in his home! My daughter has played with his daughter many times," my friend confessed. "What if he has touched her or hurt her and I didn't know anything about it? I can't believe this could happen right in my neighborhood. What should I do?"

The first piece of advice we gave this friend is one we suggest to each of you, too: talk with your children. Let them know what sexual abuse is and how to protect themselves. Then make them feel at ease talking to you about a subject that seems too "private" for words.

Sexual abuse is not a subject we readily talk about with our children because it's something we pray will never touch their lives. It's also not a subject our children are likely to ask questions about. These are two common reasons why many families don't discuss sexual abuse until after it happens.

The fact is, however, that there are several very good reasons why we should talk to our children about this topic. First and foremost, it's well known that children whose parents talk to them about sexual abuse are better prepared to prevent it from happening.

Another reason is the frequency with which this crime occurs. Although exact figures are not available (owing to the unreported and secret nature of the crime), experts believe that about one in three to one in four girls will be sexually abused by the age of eighteen. Male victims of abuse number one in eight to one in ten. An even more alarming statistic is that the mean age of the victim in sexual abuse cases is somewhere between six and nine.

Although we might sometimes prefer to believe that sexual abuse is an inner-city problem of obviously dysfunctional families, as my friend found out—it's not. Quite coincidentally, this fact was delivered to the doorsteps in my small town a few mornings later in headlines that blared "Man Says He Molested 20 Boys." Right here in this neighborhood of picket fences and shuttered houses, a local resident—known to the kids as Uncle Joey—has admitted to routinely sexually abusing young boys in his home. His latest victim is the six-year-old son of the woman with whom he lives.

We also tend to think of sexual abuse as something that happens outside "good family homes," but sadly, many children are victims of incest. Of course, because you're reading this book to find ways to protect your children, it's unlikely that you are engaged in or colluding with an incestual relationship. Nevertheless, it's something that can occur in anyone's home, among stepparents, siblings, cousins, uncles, and grandparents.

So no matter where we live or how solid our family ties, our children should be warned about the problem of sexual abuse.

When Should You Talk to Your Child About Sexual Abuse?

The best time to talk about sexual abuse is before your child is in a potentially dangerous situation. Because you have no way of knowing if or when this will happen, it's important to talk about this subject at a relatively early age. Even preschoolers are not too young.

The details of what you say will be determined by your child's age, but it's best to give children of all ages general lessons in assault prevention along with other safety lessons. For example:

- Just as you can teach young children to refuse candy from strangers, you can teach them to say no if someone wants to touch private parts of their body.
- When you talk to your children about the danger of eating or drinking unknown substances they might find on the street, talk to them also about personal privacy and the right to refuse uncomfortable touching.
- When you explain to your children why they should say no to drugs, you can include a discussion of why they have a right to say no to anyone who touches them in a way that makes them feel uncomfortable.

How Should You Talk About Sexual Abuse?

When you talk to your children about sexual abuse, it's important that you present the topic in ways that won't unduly scare or horrify them. In fact, it's unlikely that you'll need to use the term *sexual abuse* at all. Your goal is to teach your children in a positive, nonthreatening way that no one has a right to touch their bodies if they don't want them to.

This message is most easily delivered in homes where parents have already established an atmosphere that allows communication on any subject—even topics that are sensitive, personal, and sometimes taboo. It's also easier to discuss abuse prevention with children who know the proper names of their body parts, including their genitals. As you prepare to discuss sexual abuse, you might also present information from the chapter entitled "Sex and Reproduction." This will help your children get the whole picture of what's natural and desirable and what's not.

What Should You Say?

When you talk to your children about sexual abuse, you will need to accomplish two goals:

1. Give specific and accurate information that will enable your children to recognize sexually abusive behavior.
2. Teach specific ways to handle potentially dangerous situations.

To meet these goals, you can follow these guidelines:

Explain "Private Parts". "Daddy, why can't girls take off their shirts when it's hot out?"

"Mommy, why can't I come into the bathroom with you?"

"Why can't I get dressed in the living room?"

Children's questions give us many opportunities to talk about our "private parts." Without implying that parts of our body are dirty or shameful, take these opportunities to explain that the parts of our body covered by our bathing suits (the anus, the male penis and testicles, and the female vulva and breasts) are very special and private. Further explain that that's why private parts are kept covered and are not to be touched or looked at by anyone except a person's parents or a health care provider (with the parents' permission).

Explain Sexual Abuse. Children need to know that some adults try to invade the privacy of young people and that it's *not* okay to do that. There are two kinds of sexual abuse your children should know about:

Nontouching abuse includes verbal sexual stimulation, such as frank discussions about sexual acts intended to arouse the child's interest or to shock the child, obscene telephone calls, exhibitionism, voyeurism, and letting down the veil of privacy so that the child watches or hears an act of sexual intercourse.

Touching abuse includes fondling; vaginal, oral, or anal intercourse or attempted intercourse; touching of the genitals; incest; and rape.

Next, your children should know that the adults who do these things are not necessarily strangers who can be avoided by refusing offers of candy or car rides. Eighty-five percent of child molesters are people known to the child.

People we tend to trust implicitly—ministers, priests, scout masters, community leaders, teachers, baby-sitters, family friends, and family members—have been found guilty of sexually abusing young children. Recent news events have highlighted shocking cases, such as the staff members of a day-care center who were convicted of molesting children in their care, a U.S. senator who revealed that as a child she was sexually abused by "a man around the corner," a respected theatrical director who was charged with seducing some of his male students, and the heir to a pharmaceutical fortune who pleaded no contest to a charge that he sexually assaulted his stepdaughter for seven years.

Tell your children, "*no one*, not even teachers, relatives, friends, or coaches, can tell you it's okay for them to touch or look at the private parts of your body."

Explain How to Say No.   Once your children know that there are parts of their body that are special and private, talk to them about what they should do if someone tries to touch or look at these body parts or exposes his or her own private parts.

Children need your permission to take personal control of their body because generally they are taught to obey and respect adults. In this case they need to know that if they don't like what's happening, they can—and should—say no.

The most effective way a child can stop a potential assault is by saying "NO!" in a loud, firm voice and quickly leaving the situation. You can help your children rehearse saying no by making up what-if games.

Use what-if games to present a variety of potentially dangerous situations such as these:

- "What if a strange man, who says he is a policeman, tells you to get into his car so he can ask you questions? What would you say?"
- "What if a friend or relative wants you to take off your clothes to play doctor? What would you say?"
- "What if someone older wants you to touch his penis? What would you say?"
- "What if someone you know wants to rub the area between your legs? What would you say?"

Coach your children to respond to these situations with strong statements:

- "No, don't do that."
- "No, I'll tell my mother."
- "Stop, that's not okay."
- "My parents told me not to."

Once your children are familiar with this game and learn that you will play it without ridicule or shame, they may start asking their own what-if questions. This is a good sign that they feel comfortable asking you for information and support on this sensitive issue.

Give Unconditional Love and Support. Child molesters try to control their victims in three ways:

1. Coercing the child or using the power of authority
2. Manipulating the child into "playing a fun game," which results in unwanted physical contact
3. Bribing the child with favors or gifts

These techniques are quite persuasive and can make children feel as if they are in some way responsible. Assure your children that they are *never* to blame if an adult or older child tries to touch or see their body.

Convince them that it's perfectly safe and good for them to tell you about any adult or older child who tries to invade their privacy. Let your children know that molesters cajole or threaten children to keep the incident a "special" secret. Assure them that, no matter what another adult may say, they can always talk to you.

Repeat Your Message. You cannot effectively warn children about sexual abuse in just one discussion. Repetition is a necessary part of the learning process, so repeat your instructions and assurances on different occasions. After each discussion with your children, follow up a few days later with some questions that will give them a chance to voice any concerns they may have. You might ask:

"Have you thought any more about our talk about private body parts?"

"Do you have any questions about what to do if anyone touches you in a way you don't like?"

"Do you remember what you should say to strangers who offer you toys or candy?"

Listen for Unspoken Fears. Despite your assurances that sexual abuse is never the child's fault and should not be kept a secret, some children may still have trouble talking about encounters with adults that make them feel uncomfortable. That's why it's important to stay alert to behaviors that may be signals that your child is trying to tell you something.

If, for example, your normally friendly child says that he or she hates going to Uncle Bill's house, or becomes unusually stubborn about wanting to avoid violin lessons, do some probing. Ask how the child feels about an adult whose company he or she wants to avoid. Don't put words in your child's mouth, but encourage an open talk about what happened the last time the child was with that person.

What to Do If Your Child Is Sexually Abused

Nothing can prepare parents to deal with a situation in which someone has sexually abused their child. Although there is a natural reluctance to confront such a painful and disturbing event, how parents handle the situation can determine whether it will have a lasting traumatic effect on the child.

Tell the Authorities. If you become aware of any abuse—perpetrated by someone within your family or without—call 911 and report it immediately to the police. They will investigate the charge themselves and also report it to your local child protective agency. This agency is listed in the front of your telephone book, if you want to call yourself. The law requires that if either the police or child protective agency receives any report of child abuse, that agency must investigate and report it to the other.

Some parents are afraid to report sexual abuse because they want to protect their children from public exposure. Although it is not easy to make such an accusation or to prove sexual abuse, ignoring the incident can also have harmful effects on your child. If you do not report the incident to the police, your child will certainly feel that you're protecting the criminal. Your decision to keep the abuse a secret implies that perhaps you don't believe it really happened, or that the child is somehow at fault and so the authorities should not be notified. Of course, if you choose to keep the abuse a secret, you are protecting a criminal and enabling him or her to continue sexually abusing young children.

When you report suspected child abuse to the police or child protective services, you should know what to expect. A police officer will come to your home or call you down to the station to make a statement. Further interviews and investigations may result. Then a medical examination is usually mandated, no matter when the alleged abuse occurred. This examination takes place at a hospital, usually in the emergency room. If the police decide the circumstances warrant a formal charge, further investigations, interviews, and statements will be required. Finally, if the district attorney decides to prosecute, there may need to be court appearances and testimony. If the abuse was perpetrated by a relative, the child protective services will conduct their own interviews and investigation of the case. They will then decide whether or not it's safe for the child to remain in the home.

Attend to Your Child's Needs.   While the authorities do their job, there are several things you can do to help your child regain a sense of control and safety after a sexual abuse incident.

- Comfort the child. Give emotional first aid by reassuring your child of your love and by offering comfort. But don't express so much distress that your child gets the impression that this is the worst thing that could possibly have happened. The proper reaction is one of tenderness and sympathy—not hysteria or pity.
- Control your emotions. Most of us feel outrage and anger when a child has been victimized. You should discuss your feelings of anger or guilt with another adult, not with your child. In this way the child won't assume responsibility for these feelings or be frightened by your anger.
- Encourage your child to talk about the experience. Be a good listener and help the child express any feelings of fear, anger, humiliation, guilt, confusion, or embarrassment. The child may need to talk about it again and again before being able to assimilate the experience.
- Believe the child. Professional experience indicates that it's rare for children to lie about sexual abuse.
- Praise the child for reporting it. Assure your child that he or she did absolutely the right thing in telling you about the incident.
- Relieve the child of blame. Sexual abuse is never a child's fault, so don't say, "How could you let this happen to you?" Or, "You know you're not supposed to go into anyone's house when the parents aren't at home." Be very clear about the fact that you believe the responsibility and blame for the act rests solely with the adult or older child.
- Arrange protection from further abuse. Tell your child that

you are going to do everything possible to ensure that this does not happen again.

Get Professional Help.   In the case of sexual abuse, you should seriously consider getting professional help. Professional treatment, as soon as possible, is the best way to overcome the risk that the child will develop serious problems as an adult. A child psychologist can help the child regain a sense of self-esteem and relieve feelings of guilt about the abuse. Therapy can also help family members understand how to assist the child in overcoming the trauma.

The best way to protect children from sexual abuse is to talk to them. The resources and books listed below can further help you discuss this very personal subject with your children.

Suggested Resources

Childhelp
Box 630
Hollywood, CA 90028
Childhelp's National Child Abuse Hotline:
800-422-4453

National Center for Child Abuse and Neglect
400 6th Street
Washington, DC 20201
202-245-2840

National Center for the Prevention and Control of Rape
5600 Fishers Lane, Room 15-99
Rockville, MD 20857
301-443-1910

National Committee to Prevent Child Abuse
P.O. Box 2866
Chicago, IL 60690
312-663-3520

Suggested Reading

For Parents

Bahr, Amy C. *It's OK to Say No: A Book for Parents and Children to Read Together.* New York: Grosset & Dunlap, 1986.

Crewdson, John. *By Silence Betrayed: Sexual Abuse of Children in America.* Boston: Little, Brown, 1988.

Hagana, Kathryn R. *When Your Child Has Been Molested: A Parent's Guide to Healing and Recovery.* Lexington, Mass.: Lexington Books, 1988.

For Children Aged Four to Eight

Freeman, Lory. *It's My Body.* Seattle: Parenting Press, 1982.

Johnsen, Karen. *The Trouble with Secrets.* Seattle: Parenting Press, 1986.

Sweet, Phyllis. *Something Happened to Me.* Racine, Wis.: Mother Courage Press, 1981.

Wachter, Oralee. *No More Secrets for Me.* Boston: Little, Brown, 1984.

For Children Aged Nine to Twelve

Aho, Jennifer Sowle, and John W. Petras. *Learning About Sexual Abuse.* Hillside, N.J.: Enslow Publishers, 1985.

Girard, Linda Walvoord. *My Body Is Private.* Niles, Ill.: A. Whitman, 1984.

Rench, Janice E. *Family Violence: How to Recognize and Survive It.*

Minneapolis: Lerner Publications, 1992. (Includes bibliographical references.)

Spider-Man & Power Pack Child Sexual Abuse Prevention Comic Books. Chicago: National Committee to Prevent Child Abuse, in conjunction with Marvell Comics, 1984.

Terkel, Susan Neiburg. *Feeling Safe, Feeling Strong: How to Avoid Sexual Abuse and What to Do If It Happens to You.* Minneapolis: Lerner Publications, 1984.

Strangers

My family lives only five suburban blocks from our elementary school, so I never worried about my first grader's walk home with several older neighborhood kids each day. But what happened to my son one autumn afternoon illustrates the necessity and the difficulty of talking to kids about strangers.

On this particular day, Joe ran into the house breathless, eyes brimming with tears and obviously near panic. The details of his story tumbled out in disconnected pieces, but soon it became apparent that a man he'd never seen before had stalked him and his friends as they walked home. If they zigzagged across the street, the man zigzagged too. If they stopped walking, he stopped walking too. If they turned to look at him, he boldly stared back. As their apprehension grew, a woman drove up alongside the group and told the kids to get into her car. That did it. They all took off at lightning speed, each fleeing in different directions to the safety of their homes.

After hearing this story, I took my son to my neighbor's house for safekeeping, then raced back over his route looking for these strangers. What exactly I planned to do single-handedly if I found them I'm still not sure, but I was off. I found no unfamiliar faces lurking between my home and the school, but I did find a car matching my son's description parked in a driveway. Desperate for information, I employed a tactic I don't now, with a clear mind, recommend to anyone: I rang the bell and confronted the woman who answered. Here the story unfolded.

It seems this elderly woman was driving home from grocery shopping when she saw a man following some school children. She watched for a while and then decided she would drive the kids home to safety. "I'm so sorry," she confessed. "I know I frightened them even more when I told them to get in my car. But I was only trying to help."

In this scenario there was a good stranger and a bad stranger, but how were the kids supposed to know the difference? The point is that they *can't* tell the difference. Our job then, is to warn our children about dangerous *circumstances* with strangers, so they can protect themselves from the bad guys, without making them scared of the good guys.

Telling children "Don't talk to strangers—ever" is a confusing and impossible order. The message implies that all strangers are evil—all waiting to kidnap and kill little children. And yet, every new life situation involves strangers—joining a sports team, starting a new school or grade, even ordering a hamburger.

We need to be more specific about the circumstances in which children shouldn't talk to strangers and explain in detail how to handle uncomfortable or potentially dangerous situations. When we do this, we make kids feel secure and in control—not frightened.

When to Talk About Strangers

Discussions dealing with the subject of strangers should be a part of your ongoing lessons about general health and safety. You probably expound on the subject of good nutrition when your children want more than their daily allotment of junk food. You remind them how to cross the street safely when you're standing on the corner waiting to cross. In the same way, you can most effectively talk about strangers and how to handle them when the situation warrants. Here are some examples:

• If your child asks, "Mommy, why did you say hello to that lady? You don't even know her," use this opening to talk about non-threatening situations where strangers pose no danger.

• If you leave your child alone for a few moments while you run next door, explain at that time the importance of not opening the door to anyone.

• After someone drives up alongside you and asks for directions, explain to your children why you responded as you did and then explain how you expect them to handle the same kind of encounter. (Depending on where you live and how you feel about this situation, you might tell them to run away, ignore the request, or give directions without going near the car.)

Throughout each day, stay alert for the kinds of situations that you can use to teach stranger safety.

The media also give us opportunities to discuss stranger safety in the context of news events. If the news reports that a child has been abducted, for example, you can use that announcement to ask your children questions that make them think about how they can avoid a similar fate. You might ask:

"How do you think that could have happened?"

"What would you do if someone you didn't know at the amusement park asked you to go on a ride with him?"

Or, if it's reported that a child has been molested by someone behind an abandoned building, in the woods, or in a back alley, this is a good time to map out the places where your children are not allowed to play.

What Should You Tell Your Children About Strangers?

Children need to know what to do and what to say in specific circumstances. Following is a general list of do's and don'ts that covers what you should tell your children about some of the most common potentially dangerous situations. In addition, you should develop your own list of do's and don'ts appropriate to your kids and their activities and needs.

- "Never accept food or gifts from strangers."
- "Never accept rides, even if the man or woman tells you that your family asked him or her to pick you up."
- "Never play in alleys, empty buildings, houses being built, or remote or isolated areas."
- "Never go with a stranger who promises you games, toys, food, candy, or a fun time."
- "Never go to rest rooms alone, especially in gas stations, theaters, restaurants, or other public places."
- "When you answer the phone, never give information about your name or address or who is at home."
- "Never let a stranger know you are home alone. Tell the person your dad is outside or your mom is in the shower."
- "If you are home alone and a stranger comes to the door, never open the door. Talk through the door and tell them your parents are busy or asleep. Do not let the person inside for *any* reason."
- If a stranger should forcefully put a hand on you, scream. Immediately yell 'I don't know this person!' Or, if no one is around to see what's happening, yell 'Fire!'"

(Experts feel this cry brings more immediate attention because anyone who hears it will more readily run to offer assistance. A cry for help threatens a passerby's feeling of personal safety.)

How Can You Make Sure Your Children Remember Stranger-Safety Rules?

Repetition of stranger-safety rules is important because under stress children can't be expected to remember something they've been told just once. If you tell your six-year-old what to do if he or she gets lost at the mall, don't expect the child to remember your instructions when you return to the mall a week later—explain again and again.

Lecture and rote repetition of rules can, however, fail to help your children in a time of crisis. An effective way to teach your children stranger safety is by playing what-if games that ask them to think about how they would react to potentially dangerous situations. Here are some examples:

- "What if it was raining very hard and a stranger offered you a ride home? What would you do?"
- "What if a person comes up to you on the playground and says, 'My puppy is lost. Will you help me find it?'"
- "What if someone comes to the door when I'm not home and says her car broke down and she needs to use the phone to call the gas station? What would you do?"
- "What if someone you don't know calls you by name and says that your mother has been hurt and has asked him to pick you up from school? What would you say?"
- "What if you were walking home from school and someone was following you? What would you do?"

Don't be alarmed if your children give wrong answers to these questions, even after you've instructed them how to act in the given circumstance. Far better they make their mistakes playing this game with you than on the street when a stranger approaches.

Children need to know that *some* strangers are not good people in *some* circumstances. They also need to know *what to do* if they are approached by a stranger or feel endangered. This information empowers children to protect themselves and it makes them less fearful of the innumerable strangers who pass through their daily lives meaning no harm.

Suggested Reading

For Parents

Bahr, Amy C. *It's OK to Say No: A Book for Parents and Children to Read Together.* New York: Grosset & Dunlap, 1986.

Bahr, Amy C. *What Should You Do When—? A Book For Parents and Children To Read Together.* New York: Grosset & Dunlap, 1986.

Lenett, Robin. *It's O.K. to Say NO!: A Parent/Child Manual for the Protection of Children.* New York: T. Doherty Associates, 1985.

Simmons, J. L. *76 Ways to Protect Your Child from Crime.* New York: Henry Holt, 1992.

For Children Aged Four to Seven

Berenstain, Stan, and Jan Berenstain. *The Berenstain Bears Learn About Strangers.* New York: Random Books for Young Readers, 1986.

Girard, Linda Walvoord. *Who Is a Stranger, and What Should I Do?* Niles, Ill.: A. Whitman, 1985.

For Children Aged Eight to Twelve

Newman, Susan. *Never Say Yes to a Stranger: What Your Child Must Know to Stay Safe.* New York: Putnam, 1985.

Television and Media Violence

Consider this typical scene in Anyhome USA: the television in the living room is screaming with the siren cries of police cars in hot pursuit of the pimp who murdered the hooker. The television in the kids' bedroom is tuned to cartoon characters who smash, kick, klunk, punch, stomp, strike, jab, and thump their way through the half-hour show. And in the den the video game challenges the player to kill, plunder, and destroy with agility and perfect timing. Does this sound like another quiet evening at home in your house?

When acts of extreme violence occur in our homes or on our streets, we instinctively shield our children's eyes and pull them away. Yet when they occur on TV shows, news reports, or video games, we offer popcorn and front row seats. Perhaps, we tolerate TV and video violence because we forget that our children are not miniature adults in the way they view the world. We sometimes assume that our children know, as we do, that TV shows are not real. We expect children to have coping skills that are developed enough to deal with the nightly news. Unfortunately, children view cartoons, real-life dramas, video games, and the estimated eighteen thousand TV murders they'll witness before they're sixteen quite differently than we do.

Psychological Effects of TV Violence on Children

Years of research studies have established that TV violence leaves psychological marks on children in a number of ways:

- A 1982 National Institute of Mental Health study reported that "violence on television does lead to aggressive behavior by children and teenagers who watch the programs."
- Dr. Leonard Eron, of the University of Illinois, found that children who watch many hours of TV violence during their elementary school years tend to show a higher level of aggressive behavior as teenagers.
- The Position Statement on Media Violence in Children's Lives adopted by the National Association for the Education of Young Children points out that preschoolers are particularly vulnerable to the negative influences of the media because they are not yet fully able to distinguish fantasy from reality.
- The American Academy of Pediatrics has released a study stating that "sufficient data have accumulated to warrant the conclusion that protracted television viewing is one cause of violent or aggressive behavior."
- The National Coalition of Television Violence, a private watchdog group opposed to glamorized violence, warns that of Nintendo's more than four hundred games, the vast majority have violent action levels high enough to be harmful to children's psyches.

Children's Reactions to TV Violence

To verify the findings of the various research studies, just listen to your kids. Here are three reactions that kids commonly have when they're overexposed to TV violence:

Desensitization: "Man, look at that blood gush out of his head. That's great!"

TV violence can create the impression that aggression and hostile acts are commonplace and acceptable. When this happens, children stop feeling empathy for others' pain. They don't try to prevent violent acts and are slow to react to others' suffering.

Copycat activities: "Get out of my way, squirt, or I'll knock you down."

Children will imitate what they see on TV. If TV characters resolve their problems with violence, so may your children.

TV violence teaches children that conflicts are settled through force. Children who watch violent shows are more likely to argue, disobey, and hit their friends, and their problem-solving skills tend to be very weak.

Exaggerated fear: "Don't turn out the light; I'm afraid!"

TV can shape a child's image of reality. Excessive exposure to TV violence causes children to see the world as a hostile, unsafe place. This can result in what Dr. George Gerbner, of the University of Pennsylvania, calls the "mean world syndrome." This is the belief that crime and violence are pervasive parts of our world. Dr. Gerbner believes that kids don't have enough real-world information to put what they see on TV into perspective.

What Parents Can Do

There are a number of ways you can reduce the negative psychological effects of TV violence on your children. A few are listed below and you may think of many more yourself.

Cut Down on Television Viewing. Basic arithmetic supports the wisdom of reducing the number of hours our kids watch TV each day. Consider this:

- Children witness an estimated twenty violent acts during each hour of TV viewing.
- American children watch approximately twenty-three hours of TV each week.
- If you turn off the TV for just an extra half hour each day, you'll reduce your children's violence intake by seventy incidents per week!

Evaluate the Shows Your Kids Watch.   There is another method of reducing children's negative reactions to TV violence that is quite effective. Sit down and watch your children's TV shows and video games at least once. If you find that a show or game is excessively violent or glorifies gratuitous violence, ban it. Send a clear message to your kids—and to the producers of media violence—that you will not welcome it into your home.

Of course, this is sometimes easier said than done, as May Eckings found out—but it's worth the effort. "I'm pretty strict about what my kids watch on TV," May told me. "We've settled into a nice routine of watching a few selected shows each day. But one night last week, I came into the family room after giving Brett his bath and there was my eight-year-old engrossed in a real-life drama about drug dealers." As May explained it, the scene she walked in on was a brutal and up-close portrayal of a drug bust. "Suspects were cursing, police were kicking in doors, overturning furniture, and scuffling with drug dealers who were resisting arrest," she exclaimed.

When May turned off the TV, her son threw a tantrum. "Everybody at school watches that show!" he cried. "Why can't I? You're no fair," he yelled as he stormed out of the room.

Explain Your Reasons for Banning Shows.   To ease the blow of censorship, talk to your kids before you pull the plug on violent TV shows. Tell them that it upsets you to see people hurt other people, that you believe there are better ways for people to resolve their differences. You might add that just as you don't want brutal criminal activity taking place in your living room, you don't want your family watching it on TV either.

Replace these shows with programs, video games, or tapes recommended for their nonviolent nature. (See the list of recommended shows near the end of this chapter.)

Prevent Young Children from Watching the News. Many families reduce their daily violence quota by changing the time they watch the evening news. We agree with Dr. Benjamin Spock, who believes that children under the age of six should not be exposed to news shows at all. These children have great difficulty processing and coping with violence and human tragedy. There is no reason to subject them to an onslaught of nightly horrors.

If you follow the guidelines suggested above, you'll certainly reduce the negative psychological effects of media violence—and that's an admirable accomplishment. However, because we're not always around to censor the TV, because our children all have friends with TVs, and because violence is a part of our world, we can't completely shield our children from violence. That's why it's important to teach them how to critically view and evaluate television to put violence in its proper perspective.

Teaching Critical Viewing Skills

Many children (especially those under six) have difficulty distinguishing what's real from what's not. This ability is an important factor in how children process TV violence. Critical TV viewing skills can help kids understand why TV is not representative of the world in which they live, and this knowledge can lessen the negative impact of media violence.

Explain What Actors Do.   While you're watching TV to-night, tell your children: "These aren't real people. They're what's called 'characters.' The character of DJ Tanner on *Full House,* for instance, is played by an actress named Candice Cameron. It's her job to memorize lines and act out her part in front of cameras that record the scene and play it back to us."

Highlight the character and actor concept by encouraging your children to playact themselves. Let them play the role of their favorite TV character. Older children can even memorize lines to a scene.

If you have a video camera, let your children produce their own TV show. Let them choose character parts from their favorite show, write a story they want to act out, film it, and view it on the TV. If they want to include a violent scene, let them. This is another way for them to see firsthand that the violence they witness on TV shows is not real and that the characters do not really get hurt.

Later, as you view TV violence, remind your children, "TV characters pretend to hit each other like that so they don't really cause pain, like you did in your video [or play or whatever]. But if real people hit each other, that hurts."

Explain What Cartoons Really Are.   One of the delightful charms of childhood is the imaginative innocence that allows young children to believe in Big Bird and Mickey Mouse and Cinderella. But this same imagination makes them prone to the problems as-sociated with watching TV violence when they overdose on cartoon characters like Roadrunner, Bugs Bunny, the Teenage Mutant Ninja Turtles, or nearly any other popular cartoon creation. Children under the age of six need help understanding why cartoon characters don't feel pain.

While you watch cartoons with your children, occasionally ask them questions that will open up discussion on the differences between fantasy and reality. Here are some examples:

- "Is Bugs Bunny someone you would see driving a car down the street? Why not?"
- "If a real bird got blown up, like the Roadrunner, would it be able to run around again right away? Why not?"
- "Do you think there are any Ninja Turtles in our town?"

Talk to your children about their answers to questions like these, and emphasize the fantasy quality of cartoons.

You can also help demystify the life of cartoon characters by showing your children how cartoons are made. As you draw a cartoon picture, tell them, "An artist draws cartoon characters on paper like this. That's why cartoon characters can hit each other without getting hurt. If I hit this paper character, it doesn't hurt the picture. But if I hit a real person, that would hurt that person and it wouldn't be nice."

Watch Shows with Your Kids to Defuse the Tension.

You can reduce the effects of TV violence simply by being in the room when the TV is on. Studies have found that your mere presence relieves the tension children feel while viewing violent scenes. Being nearby also makes you available to answer questions like "Can that really happen?" and "Is that guy really dead?"

When you watch TV with your kids, stay alert for opportunities

to talk about violent scenes and help your children see the com-
mercial and sensationalized side of TV. Ask questions like:

"Why did he shoot that man?"

"How else could he have handled that problem?"

"Do you think a real person would act that way or do these
TV shows exaggerate violent scenes?"

"Why would a TV show want to make two people fight over
a problem instead of having them talk about it and solve it without bloodshed?"

Watch for Behind-the-Scenes Programs. A wonderful
and entertaining way to teach children critical viewing skills is
through the occasional TV special that goes behind the scenes
of a popular movie. A neighbor of ours recently praised a TV show
that showed the making of the movie *Home Alone.* The show took
viewers onto the *Home Alone* set so they could watch the director,
camera operators, actors, makeup people, and other technicians
put the movie together. They showed the actors practicing and
laughing at their attempts to make particularly hostile scenes look
realistic.

"Now my kids watch movies and TV in a completely different
way," says my neighbor. "They finally can see that line between acting and real life."

Watch for these kinds of behind-the-scenes shows, blooper programs, or even TV interviews with actors. Seeing actors out of
character helps children internalize your statement, "That character
is not real."

Violence and Tragedies in the News

The violence and tragedies reported on TV news shows present
a whole different set of problems for children. Although you can

help your children separate the violence they see in fictional shows from the reality of their world, TV news *is* reality, so it's harder for them to understand and categorize.

After watching a report of a violent event on the news, children may focus on its personal relevancy rather than the event itself. Tragic stories about children make young viewers feel especially vulnerable. A kidnapping will make children worry about their own safety; a story about sexual abuse may make them suspicious of their caretakers. News of a robbery will put them on guard.

If the news must be on while your children are around, talk to them about reports of violence and turn the focus away from your child and your family. Say something like, "What a mean thing that person did. I'm glad he was caught and locked up in jail."

You can also arm your children with protective strategies so they don't feel helpless to fend off the world's atrocities. When the news reports an abduction, for example, you can assure your children this will not happen to them because they know the family rules against talking to strangers and staying out of desolate places.

The Good News

There are some hopeful signs that the media entertainment industry of the future will rely less heavily on violence for ratings. Sega of America, whose electronic video games feature murderous villains, calamitous car chases, and bloody shoot-outs, is voluntarily rating its products: GA for general audiences, MA-13 for "mature audiences" thirteen years old and over, and MA-17 for those over seventeen. This will certainly help parents monitor their children's exposure to violence.

Also, the major television networks—ABC, CBS, and NBC— have voluntarily agreed on standards governing television violence. It's a small step, but it's in the right direction. Still, for now, TV violence is an intrusion in all our lives that we can't completely avoid.

To balance this negative side of TV, remember:

Reduce TV viewing time.

Ban exceptionally violent shows.

Talk about the difference between reality and fantasy.

Teach critical viewing skills.

Then look for shows that emphasize the positive side of life.

There are shows on the airwaves right now that model kindness, compassion, and generosity. There are shows that can enhance our children's academic and social skills, and there are shows that are just plain fun. Make an effort to find them and encourage your children to watch them.

Rated "E" for Excellent by the Experts

The following list of TV shows was selected by a team of critics, activists, and educators chosen by author Holly St. Lifer. The list appeared in *CHILD* magazine in January 1993. It will give you an idea of where to start looking for nonviolent TV programming.

PROGRAMS FOR KIDS AGED 2 TO 5	PROGRAMS FOR KIDS AGED 6 TO 12
Peggy Charren, president, Action for Television	
Long Ago & Far Away (PBS)	*Reading Rainbow* (PBS)
	3-2-1 Contact (PBS)
	Where in the World Is Carmen Sandiego (PBS)

Robert L. Schrag, professor of communication, North Carolina State University

Sesame Street (PBS)	*Wonderworks* (PBS)
Mister Rogers' Neighborhood (PBS)	*Square One TV* (PBS)
Sharon, Lois, & Bram's Elephant Show (Nickelodeon)	*The Cosby Show* (NBC)
	The Wonder Years (ABC)
Muppet Babies (CBS)	*Blossom* (NBC)

Diana Huss Green, editor-in-chief, Parent's Choice

Babar (HBO)	*Avonlea* (Disney)
Tiny Toons (syndication)	*3-2-1 Contact* (PBS)
We All Have Tales (Showtime)	*Where in the World Is Carmen Sandiego?* (PBS)

Ken Tucker, television critic, Entertainment Weekly

Sesame Street (PBS)	*3-2-1 Contact* (PBS)
Sharon, Lois & Bram's Elephant Show (Nickelodeon)	*Doug* (Nickelodeon)
We All Have Tales (Showtime)	

Thomas Radecki, M.D., chairman, National Coalition on TV Violence

Sesame Street (PBS)	*3-2-1 Contact* (PBS)
Babar (HBO)	*Square One TV* (PBS)
Mister Rogers' Neighborhood (PBS)	*Reading Rainbow* (PBS)
LunchBox (Disney)	*Bill and Ted's Excellent Adventures* (Fox)

Complaints

Here are the addresses of the major networks, if you want to complain to them about TV violence:

American Broadcasting Company (ABC), Audience Information, 77 West 66th Street, New York, NY 10023

Columbia Broadcasting Systems (CBS), Audience Services, 51 West 52nd Street, New York, NY 10019

National Broadcasting Company (NBC), Attn: Children's Programming, 3000 West Alameda Avenue, Room 246, Burbank, CA 91523

The addresses and phone numbers of smaller networks and local or cable stations are listed in your phone book.

Suggested Reading

For Parents

Gore, Tipper. *Raising PG Kids in an X-Rated Society.* Nashville: Abingdon Press, 1987.

Winn, Marie. *The Plug-In Drug: Television, Children and the Family.* New York: Viking Penguin, 1985.

For Children Aged Four to Seven

Berenstain, Stan, and Jan Berenstain. *The Berenstain Bears and Too Much TV.* New York: Random Books for Young Readers, 1984.

War

In the same way children today practice fire drills, a whole generation of us responded to the air-raid siren by ducking under our school desks, putting our hands over our heads, and praying. Every drill prepared us for instant death at the hands of an unseen, unknown, and ill-defined fiend. Over the sobs of frightened classmates, we strained to hear the sound of bombs that we were sure would crash through the ceiling at any moment.

Many who recall those air-raid drills remember that the most frightening part of all was not knowing what was really going on. Adults didn't talk openly to children about the consequences of an atomic war because, common wisdom decreed, the details would make children too fearful, give them nightmares, and cause undue hysteria. Instead, we were taught how to protect ourselves in case "something" happened.

Although the cold war has ended and our fear of missiles and bombs has subsided, war stories are still a part of our children's lives. At the time of this writing, the media are carrying front-line reports from the Middle East, Eastern Europe, Africa, and Northern Ireland. Given that warfare is as old as human history, it's a reasonable assumption that no matter when you might read this chapter, war will probably be raging somewhere in our world. Our children will always have questions about the atrocities of battle that the news brings into our homes. Now, fortunately, we realize that it's factual answers to these questions that will relieve their fears and nightmares.

How to Talk About War

It's a good idea to organize your feelings about war before you discuss the subject with your children. Among friends and co-workers you may discuss war in rather blunt and brutal terms: "We should just kick butt and get out of there," you might say, or "We should just bomb 'em till they're wiped off the map."

But is this really the message you want to give your children? As the next generation of leaders and potential peacemakers, our children should be educated about the true character of war and "enemies."

Try to focus your conversations about war on the hope for a peaceful settlement. Remaining confident about the future of the world, keep an optimistic attitude that the military and political leaders will find a way to end the war without total destruction of one side. This approach gives children hope for the future.

What to Say About War

Experts agree that it's best not to shield children from the facts. Giving your kids the freedom to talk to you and ask questions about war is the only way to meet the goal of making them feel safe and secure in their own homes.

Exactly what you tell your children about war will depend on their age.

Preschoolers basically just want to know you will take care of them. Your answers should be brief and supportive. Be optimistic that nations will learn to settle their disputes peacefully.

School-age children want more information than younger children. Don't suppress talk about their fears or avoid discussions. Use TV and print news reports to launch discussions and offer opportunities to share concerns.

There are no easy answers to questions about war. But the following examples will give you an idea of how you can balance the harsh nature of war with a reassuring hope for future peace.

"Why is there war?"

An open discussion about the concept of war can make things less frightening because it puts the threat to personal safety into a broader context. Tell your children that most often war is a political decision that's made by a nation's government to defend a country.

You might say, "When a country's existence, honor, power, or influence is threatened in some way, the leaders of that country may decide to send soldiers out to fight whoever is threatening them."

"Isn't there any other way to solve the problem?"

You may personally believe that sometimes a country must defend its honor, or you may feel that war is nothing more than a bloody game played by greedy politicians. Whatever your personal political opinions, because children are our future politicians, military officers, and peacemakers, they should be encouraged to see war as a very serious and undesirable course of action. Children should know that war is a last resort. Assure them that soldiers go to battle only after all other efforts to talk about a solution have failed.

Then encourage your children to think about ways future wars can be avoided. "If you were the president," you might ask, "how could you settle this problem in a nonviolent way?" Introduce terms like "mutual understanding," "negotiation," and "arbitration" in your discussions about alternative ways to solve national problems.

"Why are the people in that country so mean?"

We must stop teaching our children that the people in "enemy" territory are invariably treacherous, cruel, and warlike, while we are invariably peace-loving, honorable, and humane. Such black-and-white thinking will only convince our children that war is necessary and inevitable.

Tell your children, "People of all nations are both loving and aggressive. We must look for the good in others and find ways to work together in peace."

"How long will the war last?"

If the media are focusing on an international incident, it will seem to your children that war is a never-ending part of life. Assure them that the war does end eventually. Tell them, "In life, all people experience good times and bad times. The people going through this bad time of war will one day, once again, live in peace and happiness."

"Are the bombs going to come here?"

During the recent war in the Persian Gulf, many American children cried for their own safety after viewing broadcasts of Israeli children in gas masks cowering at the sound of not-so-distant bombs. If the war your children are concerned about is being waged in a country far from your home, give them some concrete information that will assure them of their safety.

First, acknowledge their fear. You might say, "Yes, I know you're afraid, and I've been thinking about this too." Then give them the facts. "But let me show you how I know we're perfectly safe from attack."

Show your children a map or globe. Point out the distance between your home and some familiar place, and then point out the war location. You might look up exactly how many miles away the war is being waged, and even add something like, "It takes twenty-four hours to fly by plane to this country. That is too far for a bomb to fly."

Then offer assurances. Tell your children, "We live in the finest, safest country in the world. You can be sure that the government and your family will take good care of you."

When Children Need Relief from Tension

If, after talking about war and giving opportunities for questions and answers, your children still seem distressed, there are some things you can do to ease the tension.

Turn off the news. Certainly there's no reason to deny the presence of war in the world, and we do want our children to know we're available to talk about the problem. However, there's also no need for our children to spend all day watching the death and destruction of war in living color.

Don't dwell on the war. If war is foremost in the news, try to keep your family conversations balanced with other concerns and occurrences. Because children will mimic your every word and deed, if you become obsessive about the subject, so will they.

Maintain your regular daily routine. Predictable routines make children feel safe; changes in routine cause insecurities. Your children will feel frightened if you halt all normal activities to monitor CNN broadcasts. They will become tense and fearful if you alter your usual commute to school or work because of unfounded fears of terrorist attack. Try to keep your daily schedule the same as it was before the news media brought war into your home.

As parents we have a responsibility to help children understand that physical conflict is not the only way to solve national problems. They need to know that trust and cooperation are possible among the people of the world. When you talk to them about war, give them the facts of the present conflict, but also encourage them to see the peaceful possibilities for the future.

Suggested Reading

For Parents

Carlsson-Paige, Nancy, and Diane Levin. *Helping Young Children Understand Peace, War, and the Nuclear Threat.* Washington, D.C.: National Association for the Education of Young Children, 1985.

Carlsson-Paige, Nancy, and Diane Levin. *Who's Calling the Shots? How to Respond Effectively to Children's Fascination with War Play and War Toys.* Philadelphia: New Society Publishers, 1990.

Van Ornum, W., and M. Van Ornum. *Talking to Children About Nuclear War.* New York: Continuum, 1984.

For Children Aged Four to Seven

Bunting, Eve. *The Wall.* New York: Clarion, 1990.
Winthrop, Elizabeth. *That's Mine!* New York: Holiday House, 1977.
Zeifert, Harriet. *A New Coat for Anna.* New York: Knopf, 1986.

For Children Aged Eight to Twelve

Dr. Seuss. *The Butter Battle Book.* New York: Random House, 1984.
Durell, Ann, and Marilyn Sachs, eds. *The Big Book for Peace.* New York: Dutton Children's Books, 1990.

References

Adoption

Jabs, Carolyn. "Adoption: When and What to Tell a Child." *Working Mother*, Apr. 1991, pp. 43–50.

Plumez, Jacqueline Hornor. *Successful Adoption*. New York: Harmony Books, 1987.

Alcoholic Parent

Al-Anon Family Groups. *Youth and the Alcoholic Parent*. New York: Al-Anon Family Groups, 1979.

American Academy of Child and Adolescent Psychiatry. *Children of Alcoholics*, 11(6) (entire issue). Washington, D.C.: American Academy of Child and Adolescent Psychiatry, n.d.

Simon, Nissa. "How Drinking Affects the Family." *Parents*, Oct. 1984, pp. 76–82.

Divorce

Voelker, R. M., and S. L. McMillan. "Children and Divorce: An Approach for the Pediatrician." *Developmental and Behavioral Pediatrics* Dec. 1983, pp. 272–277.

Drug Abuse

Board of Regents of the University of Wisconsin System and the National PTA. *Young Children and Drugs: What Parents Can Do*. Madison, Wis.: Wisconsin Clearinghouse, 1984.

National Institute on Drug Abuse. *Peer Pressure: It's O.K. to Say No.* DHHS Publication (AADM) 83-1271. 1983.

United States Department of Education. *Growing Up Drug Free: A Parent's Guide to Prevention.* Washington, D.C.: U.S. Department of Education, n.d.

Dying Child

Hurley, Dan. "A Sound Mind in an Unsound Body." *Psychology Today,* Aug. 1987, pp. 34–43.

Sheffield, M. "Don't Worry, Mom. Don't Worry, Dad." *The Catholic Digest,* Aug. 1987, pp. 82–87.

Slavin, L. A., and others. "Communication of the Cancer Diagnosis to Pediatric Patients: Impact on Long-term Adjustment." *American Journal of Psychiatry* 1982, 139, 179–183.

Spinetta, John J. "The Dying Child's Awareness of Death," *Psychological Bulletin* 1974, 81, 256–260.

Prejudice

What to Tell Your Child About Prejudice and Discrimination. New York: National PTA and the Anti-Defamation League of B'nai B'rith, 1989.

Repeating a Grade

Berger, Joseph. "Is Flunking a Grade Ever for a Pupil's Own Good?" *New York Times* 13 May 1990, p. E20.

Sexual Abuse

Fay, Jennifer. *He Told Me Not to Tell.* Renton, Wash.: King County Rape Relief, 1979.

Russell, Diana. "The Incidence and Prevalence of Intrafamilial and Extrafamilial Sexual Abuse of Female Children." In *Handbook on Sexual Abuse of Children.* New York: Spolinger, 1988.

Watson, Russell. "A Hidden Epidemic." *Newsweek,* 14 May 1984, pp. 30–35.

Television and Media

American Academy of Pediatrics, Committee on Communications. "Children, Adolescents and Television." *Pediatrics* 1990, 85, pp. 1119–1120.

American Psychological Association. *Violence on TV.* Washington, D.C.: American Psychological Association, 1985.

Cooke, Patrick. "TV or Not TV." *In Health,* Dec./Jan. 1992, pp. 33–44.

Hevesi, Dennis. "TV News: Children's Scary Window on New York." *New York Times,* 11 Sept. 1990, p. B1.

Katz, Lilian. "How TV Violence Affects Kids." *Parents,* Jan. 1991, p. 113.

National Institute of Mental Health. "Television and Behavior: Ten Years of Scientific Progress and Implications for the Eighties: Vol. 1: Summary Report." Rockville, Md.: United States Department of Health and Human Services, 1982.

Spock, Benjamin. "When Good Kids Get Bad News." *Redbook,* Sept. 1991, p. 154.

Suplee, Curt. "Mind Games." *Gannett Westchester Newspapers,* 15 Jan. 1992, p. C1.

The Authors

Charles E. Schaefer is professor of psychology and director of the Center for Psychological Services at Fairleigh Dickinson University. He was also supervising psychologist and director of psychological services, research and training at Children's Village, a residential treatment center in Dobbs Ferry, New York, for many years.

Schaefer is the author of more than twenty books, including professional books on children and adolescents as well as general books for parents.

Theresa Foy DiGeronimo is adjunct professor of writing at the William Paterson College of New Jersey and mother of three children.

Charles E. Schaefer and Theresa Foy DiGeronimo have collaborated on several previous books, including *Toilet Training Without Tears, Teach Your Child to Behave, Help Your Child Get the Most Out of School, Good Kids/Bad Habits,* and *Raising Baby Right,* which won *Child* magazine's award for the best parenting book of 1992.